Contents

JOHN MACIVER
on THE WALK AND WELFARE OF THE CHRISTIAN

JOHN MACKENZIE
on THE WALK AND WELFARE OF THE CHRISTIAN

INTRODUCTION

Remember them which have the rule over you, who have spoken unto you the word of God, whose faith follow, considering the end of their conversation, Jesus Christ, the same yesterday, and today and forever (Hebrews 13:7-8).

When the writer to the Hebrews penned these words, his purpose was to encourage and strengthen the Christians of his day. They had many discouragements to face; in a sense they were living in a time when the Gospel was fighting for its very life. But they are urged to live by faith, and not by sight; to say boldly 'The Lord is my helper, and I will not fear what man shall do unto me'.

As an incentive to faithfulness in the present, the writer urges upon them the remembrance of things past. In particular, they are encouraged to look back upon those who were faithful in delivering to them the message of the Gospel in a bygone day, who spoke unto them the word of God, and to whom was committed the spiritual rule of the church in a previous generation. But not only are they encouraged to remember them; they are also urged to emulate them, and to follow in their footsteps, considering the way in which their whole lifestyle and behaviour and service revolved around the Person and Work of Jesus Christ, who is the same yesterday, today and forever.

It is in keeping with the spirit of these wise counsels that the present volume is offered to the Christian public. The sermon notes of the Rev. John Maciver, late minister of Carloway, Lewis, and of the Rev. John Mackenzie, late minister of Leverburgh, Harris, have been in my possession for many years, and it is with gratitude to God that I am now able to make the matter of at least some of them available to a wider audience. The reader ought to bear in mind that these are sermon *notes*, and every effort has been made to present them more or less as they were written, even when translation was necessary. This means that there are some sentences which do not conform to the finer requirements of grammar, and some sermons which appear weighty in some of their points and scant in others. But it is hoped that their publication will go some way to preserving a memorial of the two godly gentlemen whose work they are.

Many of those who were nurtured under the preaching of these two servants of God are now themselves in eternity, and the passing of the years takes its own toll on the number who actually heard these sermons delivered in their original form. That does leave us now at a disadvantage, for, as any preacher will testify, there can be a great distance between the prepared text of a sermon and the actual delivery of it.

There is what Lloyd-Jones terms the element of 'freedom' in preaching, in which the preacher breaks beyond the bounds of his prepared sermon and preaches under the power of the moment. Lloyd-Jones gives this personal illustration:

> I have often found when I have gone into the pulpit with a prepared sermon that, while I have been preaching, my first point alone has developed into a whole sermon. Many times I have gone out of the pulpit realising that I had a series of sermons which I had not seen before .... What one had never thought of, or even imagined, suddenly happens in the pulpit while one is actually preaching.[1]

This freedom actually grows out of the thorough preparation of the material; but, however thoroughly the matter of the sermon has been prepared, at the point of its delivery 'there is a process of invention at the time'[2], in the words of Dabney. The ancient orator Cicero had compared this to the progress of a ship after the oars had dropped[3], ploughing through the waves as a result of previous exertion and labour.

The sermon notes on the following pages represent a little of the labour that was exerted in the unfolding of the meaning of the biblical text, as a preparation for the preaching of the Word. But the power of these sermons at the point of delivery is something which cannot be captured on paper. It is, however, certainly true that the two oarsmen on the galley of truth whose work is reflected in these pages preached in a way that was owned and blessed of the Spirit of God, and as a consequence, turned many to righteousness.

Both Mr Maciver and Mr Mackenzie had their own styles in preparation, and this introduction seeks to demonstrate this fact. But they were nothing if they were not thorough. Neither could be accused of inadequate preparation for preaching. Good sermons cannot be prepared in the last half hour of the week: they must be forged on the anvil of doctrine and shaped by the preacher's understanding and intellect. Both in their grasp of doctrine, and their thoroughness of mind in preparation, Mr Maciver and Mr Mackenzie put many to shame.

The biographical details of this introduction seek to give an historical context to the material which follows, as well as an analysis of the style and method of both men. Mr Maciver's sermons are of particular interest, because of the revival which broke out in the district of Carloway during his ministry there. The true nature of biblical revival is of great importance to the church at the current time. No concept is more misused and misunderstood throughout the professing Christian church than that of revival. The sermon notes of Mr Maciver testify to the fact that central to biblical revival is the preaching of the Word of God. The current attempts to make subjective experience the hallmark of revival, whether tongue-speaking or laughter or visions, stand neither the test of history nor, more importantly, the test of the Word of God.

In the course of the revival that broke out in New England during the ministry of Jonathan Edwards, the following points were observed by Edwards: 'the holy Bible is in much greater esteem and use than before'; 'The Lord's day is more religiously and more strictly observed'; 'the great doctrines of the gospel ... are matters of undoubted truth'[4]. These have been the hallmarks of every true revival of religion. They are not the hallmarks of the so-called revivals of the present day, where great store is laid by religious phenomena and experience. Not that the Carloway revival was without deep and lasting spiritual experience. But this was not the important issue. The central observable fact during this period of spiritual awakening was a thirst for the preaching of the Word[5]. And many souls at that time were watered through the preaching of Mr Maciver. The sermon notes show that what fed the souls of new converts and old was the marrow of evangelical theology, the proclamation of the full-orbed doctrines of truth.

The same doctrines are to be found in the sermons of Mr Mackenzie. His ministry was not attended by great or marked revival; but the same doctrines which were proclaimed so faithfully in Carloway were also distilled for the people of Wester Ross and Harris. Both these men of God were set apart for the work of the kingdom according to God's unsearchable judgements and wisdom, and their memory is blessed.

John Maciver

The Rev. John Maciver was born in Point, Lewis, in 1887. His parents, Mr and Mrs Torquil Maciver of 13 Shader, Point, were noted in their generation for Christian piety and godliness. Their family consisted of four sons and two daughters. John was the eldest son. Of the daughters, Lily, who is remembered as a beautiful Christian, passed away in what was the County Hospital, Stornoway, while Annie was to become the wife of John Mackenzie, whose sermon notes are also here recorded. The subjects of this book were not only brothers in grace but also brothers-in-law.

Mr Maciver was, for a time, a teacher in Aird School, until he began his studies in Glasgow in 1912. While he was there he became involved with the work of a Mission in Maryhill, where many exiled Lewismen and women came under these early ministerial labours. The outbreak of the First World War was to interrupt his studies, which were resumed in 1919 when Mr Maciver entered Edinburgh University. He graduated M.A. from Edinburgh, and then studied for three years at the Free Church College, before being ordained and inducted to Carloway in August 1924. Carloway was to be his only charge, and he was to labour there for 21 years until his death in March 1946. Mr Maciver remained unmarried throughout his life.

The ministry of Mr Maciver is best summarised in the tribute which appeared, shortly after his death, in the *Stornoway Gazette*:

> The power of his preaching needs no praise from any pen: the changed lives of many are an eloquent testimony. The Lord saw fit to bless his preaching abundantly, for to many it was the instrument of salvation. In their hearts he leaves a monument more abiding than any that could be carved from stone.[6]

The twin motivations which lay behind this preaching were a love for Christ and a love for souls. These are born out of the same womb, and they were much in evidence in the ministry of these two decades in Carloway. Mr Maciver loved his Lord; and he loved his people. Like the apostle Paul he could say 'the love of Christ constraineth us'.

As well as being a powerful preacher, Mr Maciver was also a faithful pastor to his people. He had sheep to feed, and he had lambs to feed, old converts and new. And the Lord endowed him with an empathy and understanding of the conditions of both. That experimental strain can be detected in his notes. It is the tune of a pastor whose heart is so bound to his people that he knows exactly what they are experiencing and going through. He was, as another tribute to him puts it,

> an experimental preacher of the first order, and frequently, while speaking of his own feelings, met one with a word in season, so exactly suited to the case that, if one told him of the state of the mind, and every particular of the situation beforehand, he could not have described them better.[7]

The present writer recalls hearing a Carloway man, speaking at a Question Meeting in Lewis, reminiscing about the ministry of Mr Maciver. He made the point that when a teacher takes a group of children out somewhere, sometimes the class can be quite unruly. All the skills of the teacher are stretched to keeping control of the pupils so that they will come to no harm. In this way, he said, Mr Maciver kept control of all the young converts in his congregation during the period of spiritual awakening and revival. With tenderness and care he pastored the flock faithfully.

At times he could be despondent and discouraged. Before his ordination he had been tempted not to enter the ministry at all. Rev M. Macaulay mentions the fact that during the first ten years of his ministry, Mr Maciver was sometimes 'very despondent' [8], although there was a regular influx of new converts professing faith at Communion Seasons. With the revival there came a new liberty in preaching, as well as fresh assaults from the devil, the enemy of all Gospel work. Nor was Mr Maciver free from physical pain, and indeed was absent from his congregational duties for a prolonged period as a result of this towards the close of his ministry.

Certain observations can be made from Mr Maciver's sermon notes. They are almost uniformly written in the same style: a page of paper is folded in two; the front page becomes page 1, the last page 2, and pages 3 and 4 appear on the inside. Very few of the notes contain sermon headings; this contrasts with the work of Mr Mackenzie, in which none of the sermons are without headings. But this is not to say that Mr Maciver's sermons lacked structure; the notes reveal that as he penned them, the preacher knew where he was coming from and where he was going.

Nevertheless, it is interesting to note how easily Mr Maciver is led to dwell on a particular point in the sermon notes. Perhaps one thought occupies him for the greater part of the study. This, it seems to me, as an objective reader of the material, betrays an element of the artistic and romantic, in which Mr Maciver's sanctified imagination leads him to the furthest implications of the truths with which he is dealing. It leads to some bold and original metaphors, as when, for example, he says that the death of Christ is a museum, displaying the glories of God (on Matthew 11:28-30), or when he compares Christ to a bright star he had himself seen in the night sky (on Revelation 22:16). This quality lends a very personal and homely touch to the sermon notes. Here is preaching of the highest quality - the loftiest themes couched in the language of the everyday.

Approximately half of Mr Maciver's sermon notes which appear on these pages were written entirely in Gaelic. This contrasts with the style of Mr Mackenzie, where, apart from an occasional word or heading, the notes were written entirely in English. The translation of Mr Maciver's notes takes us even further away from the quality of his preaching, but makes them more accessible to readers. It is recognised that no translation can adequately capture the force of the original language, but it is hoped that no injustice has been done in the course of rendering these notes into English. The fullest of all the sermon notes in my possession is that on 1 John 1:9, which appears in this volume. No other sermon is written out to the same measure of fulness, as this one; and it was written entirely in English.

Mr Maciver preached to the end. The reader is directed to Rev. M. Macaulay's history of the Free Church of Scotland in Carloway (*The Burning Bush in Carloway*, 1984) for episodes and reminiscences from the ministry of this great man of God. Although he was in worsened health, he preached twice on the Sabbath three days before he died. He lived to communicate the great message of the Gospel, and he did it in times of spiritual famine as well as in times of spiritual feasting. Rev K. Macrae notes that he listened to Mr Maciver preach in Stornoway in 1943, where 'he gave an able sermon on Luke 24:32'[9]. It is hoped that the following pages give a flavour of the ability, at both the doctrinal and practical level, that characterised his whole ministry. He died at Carloway, on Wednesday 13th March 1946, aged 59 years.

John Mackenzie

Rev John Mackenzie was born in Laxay, Lochs, in the Isle of Lewis on 11th April 1903. His parents, Annie and Colin Mackenzie, were lovers of the truth, and their home was a shining example of Christian nurturing and education. Many of the Lord's people enjoyed fellowship within its walls, and the memories of that home made their own lasting impression on the children, of whom there were ten - five boys and five girls.

The home in Laxay was not without its trials and tribulations. One young son died at the age of 6, after contracting measles, and another shortly afterward. But in the marvellous purposes of God's grace, that home was to have connections with several Free Church ministries; in 1929 Christina Mackenzie was to marry Rev. Murdoch Macrae, the minister of Kinloch from 1927 to 1961; and John Mackenzie was to become a minister in 1934. In the next generation, their niece, another Christina Mackenzie, was to marry Rev. Alex Murdo Macleod, the present minister of Kinloch [10]; and in the following generation again the present writer, the only grandson of John Mackenzie, became a minister in 1988, and his sister, Mrs Meg Miller, is presently in South Africa, where her husband, Rev David D. Miller serves in the Dumisani Bible School. Others connected with the home have held office and been in membership of the church. In this way it pleased God to bless the home in Laxay and make it a means for the furtherance of the truth at home and abroad. Of course, grace is not original, like sin, and does not flow in the family line. Yet it is wonderful to trace the finger of God in these matters, and see how the promise made to his children and their seed is fulfilled in succeeding generations.

Mrs Macrae reminisces thus on life in the home in Laxay:

> Our mothers made Harris Tweed which they had to prepare by hand ...
> All the girls had to help our mother while she was spinning. I remember
> that as she was spinning she would sing a Gaelic hymn, one of Peter
> Grant's.... We were a singing family, and one of my treasured memories
> was my father singing at family worship, and mother and children
> joining in. On week days we were given scope to enjoy ourselves like the
> other children, but Sabbath was a different day. All the chores had to be
> done on Saturday. Everyone had to be so still on Sabbath!...My father
> went to church in the morning with the older children, and my mother
> in the evening. While she was in church, my father would sit in the house
> with us and ask us each a question from the Catechism. He would begin
> with Granny who was very old, but could still remember them. Then we
> had a singing session, and off to bed.[11]

These scenes were repeated in many godly homes of the period, where
family worship was observed, and daily life was carried out around the
Word of God. John Mackenzie, brought up in such circumstances himself,
was to preach the faith lovingly and faithfully to successive generations.
The references to singing are noteworthy, as he was also to be noted as a
gifted precentor and leader of the praise.

Mr Mackenzie's early working life took him to Glasgow, where he
became an apprentice carpenter. Working in the shipyards of the Clyde
meant not only that he was surrounded by men from all walks of life, and
from whom he learnt and observed much about human nature; it also meant
that he was in the company of many of his countrymen, for many young men
and women from Lewis found employment in Glasgow at that time. This
period of his life is marked however, by the fact that it was at this time the
Gospel took hold of him in a powerful and serious way, and he professed
faith in Christ.

When he was convicted of a call to study for the ministry, he began a
course of further education in Glasgow, as a preparation for entering the
Free Church College, where he matriculated in 1931. The College was
staffed by great men of renown under the principalship of John Macleod,
Professor of Apologetics. Mr Mackenzie was to have the greatest respect
and reverence for Principal Macleod, whose photograph hung on his wall
to the end of his life.

After being licensed by the Presbytery of Lewis in 1934, Mr Mackenzie
received a call from the congregation of Plockton and Kyle Free Church,
and was ordained there by the Presbytery of Lochcarron. In addition to the
responsibilities of the pastoral charge there, he was also Clerk to the
Presbytery for a time, and Interim-Moderator of Applecross. In appreciation of his ministry the congregation marked the tenth anniversary of his

ordination with a presentation. There are still some on the coasts of Wester Ross who remember his zealous and faithful ministry.

One of Mr Mackenzie's responsibilities during the war years was as chaplain to the Naval Detachment at Kyle. Some of the sermons recorded here in note form were first preached to the naval personnel, and show how he was able to speak to their situation, and draw illustrations from the situations of the men based at Kyle. The sermon on Luke 8:22-25 is a good example of this, as he draws on the experiences of the naval personnel to illustrate the feelings of the disciples in the storm at sea. The last sermon noted in this volume, on 1 John 1:5-7, is also of interest in this connection. It was preached in Plockton and Kyle on the last Sabbath of 1945, the year that marked the cessation of hostilities and brought the Second World War to an end. Mr Mackenzie expresses his hope that peace will restore to the nation a sense of God and righteousness, but he says that he is pessimistic in this regard. In these sentiments he was a true prophet; for the life of the nation in the half-century that has passed since 1945, a nation enjoying the peace of deliverance, has been moving steadily and increasingly further away from God, its deliverer.

It was shortly after being inducted to this charge that Mr Mackenzie married, on 3rd January 1935, Annie Maciver, the sister of Rev John Maciver. The wedding service, at which Mr Maciver was best man, took place in Inverness and was conducted by Rev K. Cameron, Inverness Free North. Mrs Mackenzie was to be a true help to her husband throughout his ministry. She was a quiet, unassuming woman, and bore all the hallmarks of a truly Christian lady.

Mrs Mackenzie's piety is as noteworthy an element of the story as the ministry of her husband. She was close to the Lord, and this is seen in a wonderful way with regard to her family. Being unable to have children naturally, she and her husband decided to adopt a child. This they did on the basis of the impression made upon Mrs Mackenzie by the words of Psalm 22:30-31: 'A seed shall serve him; it shall be accounted to the Lord for a generation. They shall come, and shall declare his righteousness unto a people that shall be born, and that he hath done this'. This daughter, Lily, named after Mrs Mackenzie's late sister, is the mother of the present writer. The prophetic import of the Word of God is a sign to us of the closeness to the Lord which characterised Mrs Mackenzie all her days. She was to outlive her husband by two years.

In June 1946 the Free Church congregation of Harris signed a call to Mr Mackenzie to be their minister. This led to his induction to that charge on the 28th of August that year. There he ministered for some twenty-two years, a faithful preacher of the Word in his own congregation, and a popular

Communion preacher throughout the Free Church of Scotland. His primary interest was the proclamation of the Word. The notes which follow bear ample testimony to this. Like his brother-in-law, Mr Maciver, who passed away during the closing months of Mr Mackenzie's Plockton ministry, the burden for souls was upon him. His trust was not in man-made methods (neither in the methods nor in the men), but in the sovereign God of grace. And like the dew distilling its life-giving moisture over the soil, so he distilled the pure and unadulterated doctrines of the Reformation for the whole of his ministry.

He was also a practical man. Two aspects of his work illustrate this. The first is that in 1952 he was successful in petitioning the General Assembly for permission to sell the old manse at Ferry Road Leverburgh in order that a better and more suitable property be obtained.

A second major adjustment in the congregation's life took place in 1959. Formerly, the congregation of Harris, along with the Uists and Barra, belonged to the Free Presbytery of Skye and Uist. This created its own difficulties; for example, Mr Mackenzie was unable to attend many meetings of the Presbytery. In 1959 he again petitioned the Assembly, this time in order that the oversight of the congregation might be transferred to the Presbytery of Lewis. The record of the Presbytery of Skye and Uist states that this had been requested 'after considerable hesitation, and that he was moved to take this action solely by the geographical position of Harris which made attendance at Presbytery meetings in Skye practically impossible, as nowadays there is no direct passenger link between Skye and Harris' [12]. Because of this re-arrangement, Mr Mackenzie found himself in the unusual position of having been a member of three Presbyteries[13] while holding only two pastoral charges.

As has already been stated, Mr Mackenzie's style of sermon preparation is different to that of Mr Maciver. The notes are very full, and very ordered. The handwriting is superb, and very small. This makes it at times difficult to read. The sentences are full, with the minimum of abbreviation. There are always headings, which are always apposite and relevant. In this sense the notes are more structured than those of Mr Maciver. Apart from a word or heading here and there, they are almost all written in English. All the notes had been carefully and systematically gathered together by Mr Mackenzie himself, and were gathered under the name of the biblical book from which texts were taken. Many of the sermons in Part 1, on the Person and Work of Christ, were gathered together under the title 'Action Sermons', that is, sermons preached on the Sabbath morning of the Communion Season in connection with the dispensing of the Sacrament of the Lord's Supper.

The fact that the notes were written in English ought to be qualified by the fact that Mr Mackenzie had an outstanding grasp of the Gaelic language. His attractiveness as a winsome Gospel preacher was partly due to the fact that he was in his natural element when preaching in Gaelic. As the tribute to him in the *Monthly Record of the Free Church of Scotland* stated, 'Few could equal him in felicity of expression in his native tongue'[14]. Warm in personality - a truly Christian gentleman - he brought that warmth into the pulpit with him; not, as in the case of some, in a way that minimised the seriousness of the issues with which he dealt, but in a way that highlighted the sincerity with which these Gospel issues were presented.

One of the outstanding experiences of Mr Mackenzie's ministry was a preaching trip to Vancouver in the late Summer and Autumn of 1963. There he met many of Lewis descent and origin, and made many friends as he ministered the word. There is in our possession a tape-recording of Gaelic hymn-singing that was made while Mr Mackenzie was in Vancouver. At one point he sings a Gaelic composition, the last verse of which says:

O mo chairdean, 's mo luchd-duthcha
Ann am Vancouver tha 'n sas,
'Se mo ghuidhe is mo dhurachd
gun duin sibh ri Criosd gun dail.

(O my friends and fellow-countrymen,
Living and working in Vancouver,
My heart's desire and longing
Is that you will close with Christ now.)

As this last verse is sung, just before the tape-recorder is switched off, Mr Mackenzie is heard to say, 'Agus 'se sud mo ghuidhse dhuibh cuideachd' (and that is my desire for you too). In thus giving his seal to the sentiments of the composer, Mr Mackenzie expresses the great aim of his preaching - that men will discover Christ as Saviour and Lord.

Mr Mackenzie's worsening health led to his retirement from the pastoral ministry in 1968, when he and his wife became resident in Stornoway. When health permitted, he often preached in Stornoway. But gradually, though the spirit was willing to go on preaching, the flesh became weaker. Eventually he became a patient at the then County Hospital in Stornoway, where he died on the 18th of March 1981. He passed away as a service of worship was being conducted near his hospital bed.

The Theology
What message did Mr Maciver and Mr Mackenzie have for the world of their day? What did they preach? The sermon notes show that their message

was shaped by the Word of God. There was no intrusion of thought onto the interpretation of Scripture. The concern of both men was to let the Bible speak for itself. In their own individual ways, the Word was applied, carefully and lovingly, to the needs of the moment. What is relevant to the naval personnel at Kyle in manner and style is not put in exactly the same dress for the 'revival personnel' of Carloway. Yet the same doctrines of grace permeate all.

Central is the Person of Jesus, and His finished Work on Calvary. That is why this one doctrine is given prominence in this short collection. The sermons highlight the redemptive nature of the work of Christ, in His obedience to the Father and as the surety of His People. This word *surety*, much neglected in contemporary preaching, is at the heart of the Gospel. It signifies Christ standing as the representative of His people, bearing their sins in His exposure to the wrath of God on their behalf. He suffers vicariously; He suffers for them. This is the whole basis of salvation. There is no room for human boasting. Christ is all. Sovereign grace must do the saving, if sinners are to be saved at all.

This work stands against the backdrop of man thoroughly ruined by sin. He is undone, polluted, dead. There is no vestige of spiritual life in him. Nor is there a vestige of the divine image left in him[15]. He requires spiritual life. This is imparted to the objects of God's redeeming love and particular election. Only those foreordained to life will be brought to life. Otherwise the work of salvation will not be of grace, and God, in the typical Arminian school of thought, is made to run behind the preacher. But in the sermons which follow, it is clear that salvation depends on God's running *before* the preacher, on His love seeking out its objects, and bringing them into new life through the proclamation of truth accompanied by the power of heaven.

But none of this diminishes the responsibility of men. They must respond to a free offer of salvation. Neither preacher on the following pages was of the hyper-Calvinistic school, which diminishes the responsibility of man. They were both thoroughly Reformed, thoroughly Calvinistic, thoroughly biblical. If man is lost, it is by reason of his own neglect of such great salvation; if man is saved, it is only by divine grace. The offer of the Gospel is made to all; it is freely rejected by some, and freely accepted by others. The free rejection is the result of a will and nature vitiated and compromised by sin; the free acceptance of the gospel offer is the result of a will renewed and restored by the Holy Spirit in regeneration.

The lot of the renewed man in this world will not be an easy one. To live in obedience to Christ will mean suffering from Satan, sin and self. But grace will persevere and God will triumph. And at length there is the blessed hope – the believer can say, 'In my flesh I shall see God'.

This is the teaching of the following pages. And although some of these notes were first written some sixty or more years ago, their message is as vital today as it ever was. The reading, selecting and typing of the following notes has been a labour, but a labour of love. In seeking to place this stone on the cairn of these men of God, it is my desire that the Lord will enable us to remain faithful in our day to the doctrines of sovereign grace, so that in remembering those who spoke unto us, from our earliest days, the Word of God, we will indeed 'follow their faith'.

Iain D. Campbell
Snizort Free Church Manse
Skeabost Bridge
Isle of Skye

August, 1995

NOTES

1. Lloyd-Jones, D.M., *Preaching and Preachers*, London: Hodder and Stoughton, 1982, p299
2. Dabney, R.L. *Lectures on Sacred Rhetoric*, Edinburgh: Banner of Truth, 1979, p330
3. Dabney, ibid.
4. Edwards, Jonathan, 'Thoughts on the Revival in New England', in *Works*, Vol. 1, London 1840, pp374-5
5. Rev Murdo Macaulay alludes to this in his book *The Burning Bush in Carloway* (1984), where he says that from 1934 'The work of the Holy Spirit was from then on progressing steadily but calmly, with little external excitement, except the eager attention with which young and old *listened to the preaching of the word*' (italics mine), page 32. Again in the same volume he notes that 'the whole counsel of God was delivered from the pulpits, and no attempt was made to cater for the stirred feelings of the listeners'.
6. *Stornoway Gazette*, 1946
7. *Stornoway Gazette*, 1946
8. *The Burning Bush in Carloway*, p. 32
9. Murray, I.H. *(ed.), The Diary of Kenneth Macrae*, Edinburgh: Banner of Truth, 1980, p361
10. Amongst my grandfather's notes were the outlines of the speech he made at the wedding of Rev A.M. and Mrs Macleod, Kinloch. In the speech he states 'To me it seems a solemn and strange providence to see my niece succeeding my sister and her aunt as the lady of the Kinloch manse'.

11. From an article entitled 'Reflections' in *The Instructor*: the youth magazine of the Free Church of Scotland Volume 86:3 (December 1990), page 60.

12. Minutes of the Free Presbytery of Skye and Uist dated 30th April 1959. The geographical isolation is highlighted by the fact that Mr Mackenzie was chosen Moderator at this meeting of Presbytery in the following terms: *In view of the fact that members from the Outer Isles were present* (i.e. Mr Mackenzie and Rev James Morrison, North Uist and Grimsay), *it was moved and unanimously agreed to that Mr John Mackenzie, minister at Leverburgh, Harris, be elected Moderator*. The implication is that members from the 'Outer Isles'   w e r e not normally present.   This meeting was rather a special occasion as the Presbytery had met on this date to induct Rev Norman Morrison, brother of Rev James Morrison, North Uist, as minister of Duirinish Free Church.

13. That is, the Presbyteries of Lochcarron, Skye and Uist, and Lewis, the three member Presbyteries of the Synod of Glenelg (now the Western Synod).

14. *The Monthly Record of the Free Church of Scotland*, May 1981, page 117. The tribute was written by Rev John N. Macleod.

15. This is a much controverted point among evangelicals, but was certainly the view of Mr Maciver - see, for example, sermon number 70 on John 8:42.

JOHN MACIVER

on

THE PERSON AND WORK OF CHRIST

1. THE COVENANT MEDIATOR

He asked life of thee, and thou gavest it him,
even length of days for ever and ever (Psalm 21:4).

In the second Psalm, Christ is commissioned by the Father to ask of Him, and that He would give Him the heathen and the ends of the earth for His inheritance. Here Christ (because the words of the text indubitably apply to a greater than David), asks life of the Father as the surety of His people. But the request here appears as if the party asking were asking entirely for Himself, and for no other person. But this only manifests the closeness of the connection between Christ as surety, and His people. He made their interests His own so much, that when He asks for them, He is asking for Himself. He entered into the engagements of the divine Covenant in their behalf, and its terms depended entirely upon Him as the surety of the elect to fulfil.

From the point of view of law, He stands in this relation to the church. He claims for them, not in their name, but in His own name. He does this legally as arising from the terms of the Eternal Covenant. Christ is here pleading for the church, basing that pleading upon the work which He Himself finished. His finished work is constantly asking. It stands eternally before the Father.

This is not the work of a mere pleader. The motive which impelled Him to ask life for them is love. Here we have law and love. Love is the cause from which the framing of the Eternal Covenant emanated. But that Covenant would have to be based on law, because God though He was love had also eternal wisdom, and the honour of Jehovah had to be preserved in the salvation which was to be prepared for those who had fallen away from God. The Law of the divine Covenant was a law whereby sinners were to be redeemed from the penalty and curse of a broken law, the moral law, and yet the honour of the moral law was vindicated by this contrivance of divine love and wisdom.

What does He want? Life – that is what He pleads for. For whom does He plead this life? For His seed. What life does He ask? First, in a spiritual sense - He asks for restoration to the possession of that life which Adam lost in Eden. Man died spiritually, and this brought in natural death, and eternal death.

What is the procuring cause of the restoration of that life? Christ's death. How does the sinner receive it? Eternal death is taken away; there is deliverance from the curse. There is justification and adoption; there is deliverance from the dominion and control of sin. Spiritual death is taken away. There is regeneration and sanctification. Death is due to sin. All death, including natural death, is the result of sin. All the pain, the mourning in the world. Natural death must take its course, but it is to be conquered after it has had the semblance of victory. The souls of believers are at their death made perfect in holiness. The bodies of believers shall rise again. How glorious their victory will be. A pattern of the victory of Christ over the grave.

Do you need life? You certainly need it. Life in all its forms. Do you want it? If you do, you will get it. Why? Because Christ asked it for you before you asked it for yourself. There is no use coming to ask for life if Christ had not asked it of the Father before you asked for it. But if you want it, it is a sign that Christ has asked it for you.

He has received 'length of days'; endless life. This was not said to Adam, but it is said to the second Adam. Adam got a life which depended on himself to keep. You received a life which is in Christ's keeping, and you cannot lose it. It is a life that will win your heart for the Lord, and causes you to do your utmost yourself to retain and not lose it. Grace spurs you on to obedience, because grace is love, and its nature is to delight in God and do the Lord's will.

2. THE FAIR ONE

Thou art fairer than the children of men: grace is poured into thy lips; therefore God hath blessed thee for ever (Psalm 45:2).

The reason for which the beauty of Christ moves the hearts of those who have seen His beauty, is that the things which make Him fair tie Him to them as their Redeemer. His kindness, in this sense, is wonderfully fair. There were many things which caused Him unspeakable pain that needed to be taken out of the way, in order that He might bestow that kindness upon them. And this sheds light for them on the loveliness of His loving-kindness, that it caused Him, in order that He might be a Saviour for them, to go through pain and agony on their behalf.

There are many things which men regard as beautiful, which have no bearing on that salvation: the beauty of creation, the beauty of pictures that can be seen in Glasgow's Art Galleries. The sense in which these are beautiful has no bearing on the well-being of the individual in any way.

Natural men, who have no grace, can see loveliness in many things, yet see no loveliness in Christ. Although man sinned, sin did not rob him of the ability to see beauty in many things; but he lost the ability to see beauty in God, in Christ. Men can be filled with a sense of the loveliness of natural things, without the thought of God breaking in on them at all. But there is a loveliness in Christ which goes far higher than any of these things.

But while Christ remains un-lovely in the sight of men, nothing is so unattractive as Him; and when He comes to be seen in His loveliness, nothing, no-one is then so beautiful as Christ. Someone said, 'When I do hear the name of Jesus, it is as if a cage of singing birds was let loose in my heart'. Samuel Rutherford said, 'O fair sun and fair moon and fair stars and fair flowers and fair roses and fair lilies, but O ten thousand times fairer Lord Jesus. Alas, I have wronged Him in making the comparison this way. O black sun and moon, but O fair Lord Jesus! O black flowers and black lilies and roses, but O fair, fair, ever fair, Lord Jesus. O black Heaven, but O fair Christ; O black angels, but O surpassingly fair Lord Jesus!' Those who see no beauty in Him, hate Him. He said, 'They have hated me without a cause'. The man who hates Christ is unfortunate indeed!

There was a particular reason why the church found Him fair - grace was poured in His lips. The verse does not say that grace was poured into His heart, but into His lips. There was grace in His heart too; John says 'We beheld His glory, the glory as of the only begotten of the Father, full of grace and truth'. The kindness of God is extended to man in an effectual way, in that He deals with man's sin against God. It takes in God's especial goodness in sending His Son to save His people. And it also takes in His application of that work effectually in the souls of lost sinners.

Christ speaks to the hearts of His people, and makes them willing in a day of His power, through His Word in the Gospel. It is through the power of the truth that Christ influences for good each soul redeemed by Him. The grace that was poured into Christ's lips was for His people.

He received these people from the Father, in order that He might give them eternal life. The dead hear the voice of the Son of God in the Gospel, and He brings them spiritually to life. It is from Him that the Holy Spirit comes to them. And it is through His word that He deals with them, taking the things of Christ and revealing these things to them. There is power in the words of His lips that satisfies their soul. 'No man ever spake like this man'.

He said, 'Follow me', and those who received grace to do this, saw His loveliness, saw His Person, full of grace and truth. God has blessed Him for ever. He has blessed Him as the Mediator of His people - all of them, for ever. Christ petitions the Father on their behalf, and also speaks to them - 'I have prayed for thee, and when thou art converted, strengthen thy brethren'.

Christ in this psalm is portrayed for us as the bridegroom of the church. And it is as the church's bridegroom, as the one who is fairer than the children of men, that He chose for Himself the most un-lovely creatures that ever were. In Ezekiel 16:6, He tells His church that she was polluted and naked, unattractive and ugly. And she did not understand Him until He married her. In her sight, therefore, He is lovely because He pitied her in her ugliness. And He did this in order to make her beautiful - we have that in this same psalm. Christ's image is on His bride; she is beautiful. And she will be more beautiful still, because that image will one day be perfected. He married her because He is so lovely Himself, when she was covered in sackcloth and ashes, and did it to make her lovely.

But we also see Him here as a King. The psalmist speaks of what concerns the king. He purchased them as a King - they were under the just judgement of God. He acted as King as the Mediator of the covenant for all who were saved in the Old Testament. He fulfilled the office of a King before He undertook the office of a priest. Yet it was on the basis of the work He would undertake as a priest that the office of His kingship is secured.

Again, as King, he wishes His bride to be subject to Him. His law is in her heart. And she sees His loveliness there too - 'O, how I love thy law,' she says. Her love for Him, and the measure of loveliness she finds in Him, accords with the measure of pleasure she finds in His law, and the measure of her obedience to it.

3. THE SINLESS SACRIFICE

...he is brought as a lamb to the slaughter, and as a sheep before her shearers is dumb, so he openeth not his mouth (Isaiah 53:7).

These words are mentioned in Acts 8:32ff as being blessed to the conversion of the eunuch from Ethiopia. We are told there that Philip preached Jesus from these very words. And this shows us clearly that Jesus is in these words, for preaching, as we are trying to do. We will take the language just as it is here; there is a slight change in the wording in Acts (though no change in the sense).

A lamb speaks of innocence, inoffensiveness, pleasantness. Christ is all of these things. He is the God-man, the one who committed no sin. He had no sin in Him, and committed no sin. When we condemn sin, we are condemning what is in ourselves. And we ought to condemn it and decry it. If we do not do this until we are perfectly holy, we will never do it in this world. Those people who hate sin, and endeavour to avoid it, although they are not holy themselves, ought to condemn sin and decry it.

For this reason, Christ was a suitable Surety, because He was sinless. Sinlessness itself would not be sufficient. The elect angels were sinless, but they were not equal to this task and office. But Christ being the sinless Son of God, and co-equal with God, was suitable and able to perform the great service which the Surety or High Priest was requested to render.

He was inoffensive. He gave offence, but there was nothing in Him which should give offence. He did not offend God or the holy angels. The fact that He gave offence to men shows the depraved and evil nature of men. Holiness and purity and love was offensive to them when Christ gave them offence. It was from this that their hatred arose. It was from this it arose that they finally put him to death. What was not offensiveness in itself provoked them against Him, so that they sought His life and ultimately put the just One to death. He was condemned to death as an evildoer. This was indeed the most terrible miscarriage of justice that ever occurred in this world.

Here is an affecting scene. The innocent condemned to death as being guilty of it and deserving of it. That is an affecting incident in regard to any person in whose case it might occur. But it is more aggravating and heinous when it is meted out to the Son of God. The sufferings of Christ show both man's devilry and God's love.

This is why we should dwell upon the sufferings of Christ, and this is how it repays our trying to view them from every possible angle, because the more its lurid aspects are brought home to us, the more we realize the diabolical nature of sin and its enmity against God. In the light of this again, the wonder of the eternal love of God comes into view.

A desire to dwell upon torture and suffering apart from this consideration is not commendable. But there is nothing so efficacious to bring the sinfulness of sin before us, and as a consequence to bring the love of God into relief, like earnest and serious concentration and meditation on the sufferings of Christ. There was no other way in which the evil of sin, from which God mercifully purposed to save man, and God's love to man, could be seen so impressively and gloriously, than by His own act.

There is weakness here. The lamb is capable of being slaughtered. Christ became weak in several senses when He became man, in sinless weakness. There is the weakness of His infancy and boyhood. He was like any other child. He thirsted and hungered. He groaned in His spirit. This weakness made Him capable of dying. This made Him capable of being slaughtered. He could not die as God. The Redeemer of God's elect people would need to be a Redeemer that could die for them. Christ, as God only, could not die. He needed to die. Christ did this. He partook of man's nature.

He was crucified in weakness; yet 'the weakness of God is stronger than men'.

But the Lamb had to be healthy, without any blemish. Christ was healthy. At the age of thirty-three He was healthy in body. He was also healthy in soul. He was holy and innocent, yet among sinners. He was so healthy in His soul that He could love and keep, as a man, God's holy law. He was like the Pascal Lamb, without blemish. Christ is the Passover Lamb who was sacrificed for us. In this sense, His 'health' is His holiness, that made it possible for Him to give complete obedience on our behalf.

He was indeed a lamb for the slaughter. Abraham was asked to give up his son - to sacrifice and slaughter him. He was kept from doing so. But Christ was not prevented from being slaughtered. This was the command that God gave to the sword of His justice - 'Awake, O sword, against my shepherd'. This is the lamb for the sacrifice, for the atoning sacrifice, the 'propitiation for our sins', as John puts it. Again, he says 'Behold the Lamb of God, who takes away the sins of the world'.

He is like a sheep dumb before His shearers, and did not open his mouth. They tried to shear Him. They accused Him of belonging to Beelzebub, the Prince of devils. They sheared Him by stripping His clothes from Him. They cast lots for His vestures, and shared His clothes among them.

They stripped Him of all His rights in this world. They did not want Him to have anything in this world. They did not want to give Him anything in this world, except two pieces of wood on which they could hang Him. And they only did that in order that it might be a means of getting rid of Him out of the world. All this He endured without complaint. He did not open His mouth. The reason was that He was suffering under the justice of God, and endured it without opening His mouth to complain.

He had opened His mouth before, but now He is dumb. Now God has numbered Him among the transgressors. He is there not only at the hands of men, but at the hands of God. God has given Him over to death by way of imputing to Him the sins of His people; sinners have done so by way of regarding Him as a guilty sinner. And that is where the world still puts Him.

But in the final judgement, He will find them guilty, unless they find mercy before then. This, then, is the Christ that Philip preached to the Ethiopian eunuch.

4. THE REST-GIVER

Come unto me, all ye that labour and are heavy laden, and I will give you rest. Take my yoke upon you, and learn of me; for I am meek and lowly in heart: and ye shall find rest unto your souls. For my yoke is easy, and my burden is light (Matthew 11:28-30).

Let us notice those to whom this call is given: people who labour and are heavy laden.

There are many different kinds of labour. There is labour in this world, under the Providence of God. People may become very tired and troubled in this kind of labour, working hard for themselves and for others. Life can be one prolonged trouble, difficult and dark, like a cloudy, dark day with no sunshine. Many people spend their lives under this very kind of cloud. Such people labour and are heavy laden. Christ wants them to come to Himself. He alone can give strength according to the needs and trials of the day, and can give a back for the burden.

But there is another kind of labour, which afflicts many people, who have a special kind of burden. They are labouring for atonement, for peace between themselves and God, labouring to have their guilt removed from them, and using the wrong methods for obtaining this. They are labouring for rest (the very thing Christ promises), but in the wrong way. Christ says 'Come to me for this'. Maybe they think they are coming to Him; perhaps they are wanting the rest that He is offering, but are trying to obtain it by fulfilling certain duties. But no-one can ever find true rest that way. Only by coming to Christ can they find rest, directly to Christ Himself.

Many people put their own good efforts between themselves and Christ - their prayers, their grief over sin, their confession. They lay these things down as the price by which they will purchase rest. But Christ says, 'Come to me. Come to me with your prayers, with confession, with your grief; don't put your confidence in any of these things, but only in me. I give rest and I give it freely, without price. Come, buy wine and milk without money and without price.'

The promise is that you shall find rest. You will obtain the rest of forgiveness, the rest of atonement and fellowship with God. You will obtain the rest of knowing that you have finally reached something that is solid, that has a strong foundation, something that will endure for all eternity, an unmoving foundation for your soul. A man living in the world and for the world is like a man walking through quicksand. His feet suddenly give way, one, then the other, and there is no bottom, no foundation meeting them. Such men do not know anything about themselves. But Christ is calling them, in order that they might obtain rest in Himself.

It was in order to obtain rest for sinners that Christ came into the world. Christ and Him crucified - that is the sinner's resting-place. Believers trust to the death of Christ, and they never found such a warm, comfortable and restful bed. They lie on His death. If people can, they want to avoid death; the common experience of men is that they feel terror in the face of death; but as they look at the death of Christ, believers feel no such terror. It draws the hearts and spirits of God's people to itself.

The death of Christ is like a Museum - a place of wonders, where you see all that the loving heart of God prepared for the needs of a lost world. You will see the wisdom, and justice, and love, and power, and holiness of God in that death. His death is like a loom, in which these attributes weave a glorious robe which will cover sinners. As soon as that robe is put on them they become saints. For them there is no more condemnation. That means that there is rest for them at the death of Christ.

Christ was inviting men to come to Him that they might find rest; and the things He promised them were ready for Him to bestow, for He was to be crucified at Calvary. His death, you might say, is a factory, where the rest for His people is manufactured.

Needy souls can find a bed of rest in the death of Christ, the likes of which they can find nowhere else. Souls can lie stretched out on that bed and find rest, freedom, kindness and love.

Then there are people who bear the heavy burden of difficult trials and troubles. Like the church in the Song, they must sit under His shadow with great delight in order to find His fruit sweet to their taste. They must sit under the shade of all that He is - the perfect Saviour of God's people, the Saviour of sinners. 'Come unto me,' He says - believe in me.

He adds - 'Bear my yoke'. What is this yoke? It means that you will be ruled by the law of Jesus Christ, by His commandments as your rule and way of life in this world. 'Learn of me' - follow the example that I have left you, and desire to be ruled by the Holy Spirit.

5. THE EVER-PRESENT FRIEND

...lo, I am with you alway, even unto the end of the world. Amen
(Matthew 28:20).

Since the resurrection, the disciples have become accustomed to several appearances and disappearances of Christ. They were becoming accustomed to doing without His bodily presence until He was finally raised up to Heaven. They realised that He was parting from them. And He instructed them in the duties which they were to conduct after He was gone, and gave them a glorious promise to strengthen them in the performance of this duty: 'I am with you...'

He was not parting from them after all. There was no separation. When a person disappears bodily, there is separation. There may be memories of the past, and hopes for the future, but there is separation. In this case there was none. Christ was leaving His Holy Spirit with them. He had promised them this before His death.

Who was to be with them? The Son of God, the Omnipotent and Almighty, the all-wise, all-loving One, the Great Defender of His people. Did their lives constantly manifest that he continued with them? Did they not suffer after He was gone? What torture and pain they endured! But His presence with them was evidenced by their success in making disciples. That was the great mark by which it was known to them that He was always with them. In His Holy Spirit, He was omnipresent, and He was to be with them constantly. They were to instruct their new disciples as Christ had instructed themselves. They had commands to observe.

There is a promise here of the perpetual continuance of the truth and its power among men. But their lives were constantly in jeopardy, and were lives filled with pain and trial. The power of evil and Satan, the prince of this World, were arrayed against them. And in this world, these are a source of endless trouble. But the Lord was to be with them. These were to be the Lord's means by which He would show His presence with them. That was to be their cup, and He was with them in their drinking of it.

The Gospel, and the power of it, were to continue. Christ was here saying, 'I am the King of the Universe. I shall take care of you. You need have no fear.' They suffered, but they also succeeded, because He was with them. The Lord was there, in their success and in their suffering. Their suffering ministered their success to them. It was a factor in their success. It would have been a test to them to believe this. God was with them Himself. God in Christ had been with them, had suffered and rose again. He would be with them still.

Christ was here prophesying the growth of His Kingdom. John had said, 'He must increase, but I must decrease'. Christ would increase. He did not lose hope on account of the smallness of their number - He was going to keep them in His own hand. Satan and his temptations would come their way as Christ saw fit. The growth of His Kingdom depended on His own sovereignty as King. He would give them life to begin with, and would renew that life in them, and would watch over them.

This presence would abide, He says, until the end of the world. This has not occurred yet. The promise still stands - to the end of the world. The promise to the disciples extends to those who would come after them. The power of God is to be at work in the world until the end of the world.

6. THE DELIGHT OF THE FATHER

This is my beloved Son: hear him (Mark 9:7).

This whole incident shows us that Christ had not, and would not after this, speak a word in the world to any man, without the seal and fellowship of His Father. He says, 'As the Father gave me commandment, even so I do'. 'All things that I have heard of my Father, I have made known unto you.'

Everything that Christ said was worthy of being listened to. He was different to all other men who have ever been in the world, and He never spoke a word that was not deserving of attention. Surely He never spoke a word in the world that was not needful or profitable in some way. There are men who have spoken things worthy of attention regarding learning or education, but they might also have spoken many unprofitable and useless things too. Christ was not like this. He deserved that men should listen to His voice, and they would profit from doing what He said.

It is the Father's purpose in sending His Son into the world that men should listen to Him. Christ came into the world with a teaching given Him by the Father. And the Father makes this clear here. He witnesses to this at this very particular time, and on this solemn occasion.

'Hear him', is the Father's command. What are the aspects of Christ's Person by which He has a right to speak to men and women? He speaks to them as a Judge, as a law-giver. He will be the Judge on the last, great day. He speaks to them as a Redeemer. He speaks as Prophet, Priest and King.

The Father desires that men should listen to His Son. Men give glory to Christ when they listen to Him. The Father has respect to the glory that men will give to Christ as a result of listening to Him. In hearing Him, sinners come to listen to the Christ who is precious in the eyes of His Father.

If a man thinks little of listening to the voice of Christ, it is because He has little respect either to Christ, or to the Father. The Father wants people to listen to Christ. The person who does not do this is showing contempt and despite towards the Father and towards Christ. On the other hand, if men do listen to Christ, they are fulfilling the will of the Father. And because Christ is so great and so respectable in His sight, the Father loves greatly all those who listen to the Son, and who do it with delight and with reverence.

Let us listen to His voice before we listen to any other. We ought to attend to what He says before we attend to what anyone else says. Christ speaks to every man personally. He says 'Let the wicked forsake His way.' What does the world say? What do the flesh and the devil say? They speak differently. But Christ warns; Christ promises. He warns of the penalty of law-breaking, and promises forgiveness to those who seek Him.

Let us listen to the hope He sets before us. Do not listen to doubts and fears. Listen to Christ. It is the Father who witnesses so gloriously about His Son. His Father loves Him with great love - greater than we can understand - and His Father has great power. No change has ever occurred to that love or that power; but despite the great love and the great power of the Father, He left His Son in this world, to undergo the troubles of life, the wrath of God, the cursed death of the cross and the power of death for a time. Why? Because in this way, the purpose of God regarding the salvation of men reached fulfilment, in the death of Christ. It was not any lack of love or power on the part of the Father that left Him in agony in this world, but because Christ had become a partaker of our nature. It is this Christ we must listen to.

This is the great question - to whom will men listen? To whom do you wish to listen? If we love Christ, we will listen to Him. This is the great question - do we love Him? 'If ye love me, keep my commandments'.

7. THE SON OF MAN

For even the Son of man came not to be ministered unto, but to minister, and to give his life a ransom for many
(Mark 10:45).

Christ delighted in the designation 'Son of Man'. He had such a great love for mankind. He took delight in the humanity of which He partook. His love to mankind was to intense that to assume their nature for their redemption gave Him inexpressible joy. In becoming the Son of Man He manifested the glory of Divine love and grace. These were exhibited through the channel of His humanity.

Christ's humanity did and endured everything in accordance with the divine will, that is, the Father's will. To that humanity belonged the hands that were nailed to the cross for His people, and the side which was pierced, and out of which issued blood and water.

Christ was not ashamed of His humanity, however much He suffered, however much He was hated, abused and abased, however much He was despised. He never repented having assumed man's nature. By so doing, He rescued God's loved ones from the curse, and from damnation.

Every man is welcome to Him who is the Son of man. This was the Father's name for Him. He was not disowning His relationship with the Father when He called Himself the Son of man. God calls Him His servant in the Old Testament (Isaiah 42). He became God's servant by assuming our humanity.

Christ was like a surgeon in a hospital. There is a medical superintendent, and the staff serve him, but the doctors also serve the patients. The doctor is a servant in a two-fold sense. So Christ is the Father's servant, and He became a servant to lost souls who needed His ministering to redeem them from the curse. He was ministering to the thief on the cross when they were both nearing death. Christ on the cross was breaking the bonds of guilt and condemnation and sin. What may we not expect of Him when He is not on the cross, when He did that when He was on the cross?

When He came to minister to men, that involved His being ministered to in His infancy by His mother. He was ministered to Himself by angels, but He would not leave sinners to depend on the ministry of angels. No; there was a place where none could go but Himself. In some critical cases the doctor is in attendance himself all the time. He will not entrust the patient to anyone. Only Christ could minister to men in a specially important sense. But angels also minister to them. Yes; Christ is the ladder which Jacob saw in the dream. It connected earth and Heaven. What a wonderful servant. Christ acts the role of doctor and nurse. He was tired as men's servant, so tired that an angel was sent from Heaven to strengthen Him in the Garden of Gethsemane.

The wonder of His condescension, His humility, His love. What mother could ignore the need of her beloved child? Christ could not keep back from giving His life for His people. Imagine a father seeing his child in peril of drowning. Could he restrain himself? No. He would throw himself into the raging sea to take hold of his loved one. That was the kind of love Christ had. A love that faced the billows of shame, contempt and persecution which poured over Him, along with the hiding of God's face. The wonder of it!

8. THE CRUCIFIED SAVIOUR

He saved others; himself he cannot save (Mark 15:31).

As we contemplate these words, we must understand that they are words of scorn and mockery, hurled at Christ by the chief priests and scribes, while He hanged on the cross.

These words are both true and false at the same time. We know clearly that the words were false, that He could in fact have saved Himself; but we also know clearly why He did not save Himself. The reason was that He did not try to save Himself, nor did He wish to save Himself. He Himself made that clear. If He had wished to look after Himself, if that had been His desire, He would never have been on the cross. He might easily have avoided it. Who could have taken Him there against His will? Those who stood around Him there were the very ones He Himself had created, whose life was in His hands, and who were being kept by Him at the very moment at which they were giving Him over to be crucified. And did He not say when they came saying that they sought Jesus of Nazareth, 'It is I'? Even the natural man, who recognises truth in the Gospel, recognises that what the chief priests and scribes said was a lie.

But the very words themselves shed light on their unbelief and their wicked purpose against Christ. They are truly wearisome in their mocking. Although they said 'He saved others', what they meant was that He had saved none. They meant, 'Here is one who maintains, or about whom it is said, that He saved others. But in order to see how wrong and untrue their words were, look now at Him on the cross, and remember that if He could save others, as they say, wouldn't He save Himself from this terrible agony in which He finds Himself?' After all, they argued, who would He save before saving Himself?

The chief priests and scribes had pleasure in doing this at the cross of Christ; His death seemed to prove to them that He had not done the miracles which He performed. Had He done them, He could have performed another - to rescue Himself from the hands of those who crucified Him. Or, if He did do them, it must have been by the power of Satan. Had they not maintained that it was through Beelzebub the Prince of devils that He had put out devils? But in fact all the miracles had a bearing on His being put to death, without any effort on His own part to save Himself from death. His death, in fact, was the greatest miracle of all, and was the fountain of every miracle that took place, or that has taken place since.

Yet, despite this, they spoke the truth in spite of themselves, and in ignorance. Glorious truth was folded in their words. It was indeed true that

He could not save Himself, having saved others. The language which they used to mock Him, contained within itself the meaning and true cause of His death, and even the very heart of the Gospel. Apart from this death, He could not have saved those who had already been saved by Him. Not only so, but His purpose in dying was that thousands more would be redeemed by Him from their sins. He was called Jesus for this very reason, that He would die for sinners, in the hands of wicked men who led Him about as if He were so weak, unable to look after Himself at all.

He could not save Himself. The arrangement of the Eternal Covenant could not allow Him to save Himself. For it was a covenant of blood, that would be fulfilled in the shedding of the blood of the Son of God. It was a Covenant of Redemption, and was therefore a covenant of blood.

Since He had saved others, and intended to save more, holiness would not allow Him to save Himself. It was necessary that He should die to protect the holiness of God. Justice could not allow Him to save Himself, because the covenant arrangement was for sinners. The law of God could not allow it. The law required satisfaction for the penalty of those who were to be redeemed by His death. Justice would see to that. Nor would love allow Him to save Himself. It was love that was the cause of His death.

Christ has a Kingdom, given Him by the Father. The throne of that Kingdom over which He rules is His cross. The cross was the instrument employed by His enemies to disgrace Him. But this cross is the instrument of liberation. Here there is light, light on sin, on divine holiness, on God's mercy, and at the same time God's hatred of sin. This cross was the cost of that forgiveness.

9. THE DESERVING MASTER

And whosoever doth not bear his cross and come
after me cannot be my disciple (Luke 14:27).

There is a connection between the cross mentioned in this verse, and the cross of Christ. It does not mean a literal, wooden cross, however, although that is what the cross of Christ was.

The cross of Christ can be viewed from several angles. It was constructed of wood in such a way that Christ could be crucified on it. There is another view of the cross, however; Paul says, 'God forbid that I should glory, save in the cross of the Lord Jesus Christ'. It is the glory of the Christian. But Paul did not mean that he was glorying in a wooden cross.

What he glories in is the loveliness of the work of Christ on His cross, the worth of His sufferings as He bore the sins of lost souls. Paul views the cross from another angle too, when he says to the Colossians that Christ was 'crucified among them', meaning that the preaching of the cross made known to them the Christ that had been crucified.

What do we understand by referring to the cross of Christ? We understand several things. We refer to the sufferings, which He bore willingly. These sufferings could not be inflicted simply by the will of this world. He bore them as an act of His own will. We also understand that He had a specific purpose in dying, and in being crucified. It was not without an end in view that He underwent the pain of the cross. We mean too the depth of His sufferings - from the outward appearance, He seemed to die without hope. And that was part of His suffering. Again, we mean that behind all that He did when He bled, suffered and died, was His perfect love for His imperfect church. The stream of all His sufferings issued from His love.

Christ suffered for a reason. He had a specific end in view when He went to the cross. Had He not determined to fulfil that purpose, He would never have suffered in this way, nor would there have been any reasons for His suffering. Nor was He under any compulsion to suffer and fulfil that purpose, but the compulsion of His own free will drove Him to it.

But there were sufferings, and nothing in these sufferings but the suffering of self-denial. He denied Himself, and He did it because of love. We know that He loved the Father; but He Himself makes it very clear that the reason He goes to Calvary to suffer is because of His love for men. There was a covenant arrangement between Himself and His Father regarding the sufferings He would have to endure in connection with the salvation of sinners. These sufferings were in that covenant, just as surely as the object which the sufferings would secure. It was out of love to the Father and to those whom the Father gave to Him in the Eternal Covenant that Christ came to be a Surety, the one who would fulfil the requirements of the Covenant; and out of love for the lost He suffered.

Not all suffering is endured willingly by men. Many suffer with no sense of thankfulness. But Christ endured the heavy sufferings of the cross out of His own free-will, by denying Himself for the glory of God. He was lifted on to the cross, and suffered there for us. Had He loved His own comforts more than sinners, He would never have suffered on their behalf, and they could then never have been saved. But He Himself tells us that He did not do His own will, that is, the will that would have enjoyed comfort and freedom from pain. Christ had two wills; one that grew in love to God and men and which compelled Him to the sufferings of death, and one that would have wanted to avoid pain. He did not do His own will.

And that is where we must begin in taking up our own cross to follow Him. We too must crucify our own will, and take Christ as our example in so doing. Christ took up a cross in a way that none other could. That was the cross on which the salvation of the whole world depended. No other cross would suffice but this cross, and for this particular purpose.

There is, therefore, a close connection between Christ's cross and that of His people. It was a thing full of blessing for Christ to take up His cross, and it will be full of blessing for them also. We might even say that the cross of the church is the child of the cross of Christ. Christ denied Himself. So how are they to do this?

His people will be persecuted. They must endure this cross, and not throw it off; despite the persecution they must remain close to Christ and not forsake Him. That is what it means to bear the cross after Him, to bear a cross that is related to His. It means not to be ashamed of Christ or His glory, not to wish to be free from trouble, pain of body or weariness of mind. Where there is a true and faithful witness to God in the heart of men, such men will find themselves in danger. These are men and women who are made partakers of the sufferings of Christ. They are worthy who keep the flag of truth flying on the side of Christ, in the greatest of dangers. They bare their cross and follow Him. Only love can be behind this. They love Him, and take up their cross, because He first loved them, and took up His.

Of course, there is a sense in which believers have a cross that Christ himself did not carry. Paul says 'If ye through the Spirit mortify the deeds of the body you shall live'. He himself said that he was keeping his body in submission. Christ had no sin, although He had great sufferings. Only through the power of His cross can His people take up theirs, and battle with sin. Only in His cross can they have strength and power to bare their own.

To take up our cross is to crucify the spirit of vanity, to deny ourselves the practices of our corrupt sinful nature in every way. In this sense Christ did not bare this cross. But in following Him, His people must. We will have joy and happiness in our lives, but if we are the people of God, we will have suffering too.

10. THE GRACIOUS HOST

This man receiveth sinners and eateth with them (Luke 15:2).

This was the complaint of the Pharisees against Christ. Their complaint was no lie, but the truth - a blessed truth that was used as an accusation and a lawsuit against Christ. Indeed, the words of the Pharisees spoke as much of themselves as of Christ.

Who were the people that Christ was taking to Himself, and with whom He was eating? They were publicans and sinners. They were particularly evil people, who, because of their crimes were despised, men like Matthew and Zacchaeus. But these 'sinners' had more regard for the teaching of Christ than the self-righteous Pharisees. They recognised that they were not good people. Christ met their needs as sinners. Christ Himself said that He had not come to call the righteous, but sinners to repentance. The Son of Man came to seek and to save that which was lost.

'Sinners' is a word that well describes men. Every kind of sin is implied in the word. And Christ in the Gospel is speaking to all kinds, and calling all kinds, those whose sins were very public, and those who outwardly did not appear to be sinful. Christ calls the very worst that there are, just as freely and with the same interest as He has in those that are morally upright.

Some people think that they have sinned so greatly that they are beyond the reach of mercy. No one has any reason to think that way. No man or woman has any reason for thinking that they are too bad for Christ.

Let us consider two kinds of 'sinner':

(1) The person who thinks that he is worthy of acceptance with Christ, or who thinks that he can make himself worthy. This shows a particular opinion regarding the way Christ saves people. They think that he accepts sinners when they make themselves decent. But Christ never received sinners who came to Him with that outlook. Undoubtedly there is a reformation on the part of those who come to Him, but not so as they can put any confidence in it. That kind of thought is a sinful thought, and a sinful thought condemns a man just as surely as a sinful act.

It is a great sin to believe that a man can make himself worthy of being received by Christ. If that were possible, then Christ would not be a Saviour. This kind of opinion detracts from His glory as a Saviour. The man who thinks like this considers his own efforts as having as much merit and worth as the death of Christ, and, indeed, is saying that there was no need for the death of Christ. See how sinful this is! You say that you will receive forgiveness from Christ as a result of your own reformation of life, whereas Christ says that there is no forgiveness to be obtained anywhere but through His own death. This is making God a liar, making Christ a liar, and robbing Him of His glory. This is exceedingly sinful.

Therefore, supposing you were to confess all your sins, supposing you would cry over them and forsake them publicly, thinking that you could obtain mercy on the basis of these things, then you would be keeping from Christ the praise and reputation of being a Saviour. None of these things will do you any good. Only by trusting in Christ, as the one who died to secure forgiveness for you, by leaving yourself in His hands can you be saved.

(2) Again, there are those who think that there is not enough efficacy in the death of Christ to secure the forgiveness of our sins. This opinion too dishonours both the Father and the Son. We glorify the Father and Christ when we believe that there is this efficacy in the death of the Saviour. When we think that there is not, we are diminishing from the value of His death. The greatest sin is the sin of imagining that God cannot forgive our sins this way, however great they might be. The efficacy of the death of Christ is boundless.

And likewise, the boundless efficacy of His death is our authority to state the boundless capacity of Jehovah for forgiving sins. If there is such an effectiveness in the death of Christ, it is because the will of the Father and the will of Christ is to forgive the greatest sins. He is plenteous in mercy.

Christ intercedes for every soul who comes to the Father by Him. What greater assurance need we have that forgiveness is available for us? He is able to save all those who come to God by Him, and to save them completely. The reason is that He lives for ever, and lives to intercede for those sinners He receives.

11. THE REDEEMER OF ISRAEL

But we trusted that it had been he which
should have redeemed Israel... (Luke 24:21).

The language employed here by the two on the way to Emmaus reveals firstly the hope and expectation which they had at one time; and secondly the situation in which they find themselves now, as if they had learned that they had been deceived in respect of that expectation. And indeed, the same two were living proof that Christ had in fact redeemed Israel; the longing and the disappointment in their heart were proof of this. Although their hope had been lost and buried, they did not pass by the opportunity of meditating on it and speaking about it. There was a strong attachment that bound their heart to the hope of which they spoke, although in their minds they had made a wrong picture of it, and although Christ had been crucified and buried as an evildoer. His redeeming work nonetheless was to be seen in the longings and in the mourning they were expressing on this particular day.

No-one but a redeemed soul could be so wounded regarding the matter which caused them sadness. Those who crucified Him had crucified Him between two thieves. But He who had been crucified in the midst of thieves was in the midst of some who watched Him there, who loved Him with all their hearts; the crucifixion which gave such joy to others caused them much sorrow and sadness. As they watched Christ, they saw reproach, contempt, mocking and ridicule heaped on Him. They were not able to comprehend His eternal glory, nor the eternal redemption for them which was contained within the ugly act performed on Christ. There was no act ever performed on earth that was so wicked. It was murder. But that was all they saw.

Now the end result has spoiled the expectation they once had. There had been events in Christ's history before the cross which had given them the hope and expectation they had - the miracles which He had performed again and again, in raising the dead to life, healing the sick, for example. But more than this, they had had a personal acquaintance with Christ, which had brought home to them how natural for Him the performance of these miracles was. Had not this given them great hope? His great power had given them the expectation that He would redeem Israel.

Indeed, but if He appeared powerful in the performance of these miracles, the end of the matter seemed so weak and impotent that it seemed to belie every glorious miracle they had witnessed. And yet this was the thing about His death: that no act of greater glory had ever occurred before, or been performed by Him before now. For in His death there was a display of the glory of the Father, and the amazing grace of God, although His death was, from another point of view, the most atrocious act ever carried out. These wonderful acts they had seen were miraculous; but there is nothing more miraculous than that wicked men are permitted to carry out this violence against Him. Was it not amazing grace that now kept back His eternal power from destroying His accusers and those who reproached and crucified Him? This was grace indeed, a miracle in which there mingled love, patience and eternal power.

That was what the Emmaus disciples had failed to see on the cross. As the Psalmist puts it, 'And I will say to God my Rock, "Why me forgettest thou so? Why for my foes oppression thus mourning do I go?"'. They thought they had been forgotten by Christ, because He had been unable to save Himself. And they reckoned that since He had been unable to save Himself, He was powerless to save Israel.

But now we can see something else here. The hope which they expressed ought not to have been entertained by them at all. It grew out of ignorance. They were expecting a temporal, political redemption. And since they had this expectation, it would have been strengthened by the work of God's grace in their hearts. For it was true that He was going to redeem Israel. But the Israel He would redeem was the Israel of the covenant, redeemed through His power as the King of Grace. His intention was to establish His Kingdom on earth, by gathering a people who would be prepared by Him for the Kingdom of Glory.

But they had no right to imagine that Christ was going to be Israel's earthly king in order to free them from Rome's lordly yoke. That was an expectation without foundation. But as a token of the fact that their souls had been brought to life, and regenerated, some spiritual reality was mixed in with the hope that they did entertain. That side of the matter was from God, and it was to be fulfilled. They took with them a fleshly idea of that hope, and they were deceived in thinking that they could. That was why their hope was dashed, and they were left in despair.

In the same way, believers sometimes tend to bind fleshly expectations to spiritual hope, even though the hope that they have is indeed a spiritual one. For example, perhaps they make a picture of what the way will be like for them from the time they are converted until they reach Glory. They think they will have the same great liberty all the way. They imagine that it will only get better, and that they themselves will get better, and will reach Heaven without any temptation or difficulty to trouble them. This is nothing but a fleshly view of spiritual hope. God has indeed promised them an end to trouble and temptation, but only in the world above; these believers thought they would enjoy this here, in this world. The disciples journeying to Emmaus had seen His great miracles; they thought He would work one for earthly Israel. The flesh can build a fleshly hope on anything.

But alas! for these two, there is the discovery that they have been deceived altogether. Now their trouble begins. And for those who are believers, and who told themselves that the trouble would not come, now it most assuredly comes, and indeed, they are the very ones that need it. Now the freedom is gone, the feeling that things would only get better and better. Waywardness and corruption are lifting their head in their souls. The past miracles are not now so prominent in their thinking. They are saying - 'We thought he would redeem Israel. Were we deceived?'

Through losing their first expectations, and through discovering that they had deceived themselves, they are filled with sadness and pain. They perhaps are concerned that everything they thought they had is gone - that they were deceived about everything. Natural reason would tell them that they were indeed so deceived. But at the same time they cannot but think about the preciousness of what Christ did promise, and, if an opportunity arises, they will not be long in talking with others about it, just like the two on the way to Emmaus.

Their conversation drew the Lord to them. The breaking of their expectations drew them to think about Christ. When that happened, they had fellowship with Him. They had been disappointed, but they were in communion with Christ. It was not long before Christ drew near and showed them that the love and wisdom of the Father were in all these things that had happened to them. Now they discovered the true meaning of their hope, in the very thing they had regarded as hope-less.

12. THE LAMB OF GOD

Behold the Lamb of God, which taketh away the sin of the world
(John 1.29).

These words were spoken by John on one occasion as He saw Jesus approaching. His language speaks of a glorious, deep purpose concerning Christ and His coming into the world, a purpose which was revealed to John and which he saw it as his duty to proclaim. We can notice the name given to Christ, the service which He would perform, and the advice John gives to those who hear him.

(1) *Christ is called the Lamb of God*
John calls this Lamb *God's* lamb. This lamb belonged to God, set apart, chosen, prepared and commissioned by God for this end, that He might take away the sin of the world. It was God who had made a lamb of Him. It was because He had assumed human nature that this name was given to Him; and Christ Himself says 'A body hast thou prepared me'. This takes in His human nature, body and soul.

In setting Christ apart to be a Lamb in this way, we see both the activity of the Father and of the Son in connection with the salvation of men. The Father arranged that the Son should take away the sin of the world; He had His own part in the matter. In our nature, the Son says that He came from the Father, and says 'I have glorified thee on earth, I have finished the work which thou gavest me to do'. Father and Son have made a careful, gracious undertaking in respect of the salvation of men. No such arrangement was made to save the angels which fell. They were no more deserving of being left in their fallen condition than the fallen race of Adam. But 'he took not on him the nature of angels'. It is surely a cause of wonder to the unfallen angels that God revealed His sovereignty in this way, and indeed to the fallen angels too. It is certainly a cause of thanksgiving to men.

(2) *The Service to be performed by Him*

He was God's Lamb, then. And the designation itself tells us what He was going to do, and what was going to happen to Him in taking away the sin of the world. John had clearly been given light on the fact that Christ was going to be offered as a sacrifice.

Under the Old Testament, a lamb was sacrificed morning and night. This was an illustration of the sacrifice that this lamb was to offer on Calvary. From the beginning of the world Christ had been sacrificed by way of type, or illustration; and in the evening of the world He is to be sacrificed personally. In another sense, the Passover Lamb was sacrificed at a specific time for the salvation of men.

John's language teaches that there was no efficacy in these other sacrifices of themselves; they were only types. Many needed to be told this, and to believe it, for many were taking refuge in fulfilling their duties, and in offering the required sacrifices, without going any further than this. They needed to learn that Christ was the one sacrifice by which the Father could perfect for ever those who would be sanctified.

John received light on these matters. He saw that Christ needed to be put to death as an atoning sacrifice. 'Christ our Passover is sacrificed for us'. John saw Christ as the sacrifice before He was crucified, something that the disciples would not understand for another three years. And although He told them this Himself at that time, they still did not believe.

The name 'Lamb' takes in many things - inoffensiveness, innocence, meekness, patience, attractiveness, incorruption, health. It also implies weakness. A lamb has many enemies. 'He was brought as a lamb to the slaughter'. No other lamb was sacrificed willingly. But Christ knew He was to be sacrificed, and went meekly and patiently to it. Why? So that He could take away the sin of the world. Other lambs were tied unwillingly to the altar. But the world and Hell could not tie Christ unwillingly. Of His own free will He gave them leave, so that He could offer the sacrifice.

Christ and the Father permitted them to bind Him. While they heaped the most terrible sufferings on Him, the Father did not stop them; but at the same time He heaped His own blessing on Christ, and afterwards came out against those who crucified Him. They were sinning against the Father, yet the Father permitted it. And not only did He permit it, in a deep sense He ordained it. Christ had been delivered 'by the determinate counsel and foreknowledge of God'.

A Lamb, as we said, has many enemies. Foxes and wolves will devour them. Christ compared His disciples to lambs in the midst of wolves. In the most especial sense, this was true of Himself personally. As the lamb of sacrifice, He was a lamb among wolves. In the hand of God, these wolves were the instruments of offering the sacrifice. The God who sent Him into the world knew that His holiness and faithfulness would attract to Himself such an enmity as would put Him to death. That was ordained of old, yet God was against those who commit that act. It was a dreadful act. No act ever occurred in the world that was so terrible as the death of Christ, but no act was ever more beneficial to that world.

He was weak. That weakness came on Him because He was made a Lamb. As God, He knew no weakness. What weakness came on Him? The weakness of being in a condition in which He could die. God cannot die. As God He could not die. And yet even in this condition He remained in possession of all His divine power at the same time.

Christ was like a lamb on the altar from birth to death. Every part of His life, from the manger to the cross, had its own part to play in His taking away the sin of the world. Who can truly understand what He accomplished? We run the risk of speaking about the work of Christ as if we understood all He did, as if we had it all on our fingertips; but we can be sure that this has an unfathomable depth which we cannot measure. Surely this is what will be revealed to saints in Glory! And surely they will understand clearly there why they understood so little on earth!

But however little you know, you need to know that it was because your sins were laid on Him that you are saved. As the apostle says, 'who himself bore our sins in his own body on the tree'. Perhaps it will be life and blessing to you to know how little you understand of it; yet although it has that depth, boys and girls can understand it in a way that will bring satisfaction and peace to their hearts, and a sense of the boundless preciousness of Christ.

He takes away the sin of the world. The sin of Jew and Gentile. This was another great meaning to John's words. The Jews thought that God's favour was confined to themselves. It was revealed to John that He is the Saviour of the world. Peter needed an effective vision to bring home to him that he had to go to Cornelius to tell him about the things of God, because Cornelius was a Gentile.

How did He take these sins away? By bearing them in His own body on the cross. And it is not 'who took away' or 'who will take away' but 'which taketh away'. The present tense, so that His work, the sacrifice of the lamb, can meet with every new sin. Those who repent for all their sins, and who know what they deserve, have assurance of what His sacrifice deserves, and that the guilt of every new sin is taken away. For this reason, those who trusted in Him before He died are saved; and so it will be until the very last sinner is saved at the end of the world.

(3) *John's counsel to men*

'Behold the Lamb.' Nothing else will do. The call is to every sinner to look to Him. No-one can say that he is not here. The call is 'Behold'; this shuts no-one out. You, with all your sins. With any sin. Your hope is in the Lamb of God.

13. THE GIFT TO THE WORLD

For God so loved the world that he gave his only-begotten Son, that whoso-
ever believeth on him should not perish, but have everlasting life
(John 3:16).

This is part of the conversation which Christ had with Nicodemus on this night during which Nicodemus came to Him. The work of Christ had obviously influenced the thinking of Nicodemus. According to the light and knowledge he had, he had reasoned that no-one could perform the miracles which Christ was performing unless God was with him. Yet at the same time, in his mind he was ignorant of Christ, although he showed him reverence as one who had the Lord with him. Christ upset every opinion Nicodemus had formed before this on how man can win the favour of God.

Christ brought two things to his attention. These were the work of regeneration IN the soul (that is, being born again), and the work of Christ Himself FOR the soul. And he also reminds him of the great reason, or fountain from which all this flows, that is, the love of God, the fruit of which was the giving of Christ that men might believe in Him.

Apart from the coming of Christ, there would be none in whom sinners could believe, and faith would be impossible; and although Christ did come, that of itself was not enough to work faith in the heart of sinners either, apart from the work of the Holy Spirit. Christ brings all of this before Nicodemus.

God loved the world. That love has been revealed in Christ's being given (in the sense employed by Christ in the text), and in the work of the Spirit; and these two things make up one thing, or produce one thing, that is, the giving of everlasting life to men. Before this, death was their portion. Nicodemus had not grasped this before. Nor had he grasped the fact of God's great love for the world.

By 'the world', Christ does not mean that everyone will be saved; because it is clear that not all will be saved. But the love of God is a love that reaches everyone who ever was, or will be, saved. Those who are saved are saved for no other reason, and by no other method, but through the love of God for them. He did not die to save those who will not be saved. Christ makes it clear that this salvation will not be the portion of all men; He says that on the day of judgement there will be goats on His left hand, and sheep on His right. There will be a division among men.

Nevertheless, God does have a love that reaches to all men in a common way, a love that is disposed to friendship, and that finds pleasure in the persons of men and women, a love in which God Himself takes delight. God is love. It was this love that gave Christ. Christ came to tell men about this love, to reveal it to them. He wishes men to understand this and to believe. In believing in Him they would come to believe in and know the love of God.

Christ did not come in order to move the Father's heart so that He would act towards men in a warmer way, but to tell them just how warm His heart was, and to tell them how powerful His love for them was. It was not a case of Christ's being warm-hearted, and the heart of the Father cold. Not at all. The Father, out of love, sends Christ, whom He loves, to the world. Christ wanted Nicodemus to know, as he wishes us to know, that the coming of Christ into the world is the witness to and the proof of God's love to a lost world.

If God had given the angels whom He loved for a lost world, it would have been an evidence of love; but not so convincing or overpowering or so impressive an evidence as when He gave His own beloved Son. If He had only to give Him in the sense of sending Him into the world, that would have meant much; if He had been an ambassador, whose lot during His sojourn in the world was to be one of ease and splendour, it would furnish such an incomprehensible evidence of love. But He gave Him, His only begotten Son, to suffering and pain, and torture and agony which are wholly indescribable. His was not a life of ease or splendour, but He was humiliated, He was mocked, He was scourged. He suffered, was humiliated, received unspeakable indignities from men. But in these, He was wounded for our transgressions and bruised for our iniquities.

It is when Christ is intelligently regarded as the crowning evidence of the Father's love that men believe upon Him. We must believe on Christ or perish. And to believe upon Him, we must first regard Him as the undeniable and marvellous evidence of the love of God the Father.

It is then we have eternal life. Life that will in this world bring us to hate the sin that we loved, and to love the Lord that we hated. That is how our hearts are when we come to know the Lord. The conditions and activities of men who are spiritually alive are diametrically opposed to what they are when they are dead. In death there is the absence of what there is in life. Life is ours by virtue of the sentence of death being raised off us, and that life in our souls makes us believe in God, delight in Him, and entertain the hope that we will live with Him in His immediate presence for all eternity.

14. THE GOOD SHEPHERD

I am the good shepherd, and know my sheep, and am known of mine
(John 10:14).

Christ is here revealing Himself, and drawing attention to Himself as a Shepherd. On anyone else's lips, these words would be a sign of self-importance and pride, but on the lips of Christ they are words full of blessing and loving-kindness. For these words tell us precisely what Christ is; not only as a self-expression of His own glory, but He speaks them in order that needy sinners might be encouraged to come to Him, since there is none other suitable for them but Christ Himself. He reveals the glory of His work because He is a merciful Saviour, and because that revelation is a means of drawing needy sinners to Him.

He says, 'I am the good shepherd'. What He has declared in the previous verse sheds light on this and demonstrates it. Others do not care for the sheep. But the good shepherd cares enough to lay down His life for them.

This fact showed a strong attachment and loving bond between the shepherd and His flock. Not every flock requires that the shepherd lays down his life for them, but this flock requires Christ to do precisely this on their behalf. Nor could He be a shepherd for them, unless He undertook to do this. It is in dying for them, in laying down His life for them, that shows that He really is a good shepherd. This is what strikes us, that we see the wonderful love of this shepherd for His flock, when it is true of Him that He died on their behalf.

His love makes Him a good shepherd. He was willing to die for His sheep, and this was necessary in order that they might be saved. David was a shepherd, and a good, faithful shepherd at that. He showed that by the language he used when facing Goliath, and declared that God had saved him from the paw of the lion and from the paw of the bear when he fought with these animals in protecting his sheep. But had the lion or the bear killed him, he could not have protected the flock in his care. David was able to protect his sheep by remaining alive himself, not by dying. Had he died, the sheep he was protecting would themselves also have died. But Christ protects His flock by dying for them. So He was a good shepherd by loving them so much that He died on their behalf.

He was also a good shepherd by His suitability as a shepherd through His death. That death was of such worthiness and merit, that He became a good shepherd for them by reason of it. Someone can love another without being able to help that person in difficulty. Parents can see their children die, and sometimes dying in very tragic circumstances. The sadness of the event flows from the love that they had for them; yet despite the intensity of their love they can do nothing to prevent the death, or bring their child back to life. They had so much love for their child that, if they possessed the world they would gladly part with it in order to save their young ones, but they are helpless.

But when Christ went to die for the flock, He died for them with love far greater than the love that any parent ever had for their child. But in addition, He had power along with the love, and that power reached them through the merit and efficacy of His death. That power is glorious, for it finds its mode of working for the salvation of God's people in the death of Christ.

Christ showed obedience to God in His life, and He bore the penalty of the guilt of the sins of His people in His death. He died in order to take away the guilt of the flock. Did He not say, 'I have power to lay down my life, and I have power to take it again; this commandment I have received of my Father'.

Christ is a good shepherd in every sense. He gives life to the flock which was given to Him in the Eternal Covenant. He received them from the Father in order that He might give them life. He knows them. He knows them as the constituency which he received in the Covenant in order to die on their behalf. They are engraven upon the palms of His hands. There is not one of them at any moment outside the gaze of His watchful eye. Perhaps He allowed them to go astray until they were completely devoid of hope in themselves. But even then He knows them, and watches them. He calls to them: 'Return to me, ye backsliding children, for I am your husband, saith the Lord'. He restores our soul, and makes us walk in the paths of righteousness.

Sometimes He needs to use dogs, like any shepherd. He uses troubles, temptations, hard Providences, to bring them back to Himself. He shows them how much He cares for them, and loves them with an everlasting love. He knows them as a people who have given their hearts to Him, and who want now to be devoted and dedicated to Him. That is what they wish above all else.

15. THE FINISHED WORK

It is finished (John 19:30).

What were the feelings behind this utterance, and by what were they prompted? They were the utterance of love experiencing relief from sorrow, and a consciousness of having fulfilled a purpose which was incomprehensibly dear to the heart of Christ. He had undertaken a task whose accomplishment was to achieve an object, which was inestimably precious to Him. The task was an infinitely hard one. But now it was finished. His heart had been set lovingly and resolutely on it.

Cannot we regard this utterance as an expression of gratitude to the Father, who had sustained Christ? Thank God it is finished. And the finishing of it embodies the fulfilment of God's will in respect of atonement being made by the Son, so that the Father's pleasure in regard to the salvation of men could be executed. The Father had supported and upheld Him in all His trials and sorrows, and the Father had proved faithful and capable of sustaining Him to the end. There is here a consciousness of relief that nothing went amiss, and that the necessity of His sufferings and hard toil had forever passed away. There was victory all along the lines of battle.

The work was finished in a way which was of eternal value and significance. It was, so to speak, to have eternal repercussions. Counting on His work was the salvation of sinners by the Father. He had finished a work whose value and efficacy could never be undone. A work which was to remain enduring. To the Father His loving and zealous obedience to the law of His mediatorial office was infinitely dear. It was an utterance which indicated how dear the salvation of sinful wretches was to Him. The satisfaction He had in being now assured that their salvation was now inevitably certain. He has expressed that assurance in the words 'I, if I be lifted up from the earth, will draw all men unto me'.

Christ had such pleasure in the glorious effects of His finished work that He now spoke out 'It is finished'. He had such felicitous and heart-satisfying gratification as made Him speak it out openly. Only a thing which had the profoundest significance for Christ could make Him speak out like this. But this finishing meant as much to the Father as to Christ Himself; and it meant as much to the world which the Father and Himself loved, that He had, as it were, to speak openly thus as He did.

There was affirmation implied in these words that the power of devils and awful men in their opposition to Him and in their malice against Him had failed. By His overruling of their enmity and cruel, heartless treatment of Him, they all conjoined to achieve His redeeming purpose, by which the Father was glorified and sinners were saved.

Christ spoke these words in the moment of His deepest and profoundest misery. It was so comforting to Him. He was to be soon out of the painful state of service in which He had been before. There was no further necessity for this trying and painful service. Suffering or death was not to exact any further toll from Him. He was free from sorrow any more, whilst He enjoyed the consciousness of having glorified the Father and wrought eternal deliverance for men.

Christ did not regard His sufferings as a misfortune to Him, but as the greatest occasion of His joy. It was by them that He glorified the Father and procured all the benefits of salvation for sinners. Therefore He rejoiced in His sufferings. He did not regard His sufferings as a disgrace to Him. Now the prince of the world was to be cast out. He was not sorry that He had gone through it.

This is the language of victory. This is a declaration which has resulted from knowledge of being Victor in the struggle which so many thought was beyond hope. All was finished - Old Testament prophecy regarding Him was finished; the fulfilment of priests and sacrifices - all this was finished. The task given Him was completed. Nothing had miscarried. Everything had worked out in accord with the Eternal Plan, with the Eternal Purpose of God. As He had delight in undertaking the work, He expresses delight now that He has completed it.

16. THE APPROVED MAN

Jesus of Nazareth, a man approved of God among you by miracles and wonders and signs which God did by him in the midst of you all, as you yourselves also know (Acts 2:22).

'Jesus of Nazareth'. That was the name that was at one and the same time a name of blessing and a name of offence. But the man whose name it was was approved of God, as one who revealed God, and one who, in His work, revealed that He was the Son of God. The Father gave approval concerning Christ, and His testimony revealed that Christ was the Eternal Son of God.

How was He approved of God? How did God testify that Jesus was His Son? The answer is - 'by miracles and wonders and signs'. We could say that these are three names for the same thing. They all refer to the miracles, and the verse also says that it was by God that Jesus performed these. It is certainly true that there was power in these miracles. Nicodemus acknowledged that Christ only performed the miracles because God was with Him. As far as the power displayed in them was concerned, that power was strong enough to confirm in Nicodemus's heart the greatness of God. They brought the power of God home to him. He recognised that Christ could perform no miracle - not one - without displaying the greatness of God.

These miracles are called 'wonders'. It is a wonder to us to watch the sun rising, to be aware of the grass growing. But we lose sight of the wonder of it sometimes because it is such a usual thing, such a regular thing. What really amazes us is to see something out of the ordinary taking place, something, in a sense, 'unnatural'. In a sense it was unnatural to see five thousand people being fed with five loaves and two fishes, and twelve baskets of fragments left after this. What was all this designed to teach? Just what we have already noted - the greatness of God's power, teaching the wonder of what God was able to accomplish by His power and wisdom.

The miracles also conveyed instruction concerning God's loving, merciful, and compassionate way of working. The Bible permits us to believe that Christ performed many more miracles of healing than are recorded in the Scriptures. He was a healer. Again, we do not read of Him ever turning away any man who ever came to Him, or who was brought to Him by others. Some came to Him on their own behalf, and some on behalf of others, and never did He refuse to heal any of them. Surely this fact has much to teach us! What did this reveal but the love and kindness of His heart?

Again, we see that He wept along with the sisters at the grave of Lazarus. That showed a heart of love, of sympathy and compassion. He wept over Jerusalem after that again. He goes about doing good. But oh, how much of Hell there is in the heart of sinners! Is it not terrible that there is so much rebellion in man's heart against God? In Jesus Christ, there were signs revealed again and again of the love and mercy of God; but what did men care for that, when Jesus condemned their sins? The fact that He spoke out against their sins implanted in their hearts the poison of hatred and enmity towards Him, and they could find no relief from that hostility until they had put Him to death. He would not pass them by, but they passed Him by. Because of this, a huge, dark cloud of shame hangs over the whole world.

17. THE ONLY NAME

Neither is there salvation in any other; for there is none other name under heaven given among men, whereby we must be saved (Acts 4:12).

The end which the Word of God has in view is to correct men regarding the way by which they will be able to reach eternal salvation, or, in other words, what we call being saved. And if men do not find this out in this world, they have nothing. Despite the advancement they may make in other areas - and men may achieve much in this world - they might arrive at great honour, or reputation, or riches; but however well things may go for them in these areas, they are without the one thing needful.

Christ told Martha that one thing was needful, and that Mary had chosen the good part which could never be taken from her. Men can earn much, yet lose their soul. Indeed, the very things that men can achieve can be a means of them losing their soul. Christ asks, 'What shall it profit a man, though he gain the whole world and lose his soul?' What a great waste it is to live to the full in this world, and yet to die without having discovered salvation for your soul!

One hundred years after Mount Vesuvius erupted, men were discovering bodies in the houses that had been destroyed in the heat of its flames. These bodies were discovered in the same position as they had been in before the mountain erupted. There bodies had not changed one little bit since the time the city was destroyed. But shortly after the bodies were taken out of the charred remains, they crumbled away. This is how the happiness of the world will be when eternity breaks in on those who have lived for pleasure, fame and wealth. It will all crumble away. As long as everything goes well, the prospect of wealth and prosperity seems a good thing; but the end result will be that all these things will be destroyed. It gives little pleasure to hear this, or even to accept it. But it is the truth. And it was a truth that Christ lost no opportunity in telling to those around Him.

None of these things can save. There is salvation in none other. This implies that there is a salvation which will suit our needs, and that the only place where we can find it is in the Lord Jesus Christ. Only by faith in Christ can we lay hold of this salvation. Why is it emphasised here that this is the only way? Just because people are so ready to think that there are plenty other roads on which to obtain it. Peter was here speaking to people who had no faith at all in Christ, and who showed it by having crucified the Saviour. They were the builders in the preceding verse, who had rejected the stone which had become the chief cornerstone.

There is salvation in none other. This had reference to the healing of the lame man and who had been seeking alms at the gate of the Temple. It was also an accusation against the enemies of Christ, as if the apostle was saying, 'You have rejected Christ as the Saviour of a lost world. You crucified the Prince of Glory. You put to death the Son of God. But there is no Saviour beside Him.' It is as if he is saying, 'Yes, there is salvation in Him, even for you who crucified Him.' You would think that Peter could offer no word of mercy or hope at all to those whose hands were stained with the blood of Christ.

But Peter took courage. He knew he had authority to speak like this, to commend to them this salvation, and to invite them to come to it. Had not Christ Himself prayed 'Father, forgive them, for they know not what they do'. And the Father did that. Some of them were indeed saved, beyond any doubt. Had He not said to them to begin the preaching of the Gospel in Jerusalem? And now, in the streets of Jerusalem, Peter is lovingly and joyfully commending and offering God's salvation in Christ to them, and this despite how saddened he is that they put his beloved master to death. But Peter knows that this is the mind and will of Christ, that the salvation in Christ should be offered to all.

Peter had the right spirit, the right frame of mind. His heart reached out to them in pity and love. He longed for them to be saved by the same Lord who had saved his own soul. Peter had forsaken Him, and he stood in need of the mercy and forgiveness of God on that account. So when he tells them of the great sin they committed in crucifying Christ, he is not throwing this at them as one who was himself without spot or blemish in regard to Christ. No; he tells them so that they will come to inherit the forgiveness and kindness of God, just as he had himself.

This is salvation - the forgiveness of our sins. The renewal of our souls. It seems that the lame man was healed in a moment. He was completely cured. Christ is the great physician who healed him. And Christ is the only doctor that there is for the souls of men. In this world there are many doctors who can deal with physical ailments and problems. Some can be as good as others, or can be better than others. But as far as the souls of men are concerned, there is only one physician. This doctor is Christ, and His medicine is advertised in the gospel. It is advertised by those who preach the gospel. But they are not the doctors for all that. They do not want men to come to themselves, but only to Christ.

Paul said to one of his congregations, 'I have married you to one husband'. Those who preach, preach not themselves, but Christ Jesus the Lord, and themselves His servants for the sake of men and women. Those who preach the gospel invite men to come to Christ; and it is to Christ that men must come if they are to obtain this salvation. Not to a minister, or to a priest, but directly to Christ. Christ is the Saviour; he will heal the soul from the terrible sickness of sin.

The man was healed immediately. The people of God are not dealt with in this way - they are not made absolutely well in a moment, although health is now given to them. The poison of sin, this spiritual sickness, follows them as long as they are in this world. See, for example, when someone has an ulcer ready to be treated, the lance is applied to it, and the poison that was in the flesh pours out. But the ulcer that was treated does not heal immediately. The wound is kept open so that the poison can be removed altogether, and then it will heal.

That is how the soul of the believer is, all the time that he is in this world.

He becomes tired of the poison that affects his soul day after day after day. The soul of the believer is like a cabbage or potato field that you weed today, then tomorrow is full of weeds again. Once you have got rid of the weeds, you would not think that these enemies would raise their heads again. What do you do? You try to pull them out at the root, so that they will not rise again. But shortly afterwards you see the weeds breaking through the surface again, and you have to make another attempt at getting rid of them.

But the poison of sin in your heart keeps you looking to the blessed physician. That is the very thing that makes you desire Him and long for Him as long as you are in this world and conscious of your disease. And when the day comes when you will be healed completely, you will be eternally bound to that physician who made you whole.

Some people expect to find salvation in their own name - by their own efforts - and then they name the name of Christ along with this. But this cannot be. Others think that it was enough for them to have a godly mother or a godly father. But many children had godly parents who were themselves very wicked, and who died without showing any signs of having been saved. No; there is salvation in Christ alone, and in no other name.

18. THE UNSPARED ONE

He that spared not his own Son but delivered him up for us all, how shall he not with him also freely give us all things? (Romans 8:32).

This is the most important chapter in Romans. And I believe that this verse is the most important verse in the whole chapter. This verse talks of the Father and of the Son in a way that draws our mind to think of the love that the Father had for the Son. When the apostle uses this kind of language, and says 'He that spared not his own son', we feel that he ties to the words the thought 'Although the Father loved the Son in the way that He loved Him....', or at least that the apostle intended us to understand this.

At any rate, we understand from this that the apostle's words imply that it would not have been easy for the Father to give Christ as He gave Him because of the greatness of His love for the Son. In other words, that the Father would prefer not to have to give His Son whom He loved with an infinitely strong and eternal love. In other words, that for the Father to have given His Son was thus somewhat comparable to Abraham's feeling when having to offer Isaac.

From which it appears a legitimate inference that because of the Father's love for the Son, He would not have given Him if there were any other available means by which to achieve the end which the Father had in view, namely the salvation of His people.

If there were any other available means whereby to achieve that end, apart from the giving of the Son by the Father, then the Father might be charged with having done more than was really necessary to achieve His purpose in the salvation of His people. But can we think that God did more than was necessary to achieve that end? We can not. It appeared as if there were no other means, else the Lord would have used them to obviate His having to give His Son. Should there be other means apart from giving His Son that would suffice, the Father because of His love for the Son, would have used them. That deduction appears to be justified by the words of Christ Himself in John 3:16. He gave His only begotten son. The Apostle in our text seems to use words which lead to this conclusion, and therefore we can only stop to consider with grateful amazement the wonderful and inconceivable love which the Lord bore to His people when He would give His only-begotten for them, whom He thus loved.

Samuel Rutherford, having studied the matter carefully, once came to the conclusion that the Lord was not confined to Christ merely as the only possible means to achieve His purpose in the salvation of sinful men, having regard to the wisdom and almightiness of God. But after considering the matter after that again, he concluded that there could be no other way but by thus giving His Son.

What is implied by His giving His Son? When we were without strength, Christ died for the ungodly. The Father gave Him thus over to death for their sake. Since His children were partakers of flesh and blood, He Himself likewise partook of the same. Implied in the giving of the Father by the Son is that He prepared a body and soul for Him. And this was given to Him with the express purpose of His being given over to death. He could not be given over to death without being given a body and soul. But note too the kind of death that this was. There are some deaths that appear easy and free, without pain or trouble. But every sting that there ever was in death for His people was put into His death. His people have a glorious death. And the reason is that His death was accursed, one in which He Himself was made a curse. The curse of His people was imputed to Him, as the one who died in their place. His death was sour.

It was amazing love that the Lord gave His people, both from the consideration that He gave the Son of His love to such sufferings on their behalf, and also from the consideration of their very selves. The enormity of their guilt and degradation are measured by what He did for them, or had to do for them. For whom did the Father give Him? For those who were the devil's slaves, and this of their own free will. They hated God and rebelled against Him. 'For when we were enemies we were reconciled by the death of His Son.' If they were His friends would it be so remarkable?

The bond between Joseph and his brothers, despite what they had done to him, was quite amazing. Christ was joined to His people as their brother in the Eternal Covenant; and His love for them as their brother did not diminish, despite how terribly they dealt with Him. If Joseph had great love for his brothers, you find even greater in the Joseph of the New Testament. He is the elder brother, and He is not ashamed to call His people His brethren.

19. THE SUBJECT OF PREACHING

For we preach not ourselves, but Christ Jesus our Lord,
and ourselves your servants for Jesus' sake (2 Corinthians 4:5)

A man who is cured by a physician is obliged to relate his own experience of the physician's medical skill, when he is most earnest in proving the physician's medical ability. So believers make mention of their personal, gracious experience of God's salvation to extol the preciousness of Christ as Saviour. And when he is actuated by the proper spirit, he relates these experiences to magnify Christ's glory as a Saviour, and to attract men to Him.

Christ was hid from those who were lost, but that was no fault of Paul's, or of the other apostles. It was the fault of the darkness in themselves, resulting from their being blinded by the God of this world. It was Paul's purpose, to which he directed all his efforts, to preach the Gospel. That meant to reveal Christ to them, and if possible, to be used by the Lord as an instrument to reveal Him efficaciously to all who listened to Him.

Paul did not preach himself. He did not want attention to be directed towards himself. This folly on the part of people would break his heart, and he regarded it as a great peril that men should give themselves over to admire them, and fail to take saving notice of Jesus Christ. He only wanted to marry them to Christ.

No, the subject of his preaching is Christ Jesus the Lord, that is, the Messiah of the Old Testament. This is an official title. Christ existed always. He was the eternal God, who was God's surety and Mediator, appointed to be so from all eternity. But Jesus was His name as man: 'Thou shalt call his name Jesus, for he shall save his own people from their sins.'

Jesus was Christ's name in respect of His human nature, Christ was His name in respect of His divine nature and His human nature. The two were certainly to constitute Him as Messiah. That humanity which gave Him the name of Jesus existed in union with His divine nature.

He preached Him as the son of Mary according to the flesh. But foremost and essentially as the Son of God who partook of human nature so that He could die as the sinner's substitute. In doing so, Paul was acting in the capacity of a servant. He was doing service for sinners. He was proclaiming Christ for their good as the only Redeemer for sinful men. A servant is meant to be of profit to the party he serves. This is a service which is needed and needed greatly.

There were reasons which inspired Paul's service as a preacher of the Gospel. There was a realisation of their need from an experience of his own. His task consisted in introducing them to the most glorious of beings for their eternal well-being. A knowledge of the greatness of their misery inspired him with insuppressible earnestness to lead them to the Lord of salvation, that they might partake of the redemption which could be obtained only by exercising faith in Him. Paul's soul was overflowing with love and pity for immortal souls. All these motives of love and pity were the outcome of the power which divine grace operated in his soul. Their souls were dying of spiritual hunger, and it was none the less serious that they were unconscious of the fact. That was why he cried to them, 'We beseech you, in Christ's stead, be ye reconciled to God; for he made him who knew no sin to be sin for us, that we might be made the righteousness of God in him'.

And he mentions why he was a servant to them: it was 'for Jesus' sake'. He had a higher reason than even the desire for their good and their salvation: Jesus' sake. He has great love for Jesus. That was what impelled him, namely, the glory of Jesus; this even more than the salvation of men. That consideration had the priority by a long way. In other words, he wanted Jesus to have them for His sake, and not primarily for their own. He wanted them to be steadfast and loyal more for Jesus' sake than for their own sake. Much as he loved them and their welfare, he loved Jesus more.

It was Christ's right that He should have their allegiance, that He should have their hearts and the love of their hearts. They had no right to remain in a state of alienation, and while in that state they were giving eternal dishonour to the King of Kings and Lord of Lords. They were the King's enemies, in alliance with Satan. Paul was grieved by the disrespect shown to God, who was the sovereign of the universe. This feeling of the affront God constantly receives from sinners is uppermost in the mind of the true Christian, and takes precedence even over the pity and sympathy which the believer has for perishing sinners in their miserable plight. The two are there, but the first mentioned takes precedence because of how the claims of God are being trampled. This issues from the love of God and Christ, and from zeal to God. The glory of God comes first.

20. THE LOVER OF SOULS

The Son of God who loved me and gave himself for me
(Galatians 2:20)

The love of Christ is wonderful. It is about Christ that Paul is speaking here. The love of God and the love of Christ for sinners are co-equal. There is no difference between them. From one point of view, God's love for the angels is wonderful and glorious. But God's love for angels and God's love for sinners are not wonderful in the same sense. Christ is wonderful in every aspect of His being, and His love for sinners is more wonderful than anything else.

From one aspect, although God has wonderful love for the angels, that ought not to surprise us. They had no sin, and from this point of view it does not surprise us to discover that they were loved by Him. They were holy and upright in the state of holiness and glorious beauty in which God created them. For this reason, it would be amazing if He did not love them; although, as we said, His love for them is wonderful indeed. I do not believe that it is a wonder to the angels to be loved by God, because they would not expect anything else, since they are holy and innocent creatures, and they know it. They know that God's love for them is the outpouring of His own holy nature, and that the situation could not be otherwise. It would not be right for God not to love them. So, from these considerations, it is not surprising that God loves the holy angels; it would be amazing if He did not love them.

But the apostle uses the language of wonder and amazement, because what he is considering is a wonder to himself. What the apostle confesses here was indeed a cause of amazement to himself. Who could doubt that? Except, perhaps, men who were ignorant of God. What provoked this amazement was something in his heart, and as he speaks, he uses language that is language both of wonder and thankfulness.

The apostle certainly includes here the fact that he was loved by Christ from all eternity, and because of that love, Christ gave Himself for Paul at a particular point of time, in the fulness of time. And despite all of this, Paul was a sinful creature in the world, under the wrath of God, and in the position of being an enemy of God. God judges the heathen. And this is indeed a wonderful thing, that God loved him from all eternity, and yet he was in the position of being an unconverted man, who showed for many years that he was an enemy of God. God is the enemy of all who are outside of Christ, and He will be. His soul hates the wicked. Yet from all eternity He loves those who accept the Saviour. These are great depths.

They are sinful men and women, yet they are people loved by God, although God hates sin. He loves them in a sense apart from their sin, yet he loves them as guilty sinners, for that is what they are in His sight. As guilty sinners, they deserve only to be punished by Him. For when Paul says that Christ loved Him, he means that He loved him as a sinner, although He hates sin. Wherever you find a rational man or woman, with sin in their heart, then that person stands under the penalty of God, because sin and penalty are inextricably linked together. No sin was ever committed in this world that was not, or will not be, punished. The holy nature of God constrains Him to do this. Some say that God willed that sin should be punished, but, if He so wished, that He could choose not to punish man for his sin at all. I believe that this is wrong. God could not allow the sin of man to go unpunished. And this is what makes it so wonderful to discover that there is a love in the heart of God for guilty sinners, whom Christ loved from all eternity, and for whom He gave Himself.

21. THE RESIDENCE OF FULNESS

For it pleased the Father that in him should all fulness dwell
(Colossians 1:19).

What is this fulness? In Christ there dwelt all the fulness of the godhead bodily. That is a mystery so glorious, but which is beyond the reach of sinners to understand or reason out. This fulness of deity dwelt in Him as a child in the womb. That was God, the Eternal Son of God, as a babe, the Eternal God who had assumed human nature to Himself, and who, in assuming that nature to Himself was revealing Himself first as a human in infancy. By taking to Himself a true body and a reasonable soul, the Son of God has become man. Again, that divine fulness dwelt in Him bodily, in that His human nature was entirely holy and innocent.

But Christ has a fulness today that He did not have when He made man, our first covenant representative. He had no need of that fulness then, and nor did Adam and Eve, in their innocent condition, require that He should have this fulness. Nor would we require it, had our first parents continued in their state of innocence. At the same time, let us bear in mind, that there was no imperfection in Christ at that point; nor did there ever come a time when He was imperfect. There was no lack, no shortcoming in Christ at any time.

But the context makes it clear that there is a fulness which resides in Him as a result of His death and resurrection, the one who is the 'beginning, the firstborn from the dead', so that He would exercise sovereignty as Lord over all. It was because He died and rose again that He had this fulness. This was the Father's will. It was for this reason that the union took place between the Person of the Son of God, and our human nature: it was the Father's will that all fulness should dwell in Him. What did this fulness mean?

It meant that He took away everything that stood between Himself and sinners. All the sins and transgressions of men were removed by Him, in a way that accorded with the eternal glory of God, and His own saving favour was bestowed on His people. That is, the fulness that came to be His as Mediator, when the union between God and man was effected in His own Person. He came in order to effect the redemption of His people.

His original fulness (by which all the fulness of God dwells in Him) would not suffice for this task. And yet, apart from it, He could not be a Redeemer. He could not be a Redeemer with this fulness alone; but in order to equip Him to be the Mediator between God and man, humanity is assumed to His Person, and in our nature as the God-man, all the fulness required for our salvation dwells in Him.

He is a perfect child in the world. There was no child ever like Him. He was perfect; He was holy. He was circumcised in obedience to the law. He was baptised too. He was obedient to the will of God as the Surety of His people in respect of all these things. He suffered and died, the captain of the salvation of God's people made perfect through suffering. These sufferings were meritorious only because the fulness of deity and humanity are wedded together in His Person.

If you have a big town like Stornoway, it needs water. The loch contains plenty water, but Stornoway will not have it unless channels are made by the engineers and others. God has water for us, but that water cannot reach men and women without a channel. That was why the Father willed that all fulness should dwell in Him - that He should be a channel of the water of life to the souls of men, as the God-man, completing the work. He is the channel. He is the water of life.

That is what leaves Him now with all fulness dwelling in Him. Fulness of merit. Fulness of wisdom. Fulness of life, power and love. There is a perfect fulness of every blessing, as a result of His having assumed our nature and doing the work. All the fulness of the Spirit is there, to pour out on needy souls. The Holy Spirit is called 'the Spirit of Christ'. Christ was anointed without measure with the Holy Spirit, and the Spirit ministered to Him constantly. Now He pours out that Spirit on His church. He has a fulness of grace now, for all the needs of His people, and out of that fulness we have received. There is grace that enables us to seek Him at the beginning, and grace to go on believing in Him, and trusting in Him.

This fulness was not required for the creation of man at the outset. But it is required for our salvation. It is the fulness that He required in order to be a Redeemer for His own people. God will it – it pleased the Father. The fulness of His redemptive work existed from all eternity only in the purpose of the Father, until at last it came to be revealed in the flesh of the God-man in this world.

22. THE UNCHANGING ONE

Jesus Christ, the same yesterday, and today and forever
(Hebrews 13:8).

The immutability of Christ is stressed here as a ground of encouragement to the Hebrews to endure their trials for the faith. In a preceding passage, they were encouraged by having their attention directed to the sufferings of Christ Himself, of which their suffering was a pattern - they suffered as believers because of their relation to Him. And both Christ and His people suffered, as it were, for the same reason. The suffering of God's people for the faith in this world, from the persecution and enmity of men is the same as Christ's suffering, or, in other words, arose from the same cause. The opposition of the world was against God and was consequently against themselves because they were His representatives.

But their cause was well worth suffering for. Greater was He that was for them, than all they who were against them. He was faithful to them, and however much He permitted them to suffer for Him, it was only for the sake of trial so that they might be tested and come out as gold. It was to be a means of cleansing. They were to be purified as silver and gold. This implied their being purified in the fire of suffering, just as gold and silver were purified in the furnace.

This message, of course, was intended for a certain class of people who could appreciate it. They were a people with a past, a present and a future.

Their past was divided into two periods: the first part was that period when they were ignorant of Christ, and the later part of that past continuing into the present was a period in which they knew Christ. And they were now because of the past (yesterday) and the present (today), interested in this blessed message.

Now, how did they find Christ in that yesterday? Well, if they came to know Him, He must have conquered their hearts. They must have experienced the sweetness of His love. The wonderful glory of His blessed communion. All that they came to know of Him made them prepared to believe good things about Him. His immutability made his communion all the more glorious. The present may be dark, and part of the past even since coming to Christ was painful enough too; but yet parts of the past were sweet, and even allowing that the present might be dark, which it might well have been for the Hebrews, the sweetness would yet occur, and that in the future with greater glory.

A child does not suspect his mother's faithfulness, even if she is absent. When he cries for her, he claims the mother, and that is implied in the crying. She is his. Well, God and Christ are the believer's. The Bible says so. The believer does not have this instinct in himself, to tell him that Christ is his. This cannot but bring a measure of relief in the present, even though he cries for an absent Saviour, as the little child cries for his absent mother. If you're empty today, remember what He was some yesterday, and it was a blessed yesterday even if you have today to say that it has left you, and left you with a desire and a yearning after it. That may well give you confidence for the future. He is not fickle. Christ is the same.

This cannot be said of His people. He has the same love for His people constantly. They do not have the same love for Him. They sometimes have to mourn and lament when they consider how little love there is in their heart for Him; and although he chides their heart, they cannot get that comforting, felt love for him to waken in their heart as they would wish. At the same time, the feeling of sadness for how cold the feelings of heart towards Christ are can be a sure sign of saving grace. The love of the believer for Christ needs to be renewed constantly by the Spirit, just as the smith's furnace needs to be kept hot by the bellows. Apart from this work of the Spirit, that love would die completely.

But Christ stands in the same, constant relation towards that soul that He loves, and which is so often in darkness. He is just as loving toward that soul in the darkness as He was when there was a comforting experience of the love of the Lord. The love of Christ knows no change. Even in sorrow and trouble, that love knows no alteration. Indeed, God can use affliction and pain to bring home to us just how certain that love is.

Nor does that love change towards the Christian even when he is backsliding. Christ says to Peter, knowing that he would deny Him, 'I have prayed for thee that thy faith fail not'. He calls to His backsliding children to return to Him - this is because of love. He is unchangeable. He has the same Person, the same love, the same suitableness for the lost, the same matchless power over the heart. As far as His power to save is concerned, and His willingness to accept those who come to Him, He is the same - any sinner can come to Him. 'Him that cometh to me I will in no wise cast out'. He is the same in the riches of His grace - what He was to Manasseh, to Mary Magdalene, to the thief on the cross, to Saul of Tarsus, He still is. Many terrible and wicked men were saved, and will be, because He is the same.

He is the same in what pleases and in what angers Him. He is pleased with what glorifies Him, that is, when sinners come to Him for salvation, and who, having come to Him, bring forth fruit to His glory afterwards. 'He shall see of the travail of His soul and shall be satisfied'. At the same time, He is unchangeable regarding the things which cause Him grief. That is, sin, and especially the sins of His own people. Little wonder that their sins trouble themselves, when they have knowledge of how they trouble Him. He is the same in turning His children away from straying paths, and healing their backsliding. His is the same grace, the same mercy, and the same power to enable us to relinquish and forsake our sins.

He is the same in His treatment of men. The same in respect of His dwelling by faith in the soul. He still wins the hearts of men. He is faithful to them, notwithstanding their innumerable shortcomings. He was faithful to Abraham, to Isaac, to Jacob, to Joseph, to Daniel, to David, despite their grievous sins. The Lord would not give them up; He would not leave them nor forsake them.

In stressing Christ's immutability, the writer mentions the past, the present and the future. The first two are within the region of experience. But all are alike interested in the future, more so, in a sense, than in the present. Two great and solemn issues are to be decided in the future. The future embraces death and judgement, that is, our state throughout eternity. People are in a sense more interested in the future thus than in the past or present. What lends tremendous interest to the past, and especially the present is that our condition in the future through eternity is dependent on our position in the time now present. The future, having regard to these momentous issues, is more solemn than the past or the present. Even to the ungodly when he thinks of the future, it appears to him more solemn than the past or present. But the future is dependent on the present; the present decides definitely what the future will be. That is why we need Christ, who is the same, past, present and future.

23. THE OBJECT OF AFFECTION

...whom having not see, ye love (1 Peter 1:8).

Unlike those to whom he was writing, Peter did in fact see the Lord Jesus Christ. He regards it as quite remarkable that they should love Him without having seen Him. It is easier to love a seen person than an unseen person, so that the apostle John says 'If one does not love the brother which he has seen, how does he love the Lord whom he has not seen?'

Man's mind is so dependent upon material things, so that he finds it not easy to understand how the Lord's people can love a Saviour whom they have not seen. They don't believe it, and they don't believe that the Lord's people are honest who hold that they love Christ. How can they say they love Him when they have never had an opportunity to see Him personally or to have conversed with Him?

This is also the very reason why you find many thinking that they must see something. They cannot understand that it is possible to have a definite assurance of salvation apart from Christ making a visible revelation of Himself to man. This is the reasoning of ignorance, and results from lack of enlightenment. This teaches that we should not resort to pictures as an aid to help us to love Christ. We can see Him in a surer way than in pictures, that is, in His own truth. This teaches us also that we should not expect to see visions or any such thing. Archibald Cook remarks that he would prefer to have assurance of his salvation from the Word of God than though it were written across the firmament and across the earth that he was saved. Heaven and earth, he reminds us, will pass away; but the word of God remaineth for ever.

The Holy Spirit brings us face to face with Christ, a living Christ. He is in His word. He is a whole Christ, the Christ of God. The Christ who has made atonement. The Christ that we need as guilty, depraved sinners, to forgive and cleanse us. When that happens we see two things correctly in the truth - we see ourselves correctly, and we see Christ correctly. Without seeing ourselves, we cannot see Christ. As long as we cling to a belief in our own self-righteousness, we have not seen ourselves in the truth; and that failure to see ourselves in the truth will prevent us from seeing Christ. Let me see myself as the truth presents myself to me, and then I will realise my need. When I see my need, I will see Christ beside me in the Word as the one who provides for my need, just as Hagar saw the well when Ishmael was on the point of dying of thirst.

This, then is the cause of their love to Him - His love to them. On this depends their security. This love on His part for them begets love for Him in their hearts. How the word comes to life when the believer arrives at this stage! He reads the Bible with new eyes, with new understanding. The Word of God is alive. That person might have had a historical interest in the Bible; but now he has a spiritual interest in it. When you arrive by ferry to a town at night, you can only see in a limited measure the magnificence of the town, because it is in darkness. But what a difference it makes when the day comes, bringing light with it. The Word of truth brings that light. Do you think that if you had been on earth with Jesus it would have been easier for you to believe? Not at all. 'They have Moses and the prophets' - this is the sure word of our salvation.

Who put you into the truth? Christ Himself. You will see His beauty there as a physician. People naturally feel ill, but do not understand the nature of their disease. It is only the doctor who can tell. They appreciate the doctor's skill more especially if they believe that the fact of his understanding their trouble will enable him to administer a suitable remedy to them. His people have Christ as their physician. He comes to them. He knows their frame, their disease. He tells them their disease. His remedy is Himself. He is physician and remedy, without money and without price. He converses with them through the Holy Spirit, and manifests Himself in the testimony of the truth. What beauty, what glory there is in him as a physician!

They see His beauty as a Prophet, Priest and King. They see the beauty of His sufferings. How He died because of love for them. He would rather suffer for them than leave them to suffer eternally. All of this calls forth their love to Him, and although they do not see Him physically, they love Him dearly.

24. THE SUFFERING SUBSTITUTE

Forasmuch then as Christ hath suffered for us in the flesh,
arm yourselves likewise with the same mind:
for he that hath suffered in the flesh hath ceased from sin (1 Peter 4:1).

We are reminded here of what Christ did for us: He suffered and died. How wonderful that is! The fact is so obvious. The danger is that we become unduly familiar with it, and cease to be impressed or influenced by it adequately. If we were saved from drowning, or some other perilous plight, would it not impress us? Would it become commonplace to us? Surely not. There is nothing in the world of which a person can think that is so impressive, so majestically wonderful and gracious as the death of Christ. It should always impress us with awe, humility and gratitude. You cannot think of anything more awe-inspiring. In it, you come into contact with the infinite holiness and majesty of God, and the infinite evil of human sin. You cannot approach a holier place, and a more revealing place. By the death of Christ, men and women are saved from eternal damnation. And if a person has reason to feel indebted for being saved from drowning, much more should a person feel indebted for being saved from the deserved wrath of God.

Believers are here asked to arm themselves with the same mind. What mind did Christ manifest in dying for us? He manifested love for the Father, to God. He loved to fulfil the Father's engagements, and for that end He died. It was a concern to Him that the Father's glory should be untarnished in the salvation of guilty and hell-deserving sinners. He manifested His own immutable and uncompromising hatred to sin.

Christ manifested self-sacrifice and unexampled self-denial in His devotion to the will of God the Father. He manifested a spirit of loyal obedience. He manifested an unfathomable love for men's souls, for our own souls. That is the mind which Jesus Christ manifested to our souls, a love unto death. That is the mind with which we are asked to arm ourselves. A love unto death.

There have been many believers which showed that, and laid down their lives for Christ. Every believer is here told to arm himself or herself with the same mind that was evidenced in the sufferings and death of the Saviour. The believer must show a spirit of love to God. That is the strongest motive to hate sin, and the best antidote against the love of sin. A view and a love of God's holiness and a love of conforming thereto will make us hate sin. Christ did not need to obtain this, for He had it in Himself.

We too need to arm ourselves with a mind for the glory of God, and a zeal for the glory of God. We need to have an apprehension of the great mercy and favour He showed us in saving and pardoning us.

We must also arm ourselves with a love for our own souls. By refraining from sin we manifest the greatest and most proper love to our souls. A parent is deeply concerned about the growth of his child. We should have the same interest in our soul's growth in holiness. The Lord is entrusting us with the keeping of our souls. He loves our souls. We should love them too.

Although Christ suffered for their sins, that was not to result in their complete exemption in suffering for sin. The suffering of conviction of sin is only a grace which has flowed forth from the fountain of Christ's sufferings for the sins of His people. The suffering of repentance is a grace which has flowed from the sufferings and death of Christ. The death of Christ has delivered you from eternal suffering, the penal sufferings; but it has brought you other sufferings. The suffering of repentance is one of these, for it is written, 'They shall look on him whom they have pierced, and will mourn for him.' These sufferings are not penal. They are necessary sufferings in the economy of salvation. Without them you could not taste the sweetness of redeeming love and grace. The angels have no need of this suffering or pain to enjoy the love and favour of God. They are sinless. But to bring us into an experience of the redeeming grace of Christ, it is necessary for us. It is all peace with the angels, because they retained their original righteousness. Not so with faulty man.

'He that hath suffered in the flesh hath ceased from sin'. This is a reason presented by the apostle to show the impropriety of sinning on the part of those who profess to know Christ savingly. It cannot apply to Christ Himself, as He did not need to cease from sin. There was no sin in Him. But there was a congruity between their sufferings and Christ's. He suffered for their sins by making atonement for them. They suffered for their guilt in their being convicted of sins effectually to make them rest in that atonement which Christ made. They suffered that their suffering would produce ceasing from sin as its certain and inevitable result. They suffered so that they would have nothing to do with sin ever after, but live to the will of God, and not to the lust of man. Suffering in the flesh implies conviction of sin, which is continuous and becomes deeper and deeper. That is what causes the pain arising from a consciousness of indwelling corruption.

This penitential suffering is a grace, because it is sanctifying, and not penal suffering. Its presence in the soul has a sanctifying effect. It will itself finally vanish. There will be no need of it in glory.

25. THE EVER-LIVING ONE

I am he that liveth and was dead; and, behold, I am alive for evermore; Amen; and have the keys of hell and of death (Revelation 1:18).

John saw Christ many times in the flesh. But never did he have a vision of Him that was of such importance or of such consequence as this one. Now Christ is revealing Himself to John after having risen and ascended up to the Majesty on High. John is in the isle of Patmos, for the word of God, and the testimony of Christ.

It is clear that John saw a resemblance to Christ as he used to see Him, notwithstanding the dazzling glory which the apostle had not been accustomed to, and which surrounded Christ in this vision. He heard Jesus and he saw Him. The effect was to prostrate John before the Lord Jesus as one dead. But He laid His right hand on him, saying, 'Fear not, I am the first and the last, I am he that liveth etc.'

The first thing Christ says to John is 'Fear not'. When Christ comes near, even to a gracious man, still in this world, in an unusual way, the result is a feeling of fear and dread. That was how Isaiah was affected by the vision in the Temple, so that he fell down under the revelation given to him. He cried out, 'Woe is me, for I am undone'. The greatness, glory and majesty of God is felt by man as a weight of powerful glory and sovereignty upon his spirit, so that it brings with it, as it were, a feeling of dread and horror. For this reason, Christ had to come with comfort and reassurance.

Christ told John that He was 'the first and the last'. This brings Christ before the view of John as the uncreated God. As far as His humanity is concerned, He is born about four thousand years after Adam, and from this point of view, He was not the first. But He speaks here regarding what is true concerning His deity as the eternal God. John in his Gospel puts it thus: 'In the beginning was the Word'. He was the cause of every thing that came into existence, for without Him nothing was made that was made. The vision speaks of old age, of elderliness - His hair was white. This too points to the fact that He is from eternity. And He is to eternity. There is no end to His sovereignty, His authority, His power.

He is the living one - 'I am he that liveth'. This was mentioned for John's personal comfort, and to give him soul gladness. The vision had an overpowering effect because it symbolised majesty and might, holiness and sovereignty. John would have been strengthened and gladdened when thus comforted in these words. John trembled more before the Lord who loved him, and whom he himself loved, than before his enemies whose displeasure accounted for his exile in the Isle of Patmos. This was the Lord whom he loved, and in whom he took shelter, and in whom he expected to have eternal felicity.

It was as a man that Christ spake to John. Yet He was the first and the last, showing that He was more than man. He had no beginning. Looking back before the beginning of things, He existed and continued to exist. He lived in possession of the power which He manifested on earth. He had no more power than He had on earth, but He was exalted to a sphere of higher glory. He possessed the life and power of which He gave evidence when John saw Him raised to Heaven out at Bethany.

There was a sense in which He did not die at all, any more than the Father died, although it says 'and was dead'. There would be no value in His death if there was not another sense in which he did not, and could not, die at all. In respect of His divine nature, that is, His deity, He did not die, and could not die. He said 'I have power to lay down my life'.

But, of course, He had been dead. He says '...and was dead'. Christ states this as a truth which had been made precious to John long ago. It was, indeed, the truth which he preached and for which he loved God. It is in this truth that the roots of His love to God were fixed and it is in this soil that his love to God and Christ continued to grow. We also see that Christ Himself is not ashamed of it; as surely as His living for ever is for John's comfort and eternal good, so too was His death. His eternal blessedness depends upon both together. His death causes His ever-living existence in eternal power to be for their eternal good. This death was not a reproach to Christ but to its perpetrators. It was an eternal honour to Him. This death was in the Eternal Covenant. In the mystery of God's wisdom it was there, but nevertheless He was free from accountability for the sin of those who brought about that death.

His life without His death would mean destruction for those for whom the death procured life eternal. The result of that death is that He has the keys of hell and death. These doors are shut on John and open for His enemies.

26. THE MORNING STAR

I am the root and the offspring of David,
and the bright and morning star (Revelation 22:16).

The Lord Jesus Christ, the Son of God, here calls Himself by the name which was given to Him as He was born in the flesh. This Divine Saviour is man, along with being God. He was not always man, but He was always God; and His becoming man did not entail His ceasing to be God, not for one moment.

Christ often stressed His humanity in His references to Himself. He calls Himself the Son of Man. He seemed to have a special fondness for that name. I think it appears about forty times in the Gospels, and I think there are forty different references. And now, after His exaltation, He makes it clear that He is God and man, in two distinct natures, and one person for ever.

The name 'Jesus' signified 'Saviour'. Christ wanted to be regarded as Saviour. He brings Himself before His people in this name of Jesus as Saviour. He did not wish people to forget that He is Saviour.

He is the Lord of angels. He sent this angel to proclaim these things in the churches. Angels are His possession. He was not promised that exalted position. It was always His. The angels are His servants in seeking to execute His mediatorial work in the world. They supported Himself in the world. Angels ministered to Him, and we are told that at a certain juncture, an angel appeared to Him from Heaven, 'strengthening Him'.

What a marvellous and awesome spectacle it was to the angels to see the Lord of Glory in human nature, requiring their ministering to Him in that fashion. He seems to have sorely missed the disciples' sympathy when they slept in the garden in the hour of His bitter trials. Their compassionate sympathy seemed to have counted so much to Him in this season of unparalleled distress, had it been sufficiently strong to banish their sleepiness. But it wasn't, and Christ bewailed it in these words, 'Could ye not watch with me one hour?' Then an angel strengthened Him. But His three disciples failed Him in the garden. How weak He became as man! But the weakness of God is stronger than men.

He says that He is 'the root and offspring of David'. It was declared often that He was to descend from David, and David, Christ Himself said, called Him Lord. How then was He David's son? He was certainly both, He was David's Lord and He was David's son. These words might include within them that He was the root on which David grew, that is Christ in respect of His deity, Christ as God. So Christ is thus the root out of which David grew, and also the king of Israel from whom Christ descended according to the flesh. Other interpreters prefer to regard the reference to the root of David as denoting Christ's human nature, that the offspring of David is a repetition of the same meaning in different words. Whatever interpretation we prefer to accept, it is perfectly clear that He who was David's son was also David's Lord.

In respect of the interpretation first expressed, Christ was David's root both as the Creator who gave him natural life, and as the Creator and Communicator of spiritual life. He was the root on which everything brought into existence grew and from whom all emanated. In growing out of David according to the flesh there grew the whole company of the elect of God whom He represented before God in His capacity of Mediator for them. His becoming a root of David according to the flesh was the procuring cause of the church's redemption. Of all trees, this was the most fruitful. Its branches held all of God's people from the first saved until the last.

'Root' might also signify lowliness, and also the contempt and disregard of man. This offspring became the head of a family, an adopted family, who were black and corrupt like the devil, who first had them in his power, but who will be purified and sanctified when Christ presents them to the Father.

He is also the bright and morning star. A star is a spectacle of exceeding beauty and attractiveness. It attracts of its light. Light is inspiring and encouraging. Christ is a star in this sense. How gloriously He shines as the Father's fellow, as the adorable Second Person of the glorious Trinity. How gloriously He shines. There was a prominent star recently in the west. It seemed to me to be nearer than usual. One felt it made the night brighter than usual. There seemed as if there were a continuous moon. I felt a distinct pleasure in looking in its face at night. It seemed to dissipate gloom, and to assure that Heaven was at peace and friendly towards the inhabitants of the earth, as Heaven certainly is towards God's people on the earth. It seemed to bespeak by its light Heaven's delight in and benignity towards men.

This star seemed to outstrip all the other stars in glory. Is not Christ like this? He relieves our gloom. We see in Him the face of God. He has come like a star with warmth and light in the heavens, as the preacher of the Father. He is in a glorious relationship of friendship to the world. He has demonstrated this by shining in His salvation among men.

The shining of this star shows up the darkness in which it shines. Christ shines in the darkness of sin, and the corruption which sin brought with it. The darkness belongs to the curse and the condemnation which would reign over the souls of men for ever if this star had not come with the power to lighten all darkness.

Christ is like a shining star, something which is beautiful and attractive. It gives light and hope and encouragement. Is not Christ like this? Is not the shining of Christ, in His office as Mediator, glorious and attractive? He Himself says that He came as a light in the darkness, so that whoever believes in Him will not remain in darkness, but will have the light of life. As the Father's companion, the second person of the godhead, He was shining like a bright star. For all His greatness and glory - all that belonged to Him as God - came to shine like a star in being revealed and put to use in all His work as Mediator. He shines in His holiness, His justice, His truth, His power, and His goodness, where His mercy lies.

It was in this world of darkness that the star shone. The darkness neither comprehended nor accepted it. Indeed, the darkness did all that it could to oppose the shining of this star. And where do we see it shining? In the sky of the Scriptures. There is light and warmth there, and it sends warmth and light into the hearts of all those who see in a saving manner. There is a spiritual light that comes from Him to the mind and understanding of His people; and there is a warmth that bends the will and the affections, which melt in love to Christ.

This star was and is in the firmament of the Old Testament scriptures. Abraham saw it in the promises. This was the star which Balaam himself saw. Be sure that you have more than a sentimental interest in Christ. Close in with Him as your Saviour. This star did not shine so brightly in respect of revelation then as it does in the New Testament. It is in the firmament of the New Testament. It arose in the dark firmament of our hearts, and its light penetrated its gloom and darkness - oh what darkness that was! The darkness of the Egyptian plague was not as dark as this. But the light of truth penetrates the gloom of our hearts, brought us life, and brought us warmth,

JOHN MACKENZIE

on

THE PERSON AND WORK OF CHRIST

27. THE GREAT PROVIDER

...and Joseph opened all the storehouses (Genesis 41:56).

I come today to preach on Joseph again! I pass over the terms of imprisonment that he served by reason of his uprightness and integrity, and the marvellous deliverance and advancement that was the result. Today I propose to say a little about Joseph as he was a type of one greater than himself. Think of the marvellous Providence that raised up Joseph to save the house of Israel and Egypt from famishing. Then reflect on the indescribable greatness of the grace of God in raising up Jesus to save sinners of mankind from the tragedy and ruin of sin. Let us note:

(1) *Joseph opened the storehouses by royal authority*
It was for this purpose that he was appointed by the King. It was a fitting and appropriate appointment, because Joseph had proved himself. He was a man of exceptional foresight and wisdom. He had warned Pharaoh of the coming famine, and gave direction as to the best method of preparing for it.

Joseph was also a remarkably pious man, and he brought his integrity to bear on all the events of his life. The honour of his God was the constant aim of his life. In all Egypt there was no other man who was suitable for this high office. None could supervise the filling of the storehouses like him, and none other was entitled to open them. He planned the storehouses, and was rightly appointed to open them. He carried out the storage, and proved himself practical as well as inventive. The king could only be approached through Joseph.

How eminently is all this true of our Lord Jesus Christ! He was Heaven's appointed, and Heaven's choice for the work of redemption. Heaven's seal was upon Him, and this marked Him out as a truly unique person. The force of His person roused the forces of darkness to the utmost exertion to try to secure the failure of His plan, and on the other hand, called forth the admiration and love of the faithful. And as the king could only be approached through Joseph, no man can come to the Father but by Christ. He is the way, the truth and the life.

(2) *Joseph opened the storehouses at the appropriate time*
It was for this purpose he had filled them. As he had the foresight to prepare them, he had the discretion to open them at the appropriate time. This he did when the famine was general. Thus it was at a time when people would gladly receive and appreciate food. He did all this when he was thirty years of age. He kept the storehouses open while the famine lasted. They were

never closed while a hungry applicant drew near. The places of storage were convenient to all comers, and the hours of distribution were suitable.

The parallel is easily drawn. Think of the great antitype, the Lord Jesus Christ. He came to provide for the salvation of men. He is not only the great benefactor of all the earth - for the earth belongs to the Lord, and all that it contains - but He also opened the doors of mercy for the free outflow of the greatest and enduring riches of divine grace to the unworthy sons of men.

He came at the appropriate time. The spiritual famine was great, the need was urgent, there was none to help. The world, from a historical, moral, social and spiritual viewpoint, was ripe for His advent. It was in truth God's time, it was need's time; and the great transaction was completed at a time of life corresponding to that of Joseph - He was thirty years. By His one offering of Himself He opened the storehouses of heavenly grace; and they are open yet, and open to the famishing sons of men. The world's mad charge for pleasure will not satisfy the deep longings of the human soul, but an eternal fulness abides in Christ, and we may come to Him for the supply of all our wants. He slumbers not nor sleeps.

(3) *Joseph opened the storehouses to all comers*

All who came found a ready supply. So it is with the Joseph of the New Testament, Jesus Christ. All who come to Him receive not only a ready supply, but personal attention - something Joseph was not capable of. He had his officers, but Jesus gives personal attention to the needs and requests of all comers. So you are not lost in the crowd that throng His throne and presence.

Seekers come to Joseph from afar. And do not sinners come from far to Christ? Yes, they come to Him from the land of extreme need, where souls are famishing for want of spiritual food. Men and women flock to Jesus from every corner of the universe. We are told that during the life of Christ on earth, people came to Him from every quarter, and they do so yet.

None were refused. They had only to assert and prove their need. How applicable this is to Jesus! Yet Joseph did but sell; while Jesus gives without money and without price. All had to come to Joseph and buy if they would live. It was either buy or starve. Living near the granaries was not enough. The Egyptian was as much in danger of starvation as the Canaanite. The granaries were near and handy, but they might die with hunger if they did not buy. So it is with the Gospel provision. There is enough for all. But oh, how many perish beside the plenty! The Gospel will benefit us nothing if we do not partake of its resources. Flee then to the Joseph of the New Testament!

28. THE SERVANT OF JEHOVAH

Behold my servant, whom I uphold, mine elect in whom my soul delighteth;
I have put my spirit upon him;
he shall bring forth judgement to the Gentiles (Isaiah 42:1).

The Lord, through the prophet Isaiah, calls the attention of the church to Himself, and the revelation He was going to give of Himself in time. It is a prophecy concerning Christ, and one in which Christ recognised Himself, and claims to have been fulfilled in Him.

(1) *The Command: 'Behold my servant'*
This is God's call to His people in all ages. To the Old Testament church, the call was to consider the promise of a servant, and seek to recognise the servant promised. Thus the prophets are said to have inquired diligently regarding the meaning of prophecy - the manner and time of its being fulfilled. The Person and Work of the Servant are declared.

But this is particularly God's call to the New Testament church, to behold Him, and come to Him. Thus we are to consider Him as a figure in time, as fulfilling prophecy, in the light of His self-disclosure in word and deed, in His suffering, death, resurrection, power and exalted life. This is an exercise of soul which befits believers for the confirmation of their faith, the deepening of their spiritual life, and their loyal witness to saving grace. This is our highest good, the most suitable exercise of the soul in time. Eternity shall be a perpetual beholding. This was the Baptist's call - 'Behold the Lamb of God'.

(2) *The Servant to Behold*
His identity is declared here in several ways.

He is 'My Servant'. God has many worthy servants, of whom we read in the Bible. But He had none like this one. He was and is the Father's co-equal and co-eternal Son, not inferior to the Father, but the same in substance, power and glory. He is here called a servant, not in His personal relation to the Father, but in His surety relation to His church. Though the eternal son, yet He is the Mediator between God and men. To do this, He took upon Himself the form of a servant. He learned obedience to the will of God, and practised it as the surety of His people.

He was a chosen Servant. All God's servants are subjects of His choice, but Christ in a unique sense. He is the essence of all of God's choice, the fountainhead; in Him were all God's servants chosen. Christ was set up and appointed from all eternity as the alone fit Person to discharge the purpose of salvation. Infinite wisdom made the choice. 'God so loved the world that he gave...'.

He is a delightful servant. He was always so, but it is especially declared in the New Testament: 'This is my beloved Son, in whom I am well pleased'. The Father had supreme confidence in Him, that He would discharge His task. It was a great trust that was committed to Him, and He proved worthy of it.

He is also a sustained servant - 'whom I uphold'. God put His Spirit on Him for His work, to qualify and sustain Him in the discharge of His offices. He is also upheld as commending the Father's love. And He is an active servant; He brings forth judgement. He does that in the ministry of the Gospel, where sin is condemned, mercy declared and repentance commended. All His subjects have been brought to judgement in themselves.

(3) *How should we behold Him?*
As one worthy of being beheld. We should behold Him now, in His surety relation, in His self-offering, death, resurrection, exaltation. We should set our affections on Him. We should seek to know His fellowship through the Spirit, approach Him in the Scriptures, in our experiences, in His people. Let Him be the object of all our seeking.

The eternal employment of His church will be to behold Him evermore. If we are His, we will be made perfectly blessed in beholding Him, an exercise of which we shall never tire. What does He mean to us? What we are in time, and shall be for ever, hinges on the place we give Him, and the use we make of Him in life.

29. THE PIERCED SHEPHERD

Awake, O sword, against my shepherd, and against the man that is my fellow, saith the LORD of hosts; smite the shepherd and the sheep shall be scattered: and I will turn mine hand upon the little ones (Zechariah 13:7).

The Old Testament abounds with prophetic utterances concerning Christ. He is set before us in the promises and in the sacrificial order of the Old Testament church. His advent, birth, life and sufferings are clearly foretold, particularly by Isaiah, Jeremiah and Zechariah. In chapter 9 of this prophecy His entrance into Jerusalem is foretold and was fulfilled in detail. In chapter 12 He is referred to as the one who would be pierced, and in verse 1 of this chapter as a fountain opened. In our text the prophet tells us how this was to be accomplished. The words are profoundly solemn and affecting. May the Holy Spirit enlighten and direct our thoughts, and affect our hearts as we endeavour to consider the great and solemn truths of our text.

(1) *The Shepherd*

This could only apply to the Lord Jesus. He claimed and applied this text to Himself on the night in which He was betrayed (Matthew 26:31 and Mark 14:27). Here He is set forth in three ways.

First, we see Him as a Shepherd by His office. His official relation is that of being a Shepherd. This character is often given Him in Scripture. He is called the shepherd of Israel (Psalm 80:1), the good shepherd (John 10:11), the great shepherd (Hebrews 13:20), the chief shepherd (1 Peter 5:4) and the shepherd and bishop of souls (1 Peter 2:25). He has all the requisite qualities of a unique shepherd. As such He is claimed by God and man. Both are interested in Him. Here He is presented in His official relation to God; God calls Him 'My Shepherd'. God claims Him as His own. It was He who would set Him apart to this office. God engaged Him, gave Him a flock to tend, transacted with Him on their behalf, and held Him answerable for them. And He willingly understood and faithfully discharged the duties of a shepherd, though this implied the laying down of His life for them (John 10:18). And inasmuch as He is engaged and answerable for the flock, they have a right to claim Him and they do claim Him as their shepherd.

Secondly, He is here set forth by His humanity, described as 'the man'. He was truly a man, He had a true body and a reasonable soul. He had all the sinless dispositions of man. He was in all things like unto His brethren, sin excepted. This was necessary, because He was answerable for man, and this could only be in their nature. Without it He could not be a Saviour. Justice required that the nature that sinned should be punished for its sin. Christ therefore assumed our nature and became the surety and kinsman of His people. Someone said that He loved to try the dress on beforehand, and that was why He often appeared in human form in the Old Testament before He actually came in the flesh.

Thirdly, he is set forth by His divinity. God calls Him 'the man that is my fellow'. The word rendered 'fellow' occurs only in the book of Leviticus, and is rendered 'neighbour', one of the same blood, the same people or of the same locality. There must have been kinship or nearness to constitute one the fellow of another. Here the Lord of hosts claims for Christ the unique relation of being His fellow. Of Him alone could this be true. He was the image of the invisible God (Colossians 1:15). He was in the form of God, and equal with God. He is God (John 1:1). Thus in point of nature, property, work and happiness, He is God's fellow. And Christ Himself claimed this relationship, when He said 'I and the Father are one'. This relationship and glory remained undiminished and uninterrupted when He appeared despised and rejected on the cross of shame. There was never a moment when He was not God's fellow.

Such is the view that is presented here of Christ's glorious person. He was both God and man, and this was necessary because the cause of God and the cause of man were both entrusted to Him. Both natures constitute Him a suitable and competent Mediator between God and men.

(2) *His Sufferings*

By whom were these inflicted? It was God who said 'Awake O sword against my shepherd', even the Lord of hosts who claims Him as shepherd and fellow. It is true that men and devils were instruments in inflicting sufferings upon Him. They were early on His track; as soon as His presence in our world was heralded, hell began to conspire against Him. He was slandered, insulted, misrepresented, mocked, despised and crucified. He was wounded and pierced. But it was Jehovah, the Great Lord and Judge of all who said to the sword to waken against Him, against His shepherd, His fellow, His only Son, His well-beloved. He does not spare Him. It pleased the Lord to bruise Him. It was He in His capacity as law giver and judge that ordained and inflicted the severest blow. He was delivered by the determinate counsel and foreknowledge of God.

What were His sufferings like? They were penal, and so inflicted in justice by a sword, the symbol of vengeance. The sword is the sword of divine justice, and represents all the elements that contributed to execute the awful sentence that was pronounced as an adequate penalty for the sins of all His people. It was a terrible, devouring, flaming sword, represented in Genesis 3:24 as guarding the way to the tree of life after the fall and rebellion of man. At the sight of it, His human nature trembled, and His soul was exceeding sorrowful. It was a two-edged sword, which heaven and earth combined to inflict on the penalty sin deserved.

What were His sufferings for? Certainly not for any evil or flaw in Himself. He was holy, harmless, undefiled and separate from sinners. But as the shepherd of the flock He laid down His life for His sheep. He was surety for them, and endured what they deserved of wrath at the hand of justice. He was wounded for our transgressions (Isaiah 53:5). If sinners were to be saved, it must be at the awful cost of the surety's life and sufferings, for without blood there is no remission of sins. The law had to be honoured, and justice satisfied before sinners could be saved.

(3) *The Result of His sufferings*

The sheep shall be scattered, and Jehovah will lay His hand on the little ones. The first part of this phrase was applied by Christ to the desertion of the disciples at the time of the crucifixion. During His public ministry He never lacked for hearers, admirers and enthusiasts, but in the hour of His great trial, there is none to plead His cause. They all forsook Him and fled, and in that terrible hour the shepherd stood alone. He trod the winepress alone, and of the people there was none with him. They could have no share in His work at any stage of His official action. He stood alone from beginning to end. This does not excuse the desertion of Him by the disciples, who forsook Him. But none could stand in the presence of God's fierce anger but Christ alone. Only that He stood there, the sword would have fallen on us.

He will lay His hands on the little ones. This sometimes indicates divine action by way of judgement, and at other times by way of gracious influence. The latter is meant here. He will lay His hand on them to bless them, to impart to them the blessings of Christ's purchase. He will forgive, save, justify, adopt them and supply all their needs. He will restore them from their falls and wanderings. He restored Peter, and will do so for His people till the very end of time. He will lay His hands on them to keep them by His power. They are among enemies and exposed to dangers. They need His preserving care. He will also lay His hands on them to use them in His service and to His glory. He has entrusted the affairs of His kingdom on earth to them.

Here then, is God's way of salvation. He provided a Saviour, proved Him, approved Him and commends Him to sinners. In Him is shelter from the storm of divine wrath. There is no salvation apart from Him.

30. THE DESIGNATED SAVIOUR

Thou shalt call his name Jesus; for he shall save his people from their sins
(Matthew 1:21).

These are the words of the angel to Joseph, to explain to him the nature of the mysterious providence which perplexed his mind, and caused him resolve to put Mary away secretly. The mysterious event is explained to him by the name he was directed to give the child born of Mary. The deep things of God can only be revealed by God Himself by some agent. Angels were often used for this purpose in the Old Testament, but under Gospel light the church has the secret of the Lord in the written word; even then only the

Holy Spirit can disclose its inner content. This He does in the ministry of
the Gospel. The name here given opens up God's purpose of redemption,
and we may look into it. Let us consider:

(1) *The Name*

His name is to be 'Jesus'. Usually names are given to distinguish men from
one another, and are given in honour of the living or to commemorate the
dead. But in the Bible names were given for a much higher purpose; they
were usually declarative of character and work, or associated with notable
events.

The name Jesus is the Greek for the Hebrew name Joshua. There were
two men in the Old Testament with this name: the successor of Moses who
led Israel into Canaan; and the high priest of the second Temple after the
return from Babylon. Both these men were associated with great deliver-
ances in the history of Israel, and both were types of Christ and His work,
who is the captain of salvation for His people, and the high priest of our
profession.

The Saviour had many names ascribed to Him in the Old Testament,
which are appropriate and applicable to Him alone. He is called wonderful,
counsellor, mighty God, everlasting Father, Prince of Peace. He is called
the Branch, the root of Jesse, the ancient of days. But the name by which
He is especially distinguished is Jesus, because it embraces all the others.
The unique greatness of Jesus is announced by the names given Him of old.
It was fitting that His identity as the Son of God be announced beforehand.
But the Person named 'Jesus' is both the Son of God and the Son of Man,
God manifest in the flesh, the wonder and miracle of the ages. He is the
eternal son. He is the Son of Man by the Father's appointment, and His own
assumption of our nature, not by natural generation but by special concep-
tion. This is a great mystery, one upon which natural reason stumbles.

The name 'Jesus' was God-given; it was not left to Joseph and Mary's
choice. It was announced before His birth because the name must answer
to His character and work on earth. It is a name above every name, and every
knee will bow at it and confess that He is Lord.

(2) *His Work*

His name implies the nature of His mission and work among men. He is the
Saviour. This is the greatest even to be heralded in time - that there is a
Saviour, and such a Saviour!

Whom did He save? His people. The Jews are so named in the Bible.
They were His own peculiar people from Abraham down through the ages,
set apart from other nations by His call, laws, service and privilege. He was

their saviour in adverse circumstances. To them He gave revelation of Himself in promise and type, and among them He had ornaments of grace. But the name 'His people' has a wider application. Many of the Jews rejected Him and perished through unbelief. It is evident that the term extends to all nations, for in John 3:16 we read that 'God so loved the world', so that it is clear that His people are among all nations. They are his covenant people, given Him by the Father to redeem them. He becomes answerable for them in that covenant arrangement.

He saves them from their sins. The people whom Christ undertook to save were sinners. What does that mean? To answer this we must consider what sin is - a want of conformity to and transgression of the law of God. Sin is a coming short of what God requires, and a rebellion against His authority. So we see here God's great mercy in devising a means for their salvation, and the amazing condescension and love of Christ in undertaking their salvation. They were His enemies, yet He undertook their salvation in order to make them His own. What love! He who was rich became poor for their sakes to make them rich - He came to save them from sin, from its desert, guilt and dominion and make them to Himself a bride worthy of His affection. He reforms and transforms her, giving her high and holy principles, and will finally present her without spot, redeemed by His grace.

How does He save? By making atonement. He engaged to answer for her in relation to the requirements of the law and the justice of God, and so rendered on her behalf such obedience and love to the law as honoured it, and by His self-offering satisfied justice by enduring her punishment and dying her death. He brought life and immortality to light. By the operation of His Spirt He saves from the bondage and dominion of sin. In regeneration, justification and sanctification He makes her to participate in the blessings of His purchase. Again, He saves by the supply of grace and power that enables them to overcome their sinful nature. He rules and defends His people from all their enemies: to save means to defend as well as to deliver.

What are the evidences that they are His? He describes them as people who do the will of God. They are made a willing people in a day of His power, willing to seek the Lord and renounce all other lovers. They obey His commands. They are separated from the world and consecrated to His use and service. This is the life of faith. We have no right to believe we are His unless sin has lost its sway and attraction. Since Christ saves from sin, He establishes a dislike for it in the heart, thus believers groan under its burden. Yes, salvation is on this name Jesus!

31. THE GOOD PHYSICIAN

But when Jesus heard that he said unto them, They that be whole need not a
physician, but they that are sick
(Matthew 9:12).

In this context, we read of Matthew's call and the feast he prepared in
honour of his Master. To this feast he invited his old companions, probably
in the hope that they too might receive a blessing from Christ. The
Pharisees, who were looking for an opportunity to accuse Him, said to the
disciples 'Why does your master eat with publicans and sinners?' They
thought that if He were righteous, He would not be in such company; they
could not see how He could mix with such a class and remain untarnished
by their sin. In our text He tells plainly that His business is with such, and
thereby teaches one of the most fundamental doctrines of our faith. This is
one of the most blessed and pregnant statements we have in the Bible, and
is indeed the substance of what is taught therein. He employs an ordinary
experience of men, not simply to defend Himself against the cavil of the
Pharisees, but also to illustrate great spiritual truth.

(1) *The Sickness*
The reference is to the condition of men as sinners. Various figures are
employed in Scripture to describe the sinner's state - it is represented as one
of guilt, transgression, wickedness, rebellion and misery; here Christ terms
it as sickness. The nature of the sickness is diagnosed and defined as sin in
verse 13. That is the disease that is active in the soul, and from which springs
all the troubles in the world. Its dreadful corruptions are seen in wrecked
lives, ruined homes, in discord and misery among men. It is the most
loathsome and devastating sickness in the world.

It is a universal disease. It is not limited to any area, it is co-extensive
with the universe. It affected men and angels, and brought the universe itself
into the bondage of corruption, from which it groans to be delivered of God.
Heaven alone remains free from its taint and degradation. All men are
suffering its baneful influences, for all have sinned and come short of the
glory of God. There is none that doeth good, no, not one.

It is a deep-seated disease. It is not simply a matter of behaviour, it has
penetrated to the very core of our being. Nor is it weakness inherent in
human nature - as the apologists for sin assert; but rather a dreadful plague
and malignant poison, which entered the citadel of the soul, and rendered
the heart the nursery of evil habits and deeds, for out of the heart springs evil
thoughts and acts. The Bible speaks of sin not only as guilt, but as

indwelling power, moral defilement, by which the faculties of the soul are rendered incapable of performing their proper function.

It is a fatal disease. The wound is mortal. The wages of sin is death. Human skill cannot arrest its steady progress; no earthly medicine can stop or cure it. It is sin that rendered man mortal. Some laugh at this idea, but God has made this so clear that there is no reason to doubt it. Science has done much to alleviate the sufferings of men, but the discoveries of science cannot prevent death. But deadly as sin is, it can be cured - there is an effective balm in Gilead, and a physician there.

It renders man unconscious and leaves men indifferent to the only cure their soul needs. There is such a thing as sickness of which those who have it are not conscious, not only in its first stage, but in its steady progress. Men are dying because of sin, and do not know it. They think they are whole, and have need of nothing; yet they are the subjects of a most dreadful disease. Sin has a stupefying effect on the mind and senses, renders you unconscious of injury. Ah friend, you who are unconscious of and unconcerned about your danger, let me tell you that you are sick, and your case is desperate. But there is also such thing as conscious sickness, when the patient fully realises his condition and danger. The nature of his trouble has been diagnosed, the X-ray leaves no doubt of the advanced stage of his complaint. So it is with the enlightened sinner - his case is clearly defined, his wound is painful and he sees his danger. He blames only himself. But there is a physician and to Him he comes.

(2) The Physician

And what must we say of Him? Well, there never was His like. And there never will be. He is unique and has no peer. What is His name? What are His qualifications? They must be stated.

His name is Emmanuel. That is a most significant name. It signifies 'God with us'. He is Jesus Christ the Righteous. These names represent His qualification to deliver. He is suited to our case.

He was appointed by the highest authority. Although He was not recognised by the state and church authorities of His day - He was rejected by both - yet His credentials are sure, and bear the seal of the God of Heaven. He knew and He alone could measure the depth of degradation to which man fell, and in exercise of grace He provided the only effective answer. He appointed His own Son, the God-man, to be the Saviour of sinners. He has the necessary qualifications. He was trained in no famous school or university, yet His qualifications are so marked that they arrest the attention and admiration of all who consider Him. He is our kinsman, surety, Saviour. He submitted Himself to all the tests that the law required, and was qualified by His satisfaction and triumph to be an all-sufficient healer.

He has the necessary skill to deal with ailments of the deepest dye. He provided an effective remedy in cases where human skill failed, and restored cases considered hopeless. But He is not so much the healer of the body as the healer of the soul. It is true that the body will ultimately share the salvation which He imparts, but it does so first because the soul is saved. He knows the patient's trouble, whatever its nature, be it a wounded conscience, a contrite heart, a burdened spirit, a running sore - He has the remedy.

He has the power or ability. Men, however skilful, have their limitations. They lack ability or power. There are times when men are utterly helpless, but He is never at a loss. He has the necessary resources at His command, and is able to save to the uttermost all who come unto God by Him. He is an incomparable healer. He never refuses an honest plea for help. His terms are reasonable and easy. His medicine is effective and free. He gives free service, personal attention, constant supply of healing medicine. We are sick creatures, our case is helpless and our condition serious. We must consult the heaven-sent Physician. Millions have benefited by His healing balm; why should we perish through failure to consult Him? Sometimes in visiting a surgery you have to wait hours, wait your turn and then at last be told that nothing can be done for you. But if you come to Jesus, you receive personal attention and an effective cure.

32. THE JUDGED ONE

While the Pharisees were gathered together, Jesus asked them saying, What think ye of Christ? (Matthew 22:41-2).

It is an undeniable fact that Jesus occupies a place in history all His own. The question of His identity has been debated down through the ages, and He is still the subject of investigation and acclamation. Even when His identity is established, and acknowledged, many other questions arise concerning Him, and the place which belongs to Him.

During His sojourn in this world, He was constantly harassed with questions of various kinds, and He always gave the correct answer. The Pharisees were particularly hostile to Him, without just cause; and here we see one of them, a lawyer, questioning Him regarding the Mosaic law. Jesus answers with ease, clarity and authority. He, taking advantage of the opportunity, posed a question Himself to them regarding their views of the

Messiah, which rather embarrassed them, so that from that day no man dared ask Him any question. As this question is still relevant for us, we may examine it together.

(1) *The Question: 'What think ye of Christ?'*

This is the question of questions. There is no question greater, or more momentous. It has occupied the best thought of all time, and it is still as fresh as ever, not because the answer is obscure, but because it is relevant to every age. It is a question which requires looking into, because it is of vital importance what views we have of the Person mentioned. It is the greatest, most interesting, and most profitable question that could possibly engage the human mind.

Some try to evade it, saying that Christ is of no great significance to them. They do not think He merits any more thought than other figures in history. But such an attitude ignores essential facts, and is the result of not having given sufficient thought to assess His work. Others are hostile to the principles and truths advocated, and they reject Him in the same spirit as those who crucified Him. But the truth is that we cannot afford to ignore Him, because we cannot get rid of Him. Those who crucified Him thought they got rid of Him. But did they? No! He came back on them with even greater authority and power. He meets us too at every turn in life, at times more than others - in providence, the Gospel, the reformed lives of men and women who have felt the dynamic attraction of His love.

(2) *Its content   Christ is the subject of the question, and it concerns His identity and worth.*

It matters a lot what we think of Him, and what place we give Him. Some deem it necessary to have fixed, well formed thoughts of Him - they think they can play fast and loose with Him. But it is evident from the question that it is highly important what our views of Him are. We are not at liberty to think of Him as we please - our thoughts must be governed by the facts.

All right thinking about Christ must have respect to the scriptural and historical facts about him. These are our sources of information about Him. He is found in the Old Testament scriptures; and their record of Him must be unreservedly accepted and defended. No doctrine of Scripture concerning Him can be sacrificed, because each is as vital to Him as the organs are to the human body. Take from a man a hand or eye and you injure him; take his head or heart and you finish him. So with Christ. Many do Him grave injustice, but to deny or reject the attributes ascribed to Him in Scripture is to do Him great dishonour.

The historical facts about Him answer in detail to the prophecy of the Old

Testament. He was born of a virgin (Isaiah 7:14), in Bethlehem (Micah 5:2), was brought up in Nazareth and suffered and died according to Isaiah 53.

Who is He then? What do you think of this Person - whose son is He? In Scripture we find Him designated in a twofold way - the Son of Man and the Son of God, not as contradictory, but as complementary terms. Thus He is called David's son, and also David's Lord. He is the Son of God essentially, unchangeably and eternally; and the Son of Man by the assumption of our nature, God manifest in the flesh.

What sent Him here? He came to seek and save the lost, to redeem by His own self-offering, sinners of mankind. He came to the Jews first and to them He proclaimed in the most unmistakable terms that the compass of His love embraced the entire world (John 3:16; Romans 5:8). Christ, by His death on Calvary, secured the salvation of His people.

What proofs do we have of His saving power? Many! There is His resurrection, which is as much a fact of history as His life. It is proved beyond doubt, and changed the whole complex of world history. Then there is the advent of the Holy Spirit at Pentecost, the existence of the Christian church, and the experience and testimony of believers. These are men and women who have witnessed this saving power in their own lives. Theirs is the living and exalted Saviour, by whose power they live, and by whose wealth they are sustained.

(3) *Its Application.*

This is a matter of vital personal concern. It concerns you and me - 'What think *ye* of Christ?' Not, 'What do others think of Him?', but 'What do *You*?'

What is your estimate of Him? His Sonship is established, His work described and His claims asserted. What place do you assign Him? Here was the most wonderful Person who ever appeared on the stage of time, whose advent changed our reckoning of time, and whose birthday shook the earth into a new era. What place do you give Him? Scripture gives Him the place of Saviour. That place He merits, fills and seeks. Will you give Him that place? There is salvation in none other. Will you not make personal business with Him, who is waiting to be gracious? He gives a full and free salvation.

This is not a trifling question. Your conduct towards Christ determines your destiny. Do ignorance, prejudice, indifference hinder you? Today he invites your inspection, and pleads your acceptance. Tomorrow He may inspect you, and assign your destiny. He, the judged today, will be judge tomorrow. What think ye of Christ?

33. THE RETURNING KING

When the Son of man shall come in his glory, and all the holy angels with him, then shall he sit upon the throne of his glory, And before him shall be gathered all nations, and he shall separate them one from another...
(Matthew 25:31-2).

Gentlemen, this is a very solemn passage. So unspeakably awful are its contents that we almost shrink from their consideration. Some people try to avoid thinking of anything which may disturb their peace of mind, or cause them anxious thoughts. They want to be happy, they say, hence they try to avoid being serious, and they intentionally shrink from examination of their relation to God.

But that is not the way to settle our affairs with Him, nor is it fair to ourselves. It is simply closing our eyes to all danger, and leaping forward into the dark without any regard to the consequences. God would not have it so; hence He warns and counsels, and has provided us with a revelation, and the means whereby we may attain to real happiness and blessedness. This passage was spoken by Christ, and in it He mentions several things that deserve earnest attention. It was on the eve of His death that He addressed the disciples in this way.

(1) He tells that He is to come again
The time was drawing near when He should leave this world and go to the Father. Now He informs the disciples that He will come again. This passage does not refer to the resurrection; on a previous occasion He had told them that He would rise from the dead, but none of the things mentioned in this passage were to accompany the resurrection. It refers to His second coming, His coming to judge the world and its people with equity.

He will come as the Son of Man. This is a fact which proves that He has human nature in His exalted position on the right hand of God. This is an assurance of salvation to believers, and a pledge that their nature will one day inherit the same exalted position, for they shall surround the throne of God and of the Lamb. When Christ shall appear again, it will be as the Son of Man, to prove that all judgement has been committed to Him by the Father. In the very nature in which He was despised, rejected and crucified He will come to judge.

And He will come in His glory, that is, in the full display of His personal glory as the Son of God. That glory He concealed within the garb of His human nature during His state of humiliation, except on a few occasions when He revealed it to His people. In His miracles He revealed the glory of His power, but it went largely unnoticed. When He comes the second time, it will be in the full splendour of His glory. But along with the glory which is His essential and personal possession, He has another glory, the glory which He secured by His passion - the glory of purchasing the church.

He will come with the holy angels. They are His attendants, and the ministers of judgement and justice. They attended His first coming with song, and they shall attend this second coming with the glory of triumph. And every eye will see Him - yours and mine. All will be very public.

(2) *The Method of His Administration at His Coming*
First, all nations shall be gathered before Him. This means that His second coming shall not be limited or local, as was His first. As God He is omnipresent, and so shall appear to all the nations. Who shall stand or endure it?

Secondly, He shall regard only two classes of people: the good and the bad. These two He shall judge in the light of their treatment of Him during their earthly pilgrimage. The good shall hear His welcome home - 'Come ye blessed...'. They shall appear before Him as blessed. They will be publicly acknowledged as such, and their eternal security and felicity will be secure. They shall enter on the inheritance prepared for them. But the bad shall appear before Him with a curse, the curse of the broken law, and of their failure to love Him, for Paul says that those who love not the Lord Jesus Christ are cursed with a curse. They shall be judged as such, and shall depart from Him with a curse. What a dreadful thought! We must not ignore it, lest we meet with the fate of the bad.

This should lead us to enquire how we treat Jesus now, for let us be certain of this - according to our treatment of Him here, shall be His judgement of us at His coming.

34. THE TRIED CHRIST

And Jesus stood before the governor... (Matthew 27:11).

This is a solemn scene, in the light of which we feel the blush of shame on our face for the despicableness and lowness of man. Yet it is a scene which is fraught with significance. Here we see the Prince of Life on trial before men, and rejected by them, while in it all, He was discharging His assigned task. Here too we see an exchange of places, which is a forecast of things to come, when the judged becomes the judge, and the judge the judged. It is a scene which is still enacted and perpetrated in the world, when the question of Christ's identity is lightly dismissed. In the light of all this we may well consider our own treatment of Christ.

(1) *Christ before Pilate*

Our Lord had been betrayed by Judas into the hands of sinners, who had previously resolved on His death. His life and teaching censured their customs and views, and they hated Him without cause. This shows how indifferent a Gospel-hardened people can be to the claims of Christ.

They had been seeking occasion to formulate charges against Him, that would give a show of justification to their resolve to kill Him. The high priest sought false witnesses against Him, but they were so contrary to each other that their witness could not stand. Then the high priest intervened and asked 'art thou Christ, the Son of God?'. To his obvious amazement, Jesus replied 'Thou hast said'. Instead of acknowledging His claim of right, or seeking further light, he declared Christ a blasphemer and this became a sufficient reason to put Him to death. So they resolved to crucify Him, and thus make Him a public spectacle of shame and disgrace, but as they had no legal right to execute their sentence, they deferred the matter to Pilate for confirmation and execution.

Thus Christ appeared before Pilate, the Roman Governor, on a twofold charge of high treason and blasphemy, which Pilate proceeded to investigate. The Jews accused Jesus of claiming kingship, refusing homage to Caesar, and perverting the people. To this charge Pilate, naturally, gave particular attention to asking Him, 'Art thou a King?' Jesus answered, 'Thou sayest', adding that His kingdom was not of this world, and that the purpose of His mission in the world was to establish it. Regarding the charge of blasphemy, Jesus was equally emphatic and clear, saying 'Thou couldst have no power against me except it were given thee from above.' It is worthy of note that Jesus made no effort at self-defence against the false charges, but acknowledged the truth of His Sonship and Kingship.

Before Pilate, Christ's manner and bearing were worthy of His Person. He appears with the utmost composure, there was no agitation, as is customary with guilty men on trial. There is no confusion of thought or speech; what He says He says plainly, clearly and firmly, with obvious authority. There was no evidence of fear, but a calm nobleness, and a resignation which puzzled Pilate, causing him to say that Christ was innocent.

Why did Jesus submit to such humiliation at the hands of men? Because this was the way in which He was to achieve the purpose of His coming. Thus He voluntarily submitted to the shame and suffering of death, as the essential ingredients of the cup which was given Him to drink as the surety of His people. He was not suffering by compulsion but by consent, not a passive sufferer but an active agent. He bore the penalty of our sin, and both His submission and activity imparted such value to His obedience and endurance as was adequate satisfaction to justice, and thus adequate to secure the redemption of His church.

Such is the scene that we see before Pilate. Jesus was not a helpless victim, the creature of circumstances over which He had no control; but an active agent in full control of the situation into which His assumed duty brought Him, in order to save the lost.

(2) *Pilate before Christ*

As we look at the scene, we see that Christ was not the only one on trial. Pilate is also on trial, so that the judge becomes the judged. The contrast is clear. Christ honourably discharged His assigned task and earned it glory; while Pilate brought shame and eternal discredit upon himself.

Pilate presumed to judge Christ according to worldly policy, only to betray himself as a moral weakling who hadn't the courage to enforce his own sense of justice. He pronounced Jesus innocent, and yet handed Him over to be crucified.

His desire for popularity and to be in court favour weighed more with him than the place and honour of Jesus. In all this he discloses himself as a cruel, principle-less slave to worldly considerations which miserably failed him at last. He is said to have lost the favour of the court, was disgraced and ended his own life, like Judas, haunted by his misdeeds. But he not only betrayed himself - we actually see him under judgement; Christ looked upon Pilate, with a searching eye which pierced him through, and we see him becoming a self-conscious and unhappy man.

Christ so impressed him as to produce in him a twofold effect. First, he marvelled. He investigated the charges, found them invalid, declared Christ innocent, and proposed to release Him. When falsely accused, He made no defence, when reviled, He answered not: Pilate is amazed - he does not understand this man. The prisoner's bearing astounds him; he tries to humble Him, but he is only humbled himself - he is clearly a puzzled man.

Secondly, he was alarmed. Generally prisoners are afraid of their judge, but here the presumed judge is afraid of his prisoner. Three factors contributed to his concern and fear - Christ's obvious greatness and omniscience, His claim to deity and the warning message which he had received from his own wife. But Pilate tried to evade his responsibility. He proclaimed Christ innocent, wished to release Him, and sent Him to Herod; but when the Jews clamour for Christ's death, he will neither release Him nor condemn Him, until they question his loyalty to Caesar, and then he gives Christ over to be crucified. But even then he tries to escape from his sense of wrong by putting the blame on the Jews, and washing his hands in innocence he showed he was a guilty man, and an unhappy man.

So it is still. Men cannot get rid of Christ with a wave of the hand. He comes again and again, until they either break down in grief over their sin, and become His friends, or else through hardness become doomed like Pilate, who was finally assigned his eternal place by the very Christ whom he scourged and crucified. We must all decide what to do with Christ, and do so in the light of the fact that He shall decide at last what to do with us.

35. THE SON OF MAN

For even the Son of man came not to be ministered unto but to minister, and to give his life a ransom for many
(Mark 10:45).

The occasion of these words was the request of the sons of Zebedee, through their mother, for prominent positions in Christ's kingdom. Such positions are secured among men by those who seek them in good time. So they would not be slow with their request for eminence in the kingdom which they assumed He was to establish in the world. This ambitious spirit, while it may be legitimate in the natural sphere, is dangerous and unbecoming with respect to the kingdom of Christ. His is a spiritual domain, and its regulating principles are not conflicting, oppressive and ambitious, but equality, agreeableness and service. Real greatness is characterised by ungrudging service to our fellows. This is illustrated by His own example - He came to minister and give His life. Here we have one of the most profound statements bearing on our Lord's mission that is on record, and yet it is so clear that it requires no great mental effort to understand it. He tells us certain things about Himself which may be considered with profit.

(1) *His Character - The Son of Man*
This designation is exclusively employed by the Lord Himself. Ezekiel is often addressed as 'son of man', but never as THE son of man. Jesus alone spoke thus of Himself. The disciples never employed the designation themselves; the only reference apart from Christ is when Stephen at his death said that he saw 'the Son of man standing on the right hand of God' (Acts 7:56). The words would be unbecoming on the lips of mere men, but were profoundly significant from Him.

He was a real man, possessing a true body and a reasonable soul, in all respects like unto His brethren, sin excepted. He was the ideal man, the perfect man, a unique man. There never was His like before, and never again shall there be one like Him. He was holy, harmless, undefiled and separate from sinners. This was asserted by His friends and admitted by His enemies. All that is true, but He does not speak of Himself as the real or ideal man. He employed this name because it suitably expressed His connection with His people. It is official rather than personal, for it is personal only by reason of official action.

Hence, He speaks of Himself as having come - 'the Son of man CAME'. He thus claimed an existence prior to His coming, and that He actually acquiesced in coming. This could not be said of any other. The second Person of the glorious Trinity became man - God was manifest in the flesh, God and man, in two distinct natures, yet one person for ever. It is true that He was given and sent by the Father, but it was He, the Son of man, who came. He was willing of Himself to do this. He came to be what He was not, and ceased not to be what He was. And this was His own act.

He evidently took delight in referring to Himself as the Son of man. This is clear from the fact that He employed it some eighty-four times. He thus presents Himself in His official relation to His church for only by becoming man could He effect His purpose of mercy concerning her. It was necessary that He should emphasise this; efforts were made in the church to deny His human nature, but He established it for all time, and established that His human nature is as necessary to us as His divinity.

(2) *His Mission*

The Son of Man came not to be ministered unto. He might have come requiring ministration, and had He done so, He would have been acting justly. He is the Creator, to whom all honour and homage is due. And had He so appeared, to require of us our due, we should have no standing-place before Him. But He did not thus appear, in the display of His majesty and honour.

Nor did He appear in the pomp of royalty and the glory of earthly splendour, as many expected Him to come. They expected His appearing in the form of a mighty prince, requiring their assistance to establish an earthly kingdom. He did not come seeking ministration, not to be waited on. There is a sense in which He has no need of our service! Thousands of angels are His chariot.

But what He did not require was lavishly and lovingly bestowed upon Him. Angels waited on Him, and ministered to Him at His birth, and throughout His earthly career; wise men opened their treasures to Him who was born King. The shepherds joined in angels' song and sang His praises, and His redeemed people ministered to Him of their substance. Yet in His humble form, He was unrecognised by the multitude, 'he came unto his own, and his own received him not'. He would wash the disciples' feet, but asked not that it be done to Him.

He came to minister. This is the positive aspect of His mission among men. For this purpose He assumed human nature, for in that nature alone could He discharge the duties of His office.

For whom did He minister? Not for Himself, but in an official capacity for others who could not minister for themselves. He allied Himself with men in their sin-ruined state, became surety for them, entered into their legal obligation and made Himself answerable for them.

To whom did He minister? On behalf of His people, He ministered in things pertaining to God. Thus His immediate action and ministrations were Godward. God was the primary object of His ministration, He ministered obedience to the law, and satisfaction to justice. He ministered that love, devotion, honour and service which men should have rendered to God, as their Creator, preserver, governor and judge. He alone was competent to answer thus. In the very nature that sinned, God received from Christ the surety the required honour and satisfaction.

But He also ministered to men, not only for them but to them. He ministered to their physical needs, by works of healing, feeding thousands, delivering them on the stormy lake. And He does so still, by preserving and feeding. He also ministered to their spiritual needs. He could and did forgive sin, and assured His people of a peace that the world could not take from them. He did so when on earth, imparting the blessings of spiritual life, while as yet His work was not complete. He has not ceased to do this; in His exalted state He now discharges a work for His church. He is active in the interests of men now.

(3) *His Death*

This was the crowning act of His ministration for His people and the high purpose of His advent to our world. His service was utterly unstinted, and He would go the whole length with it.

He gave His life; not simply His obedience, love and best service, or His energy and time, that is, His life from beginning to end, He did more. He actually gave it in death, and thus gave the most precious thing He had. But that was required, and nothing less would do. Life was required by offended justice, and it must be offered if satisfaction is to be procured.

He gave His life as a ransom, that is, the price to be paid for the deliverance of His people. They deserved to die, but, as Paul says, 'Christ hath redeemed us from the curse of the law by being made a curse for us'. The ransom is paid in exchange for the liberation of captives, or for culprits, that they might go free.

And He did it. He alone could do it. He was not deprived of His life, robbed of it, forced to die. It was voluntary - no man takes it from Him; He has power to lay it down, and power to take it again. He alone could dispose of His life, for it was His possession. He had life in Himself. Thus He was the offerer and the victim offered. Humanly speaking, no man has a right to dispose of His life; he is answerable for it, and the law would take charge of one who was reckless with it. But it was not so with Christ; His life was His own, it was not derived, He had it in Himself. This was His own act, He is active in suffering, in dying, and in death, active while acted upon. This is what was implied in our redemption; the price for it was life.

This was for many. Not a few, but a great company which no man can number; without respect to class, colour or clime. Blessed indeed are those who experience His redeeming power. Here is a view of the Saviour, one worthy of our trust, love and devotion. Come, behold what He did. Think of what He expects. He gave Himself for us. What do we give to Him?

36. THE HERALDED CHILD

Glory to God in the highest, and on earth, peace, good will toward men
(Luke 2:14).

Christmas is again at hand. Great prominence is given throughout the Christian world to the celebration of Christmas, despite the savages and horrors of war. It is to be feared, however, that greater prominence is given to the celebrations than to the significance of the glorious event which occasions them. Christmas has a message, and it is the message rather than the celebrations that deserves attention.

The time had come, according to the determined counsel of God, when His plan for the salvation of men should be revealed. Promises had been given of old, and types were instituted bearing on the manner and time of the Messiah's advent. Here the angels of Heaven herald His appearing among men. Three statements in the angelic song deserve consideration.

(1) *Glory to God in the highest*
God is recognised as the moving cause and active agent in this unique and marvellous event, which inspired the song of the angels. The message was

no sooner announced by one angel, than suddenly there was a chorus of the heavenly host praising God.

Glory is ascribed to God, for the praise of man's redemption belongs only to Him, and angels, though not immediately interested in it, yet desiring with holy wonder to examine it, will celebrate it to His honour. The wondrous event announced was designed not only to promote the glory of God, but also to express that glory. Nowhere is the glory of God more strikingly exhibited than in the giving of His Son to die for man's redemption.

The love and mercy of God designed this unique favour, and His marvellous wisdom contrived its revelation in a manner which is in harmony with the requirements and honour of all His glorious attributes. It is in every conceivable respect worthy of His greatness.

Other works of God are for His glory, but the redemption of man is for His glory in the highest. The words 'in the highest' may mean that He is to be glorified in the highest strains, in the highest possible manner; or that He is to be praised in the highest heavens. There He abides, and occupies the throne of Glory, and there angels minister to Him with praise and honour; there too the ransomed and glorified saints adore and praise Him for His wondrous love. Oh that men on earth would join the angels in song of praise to the highest God who dwells in the highest!

(2) On Earth Peace

It was a disordered world, a world lying in wickedness, into which Jesus came. It was a world at war with God. Men had rebelled against His rightful authority; and the marvel is that He did not manifest His just displeasure against them. That is what men deserved, and it must have astonished the angels that men were not to suffer the fate they deserved, and which is the irretrievable portion of fallen angels.

But more - the world itself was harassed with strife. The Romans were gradually extending their subduing influence over the conquered nations. There was strife and war and unrest everywhere. The people among whom Jesus appeared were vassals of Rome, and we read that at this time an order had gone out from Caesar Augustus over the whole earth, to tax the earth.

It was into such a world that Christ came. And what a cold reception He received. There was no room for Him in the inn. His first home was a stable, His first cradle a manger. He was obscure and unknown, yet His mission on earth was designed to establish peace in the world. He was predicted as the Prince of Peace (Isaiah 9:6). He came to reconcile Heaven and Earth. So we read that He made peace by the blood of His cross. By the once offering of Himself He removed the barrier between God and man. He came to bring the rebellious sons of men into a state of peace by the subduing influence of His grace and spirit. He makes a people willing in a day of His power. We see this happening on the day of Pentecost, and in the case of Saul of Tarsus on the Damascus Road.

He makes peace by disposing men to lay aside their differences to each other and seek each other's welfare, and so banish envy, malice, pride, lust and covetousness, the cause of disharmony on earth. He broke down the middle wall of partition between Jew and Gentile, and made them one in Himself. In Him men the world over, whatever their creed or colour, have a common Saviour if and when they turn to Him.

He also makes peace by diffusing the principles of universal peace among all nations. This He does by the ministrations of His word and church. If the Gospel of Jesus should universally prevail, there would be an end to wars and rumours of wars. This is the only cure for the ills and wrongs in the world.

But before peace on earth could be accomplished, the Lord Jesus made it quite clear that the world had to endure the ravages of war, until men should gradually learn the folly of it, and so embrace the reign and administration of Christ, for only then will the world enjoy lasting peace. In our own day the world is engaged in mortal strife. Such horrors have never been known in the world before. The inventions of man's genius have turned out to his own destruction and misery.

War is waged in the sky, on the sea and beneath it, and on earth. War is not only remorselessly prosecuted, but oppression and murder are viciously exercised for the extermination of races, and the perpetrators of these terrible deeds boast of a new order. Does not this seem a contradiction of the text? Has Christ failed in His mission? Surely not! If men would only embrace the religion of Christ, and regulate their lives according thereto, then we would have no war, and peace would reign on earth. Never in the history of man did the world need the Christmas message more than now. Christ came to establish peace on the earth, but this was to be gradual. God is in no hurry with the execution of His plan for the world, which shall be gloriously accomplished in the appointed time and way. Indeed, Christianity has already contributed largely to change the attitude of nations to war. Once nations gloried in war, but wherever Christianity has thrived, there is a decided change of attitude, and a keen desire for the total abolition of it.

(3) *Good-will towards men*

The gift of the Saviour is an expression of good-will or love towards men, and for this the praise, honour and glory is entirely due to God. The work of redemption is uniformly represented as the fruit of the sovereign love of

God. No words can express the greatness of that love. It is unique in its character and glorious in its exercise. It can only be measured by the misery, helplessness and danger of man, by the extent of the sufferings here and hereafter which would be his portion had not the mercy of God intervened, and by the eternal honour and happiness to which the ransomed soul is raised. All these are, of course, meantime beyond our comprehension, but shall be appreciated in the world to come.

The Gospel provision is principally for the good of men as individuals and not merely for the good of nations as such. The Kingdom of Christ is composed of individuals out of nations, although He favours nations and uses them to execute His purposes. But the day shall surely come when nations will hasten to His call.

It is sad to think that men, instead of responding with gratitude and love to the good will of God, actually oppose it. It was so with the world of Christ's day, and it is so still. Many treat it with contempt. But in spite of it all, the living Christ reigns to bestow the blessings that He secured by His death. Let us then echo to this angelic song. Let us have the same prayer and song of praise.

37. THE WITNESSING CHILD

And Simeon blessed them and said unto Mary his mother, Behold, this child is set for the fall and rising again of many in Israel: and for a sign which shall be spoken against; (Yea a sword shall pierce through thy own soul also,) that the thoughts of many hearts shall be revealed (Luke 2:34-35).

These words were spoken by godly Simeon to Mary concerning Christ. They were prophetic words, declaring the place which Christ would occupy in the esteem of men down through the ages. It is a solemn truth that He stands in such a relation to men, as to condition them for time and eternity, in terms of the place they give Him.

The words call us to consider the wonder and miracle of the ages - 'Behold, this child...'– He was a unique child. The Son of God is found in human nature as a weak child. This was foretold by the prophets (Isaiah 7:14, Micah 5:2-3), and to Mary by the angel, with His name and identity. According to the text, the coming of Christ would have different effects.

(1) *Many will fall*
This does not mean that they had not fallen before, for all have fallen. But it does mean that by rejecting Christ there is a further fall, the first from the

law, the second from grace. This is so by stumbling at the truth concerning Him.

It is true concerning His Person. The mode of His entry into the world is questioned by men. The truth is that Christ did not come into the world by an ordinary course, and so reason stumbles at and rejects the Virgin Birth as incredible. Then His identity is questioned. That God should be incarnate is inconceivable! He is placed on the level of ordinary childhood. This was reported in the press recently, as an attempt to discredit the Person of Christ. Against this we protest; as these truths are denied, so our Saviour is dishonoured. They are basic to our salvation. But the truth stands, and the truths about Christ are essential to salvation. They present God providing a Saviour suited to all requirements, suited to man's condition and to God's exactions. Man's Saviour must be holy; hence the Virgin Birth. He must be Divine, to discharge the work committed to Him. These are the articles of our faith, which are revealed and declared as essential to His work.

The Jews stumbled at His identity, His humility and obscurity. They rejected Him, as He did not answer to their preconceived notions as a mighty deliverer, though He gave abundant proof of His advent. But He was an offence.

Men still stumble at His identity. They also stumble at His teaching. They are offended at His presentation of God, of Himself, of man in his helplessness. They consider themselves as being wiser than Christ and the apostles, but they only destroy themselves by their blindness and ignorance.

They also stumble at His death. They reject its atoning and vicarious aspects. They say that death was His end, as it is the end of others. But what of the resurrection? That too they reject, and try to explain away. But the resurrection is as much a fact of history as His death, and the one is as unique as the other.

This stumbling is called a fall. It is a fall in respect of the privileges men have. Those who have the Bible and hear the Gospel are highly privileged. Like the people of Capernaum, they will be cast down to Hell if they do not repent. It is dreadful to think that privileged people reject Christ even in the fact of the evidence of truth concerning Him. Such indeed is a fall from grace; to such the Gospel is a savour of death. What falls is not where it was, but is much worse. The only remedy is repentance.

(2) *Many shall rise*

In John 1:10 we are reminded that not all reject Him. To those who receive Him there is the blessing of adoption as the children of God. That is the highest honour that can be bestowed, in time or in eternity. They rise in Christ.

This is true of all who, by faith, receive Him as Saviour. They are accepted in Him, and are given the rights and privileges of the children of God. They rest in Him, feed on Him, live by Him, and live in Him. They receive Him as presented in the Gospel in His Person and Work.

The words imply a quickening, a resurrection. By nature all are dead in sin; but Christ quickens them by His Spirit and brings them to life. Hence He is called the resurrection and the life. He gives them the Spirit of life, and the graces of His Spirit. By His indwelling they are renewed in heart and life. It is the raising of the poor and needy to honour and wealth. Christ exalts as only He can. In Him they are new creatures, delivered from the power of sin and slavery.

This is true of many - of all who experience His resurrection power. They are not a few, but many. We may think them few, for so they appear. But we must not limit divine power. The life they live is evidence of their resurrection, and of this they testify. The life they now live in the flesh they live by the faith of the Son of God (Galatians 2:20). The Christ of the Scriptures is alone the basis of life, hope, and comfort for time and for eternity. By His death He secured salvation and likes to bestow it.

(3) Christ is an abiding witness

He will be 'spoken against'. He is said to have been sent for this purpose, as His witness has a twofold effect, of falling and rising. It is by Him that we will either stand or fall.

Christ stands as an abiding witness to the truths relative to His Person and Work. He declared His identity and the nature of His life's work as a ransom for many. He clearly foretold the order of events just as they occurred, regarding His death and resurrection. He also foretold the coming of the Holy Spirit to convince and convert. Thus He was, and is, His own witness, still proving Himself in the life of His church.

He is spoken against. This is His lot from His advent until the end of time. Why? Because men of dark minds understand Him not. They are offended at His Person, teaching, claims, principles, death and resurrection. But there He stands, as His own chief witness, and He will have the final say.

Thus, by His witness, He distinguishes men. By Him we stand or fall. We are judged in terms of our relation to Him. The place we give Him, is what places us. In this light we must assess our standing with God. In Christ alone is salvation for sinners and sanctification for saints.

38. THE FULL CHRIST

And of his fullness have all we received, and grace for grace
(John 1:16).

A story is told of an English woman, a factory worker, who had never seen
the sea. When she went on her first excursion to the coast, and saw the vast
expanse of the sea, she stood amazed, and exclaimed, 'At last, here is
something of which there is enough'. This certainly holds true of our text
today. The apostle John speaks with even greater wonder of the fulness of
Christ, because he was aware of its length and depth.

(1) *Christ's fulness*
This is in truth a great deep, which no creature can fathom in time or eternity.
As one put it, 'if it were not too vast for my understanding, it were too limited
for my need'.

It is true of His Person. In Him dwells all the fulness of the Godhead.
The fulness of omnipotence, omnipresence, wisdom, power, justice, holiness and mercy. The attributes of His Person make up a grand total, and
what is more, these things rested in Him unchangeably and efficiently, even
when He was in this world, though unseen by men.

There was also fulness in Him in respect of His manhood. He was in every
sense the Son of Man, sin excepted; He was the perfect man. In this sense He
was as Adam was before the fall, though in respect of His Person He was
both God and man. He was the perfect man, in nature, meekness, sympathy,
steadfastness. He was kindly and just in all things. In Him there was all the
fulness of a sinless, perfect nature, yet in all respects He was truly man.

But there was in Him an acquired fulness, as Mediator between God and
man. He engaged on a work of salvation which necessitated the right to
supply the undeserving in a manner consistent with justice. Thus by His
perfect obedience to the law, and His satisfaction to divine justice, He
secured and opened an everlasting fountain of merit, and now, as the risen
Saviour, He has a fulness of saving and cleansing power. He bestows the
fulness of the Spirit, that was on Him, and whom He promised.

His is a fulness of grace, earned by Him. He has a fulness of pardon, of
peace and of rest. It is an abiding fulness. From it, saints in all ages have
been supplied, and now it is as full as ever; there is no abating of His fulness.
Earthly fountains become exhausted by demand; not so here. He is as full
as ever. The largest fountain gets depleted in dry weather, but His fulness
is unaffected and unchanging. This is a fulness of atoning merit, and of
justifying and sanctifying right.

(2) *The Supply*

John says that we have received out of this fulness. Not only the apostles, but believers in all ages and places have done so. If they received from Him, they must have been empty before they came to Him. Ah yes they were, and such is the condition of all believers. They know not what it is to be drawing on a fulness which never fails. In Christ there is full pardon, righteousness, right and riches, all we need now and for ever.

And, says John, we have received 'grace for grace'. There are different interpretations of this. Some have taken it to mean 'grace in the room of grace', and apply it to the Gospel dispensation, instead of the former dispensation. Others read it as 'grace for the sake of grace'; since all the favours we receive have their root in the free and sovereign favour of God, we see here cause and effect. This is certainly true. Others take it as 'grace upon grace', the fountain ever flowing like a torrent, with a constant supply, heaps of grace. Others take it in the sense of 'grace given resembles grace in Him', but the words imply more than likeness. Others say it is 'grace answerable to the grace given to us', according to His fulness and according to their need. In Him is the answer to all our needs.

All these views have in them an element of truth; and taken together may give us a complete view of His fulness. It we receive grace, it is because of His grace, it resembles His grace, it is grace upon grace, and the answer to grace. It is all out of the abundant fulness of God.

And what grace do we receive? Faith, hope, love, repentance, sorrow, humility, joy - and all the attendant fruits of His salvation. Here is the germ growing into bloom. There is preserving, sustaining and enabling grace. This is indispensable. Have you received grace? Then go to the fulness and keep at it. We need grace to receive grace, to make use of grace and to live by grace.

39. THE OBEDIENT CHRIST

And this is the Father's will which hath sent me, that of all which he hath given me I should lose nothing, but should raise it up again at the last day. And this is the will of him that sent me, that every one which seeth the Son and believeth on him may have everlasting life: and I will raise him up at the last day (John 6:39-40).

The Lord Jesus speaks of Himself as sent of God as the provision for the spiritual needs of man, needs deeper than those for which the manna was sent. He here speaks of Himself in relation both to God and men: He came not to do His own will, but the will of Him that sent Him, that is, the Father. He is thus the Father's servant doing His will, and He discloses the content of that will in reference to men, even their salvation. We may consider three things.

(1) *The Will of God*

This is a great deep which we cannot fathom. It may be defined as that perfection of His Being by which He resolves to act both towards Himself and His creatures in a manner consistent with all He is. It is the basic cause of all things, the reason for which they exist.

It is evident that God has a will which He exercises freely and sovereignly. This is spoken of as the general will of God in respect of unseen and revealed things, but is distinguished as His secret and revealed will. The former regards His decrees, His secret purposes known only to Himself, concerning what He foreordains or permits. The revealed will we have in the Bible by way of precept and provision, and it is this we are particularly concerned with.

His revealed will is seen in creation and providence - the government of God by which things He causes to be are preserved under the control of given laws. It is illustrated in human experience, which shows clearly that man is subject to a will other than His own. We order and plan and matters turn out differently; not because plans miscarry, but because they were willed otherwise. Yet within the compass of that will we are free agents, not under any compulsion.

We see this illustrated also in Christ. It was God's will that He should come, and in compliance thereto He came, and He came to execute God's purpose in all its parts. There never was a conflict of will between Him and His Father; He says 'To do thy will I take delight'. His entire life was dedicated to performing the Father's will. Here He defines it.

(2) *The Salvation of Men*

There are several points to note concerning this. Who are to be saved? Those whom the Father has given to Him. When? Before the world was. God established a covenant with His own Son on their behalf, in terms of which they were given Him, committed to Him, to answer for them in respect of their obligations to God as a law-giver. They were given to Christ in covenant; they were also given in promise, on condition of accomplishing the salvation. Here we have the doctrine of election clearly set forth, by Christ Himself, and nothing can erase it. It is a doctrine not to be shunned, but loved, for which God should be glorified.

This ensures their salvation in Christ. They are given to Him. He secured salvation for them. He lives to ensure the application of His purchase by the Spirit; they are operated on, and made willing by His power. They come to Him and are welcomed, received into favour and fellowship. They shall in no wise be refused, since it is for them that salvation is provided and intended. The value of His offering ensures their complete salvation.

It ensures too their perseverance to the end. They are kept by the power of God unto salvation. The nature of the life imparted ensures this. Hence the apostle says, 'Who shall separate us from the love of Christ?' None perish of those given to Him, else He would not be a Saviour.

(3) *The Resurrection of Men*

Christ redeems sinners as complete persons, soul and body. Both shall share in the resurrection of life - He shall raise them up at the last day. Christ Himself is the firstfruits, and His resurrection ensures theirs.

They shall all share the inheritance of the saints in light, wholly conformed at last to the pattern designed - they shall be like Him. We cannot now conceive of that; we can think of what He was, but not of what He now is. This shall be eternal, and none shall tire of it. These glorious words speak of a counsel which cannot be changed, a calling which cannot be resisted, an inheritance which cannot be defiled, a foundation which cannot be shaken, a seal which cannot be broken, and a life which cannot perish.

40. THE LIVING BREAD

I am the living bread which came down from heaven: if any man eat of this bread he shall live for ever, and the bread that I will give is my flesh, which I will give for the life of the world...He that eateth my flesh and drinketh my blood, dwelleth in me, and I in him (John 6:51-56).

This chapter records some of Christ's wonderful doings and sayings. Among His sayings here we have the most extraordinary of them. In it, He presents Himself as the only answer to human need. It is a claim which He alone could make, and the more we consider it, the more we see how true it is. Truly, never man spake like Him, and there is little wonder though natural men should regard His sayings as hard, and be offended in them. We need the faith which is His own gift to apprehend the significance of these statements.

(1) *What He says of Himself*

'I am the bread of life'. This is figurative language by which He presents Himself as the answer to all our spiritual needs. He tells us where He came from: from Heaven, in contrast with natural bread, which is of the earth. This is Heaven's bread, heavenly in origin and nature. He speaks of Himself as given, as sent by the Father, and calls Himself the bread of God (v.33). Bread is prepared, and is composed of the ingredients necessary to sustain life. This is indispensable and useful. So Christ was prepared; and a body was prepared for Him. He is the corn of wheat which fell into the ground and died, and was thus divinely prepared, ground, kneaded, baked in the fire of sufferings which renders Him suitable bread. He is God's bread, prepared and recommended by Him.

In respect of this preparation He speaks of His flesh, or human nature, as the bread. This is because it was in His human nature that He had the means to discharge our obligation and thus stand as the answer to our spiritual needs. Thus we are to think of His flesh or human nature as vested in His Person. His blood represents offered life - 'the life of the flesh is in the blood'.

He also speaks of Himself as living bread. He came to us as living and containing life in Himself. In this He differs from natural bread, or even from the manna, which required living human beings to put them to use; Christ has life in Himself, life which He imparts and sustains, 'for as the Father hath life in Himself, so hath He given to the Son to have life in Himself, and hath given Him authority to give life...'. He is the living bread in this twofold sense. First, He gives life. He alone is the giver of life, because He has it in Himself, and has the right to give it. This is true of Him naturally and spiritually. He gives natural life to all flesh as Creator, and He gives spiritual life to His covenant people, for whom He engaged to earn it. It is earned life, in the sphere of His sufferings and obedience to death. His death is its price. The life which issues from His death is spiritual and eternal, and in this it differs from the life which Adam possessed. This life He lives to bestow, and does confer on His people.

But, secondly, He sustains the life He imparts. He is indispensable to all life, because He has it in Himself - nothing lives of itself. This is true of natural life itself - He alone preserves in being the creation and all His creatures. Regarding the spiritual life which He confers on His people He says 'He that believeth on me shall never hunger. If any man eat of this Bread he shall live for ever.' This is surely a life worth seeking, having and living.

(2) *What He means by Eating*

This is not meant in a literal sense. It was thus that the Jews understood Him.

But this was prohibited by law, and so was any contact with the dead, both of which incurred ceremonial uncleanness. Hence it is not surprising that they enquired, 'how shall this man give us His flesh to eat?'. So they were offended in Him. But He made it clear this was not the sense.

Nor is it meant in a sacramental sense. This is the position of the Roman Catholic church, that the body and blood of Christ are present, and eaten, in the Mass. This is unreasonable and unscriptural. The body of Christ is glorified at God's right hand, and it is incapable of such distribution.

The eating of Christ as the Bread of Life is an act of faith. This He made clear enough - verse 47. Faith means coming to Christ and receiving Him. It implies a sense of need. Only the needy come to Him. There is an awareness of our impoverished state, and also a desire akin to hunger and thirst for Christ as He is presented in the Gospel.

There is also in faith an apprehension of Christ's fitness and value to our need. The God-man is our Saviour, answerable and adequate to our case. In His human nature He identified Himself with us, assumed our liabilities in His surety-relationship to us, and in our nature He met our obligations. This He could do only in our nature. His blood represents His self-offering as an adequate satisfaction to justice. So Christ in our nature becomes meat and drink to the believing soul. In Him we find the full answer to our case.

Again, eating of Him is to receive Him, and so make Him our own, the only worthwhile possession, in whom we rest and delight. Eating implies assimilating, feeding, feasting, being satisfied with all He did as Saviour. Again, eating is pleasurable, nourishing and satisfying. These distinguish the believer. What food is to the body, Christ is to the soul. He is indispensable; nothing is so beneficial or more excellent.

(3) *Eating of Christ implies life*

Apart from Him there is no life. He says 'If ye believe not that I am He ye shall die in your sins'. He alone gives the life we need. This life is not natural, but spiritual life. We have natural life from Him already, for it is in Him that we live, move and have our being. We should value His sustaining and preserving care. But He gives life that is spiritual, and life that is eternal. This is what we have in Him. He gives us a legal standing before God, in that He has saved us from the curse of the law. This life He won by dying, and puts to our account in justification. He imparts this life to us in regeneration, by which the soul is quickened spiritually, in virtue of which faith becomes operative and reaches out to Him. This life evidences itself in a life of faith, obedience, love, repentance and reform.

This life is eternal. This is true of its nature and duration, and is so by reason of the fact that Christ, who is our life, dwells in us. We have it both in right and in possession now. And at death it ensures full entry on a life of unbroken fellowship in Christ's likeness. He is the answer to our need. Without Him we perish. Have we tasted of Him?

41. THE DRAWING CHRIST

And I, if I be lifted up from the earth, will draw all men unto me
(John 12:32).

Jesus comes to Bethany, and is entertained to supper by Martha, and anointed with costly ointment by Mary. Here He defends Mary's action and all the actions of love towards Him against the callous accusers and fault-finders. Then we read of His triumphant entry into Jerusalem, in fulfilment of prophecy. Among the crowd that thronged around Him were some who witnessed the raising of Lazarus from the dead, and they testified to what they had seen. For this reason the people gladly received Him. The Pharisees said 'Behold, the world is gone out after Him'. That was the language of fear, but it will be actual fact. There were some Greeks present at the feast who expressed a desire to see Jesus. Philip and Andrew told Him this, and this occasioned the address in which our text is found. The shadow of the cross was already in view and felt; His soul is greatly troubled, for the hour was come. Yet the Saviour looked through the thick darkness of the cross, and in it saw His victory. Being lifted up, He would draw men to Him.

(1) *The Uplifted Christ*
We may consider, first, the One uplifted: the Lord Jesus Christ. He is one who was both loved and hated. He was loved by God, the disciples, Mary, and many more. His people in all ages love Him. But He was also hated; not because He had injured anybody, but because His life, words and actions censured the carnality of men. He was hated especially because He made certain claims - that He was the Son of God, the expected Messiah, claims which were true. For He was indeed the Eternal Son, and not one of God's many sons. He was the Second Person of the Trinity in human nature, the surety and Saviour of His people. He was one who came to seek and to save the lost. And yet He is treated by the majority with the utmost hatred, and this found expression in the desire to kill Him. The world had gone after Him; therefore He must be disposed of, and that in the most degrading fashion - by crucifixion.
He was thus uplifted *on the cross*, held up to the scorn and ridicule of the

world. He saved others, but Himself He cannot save. There you see Him uplifted and hanging on the cross - between Heaven and Earth, as one rejected and not worthy of either. That was the meaning of the cross, and in reality it was true. He was rejected by earth's proud ones, crucified by the choice and desire of the majority. But as the surety and substitute of His people in suffering and dying for them He is not favoured by Heaven either. The displeasure and wrath of the Eternal God against sin is displayed against Him. Picture the scene - the sun withholds its pleasant rays, the world is in darkness, thunder rends the heavens, the earth quivers, rocks are ruptured, while the sin-bearing substitute suffers what the Eternal Judge deemed necessary for the vindication of His own honour and the salvation of His people. Yes, He is lifted up on the cross, as an object of ridicule and shame, and He must go lower, to be buried and sealed in a tomb, and that was to be the end of Him, as far as the enemy was concerned. But was it?

He subdued death, rose triumphantly, and now this Christ is uplifted *to God's right hand*. In a place of favour, honour and prominence. It is a position of complete triumph, a triumph achieved under the most disadvantageous circumstances of the cross, yet achieved over the mightiest foes of God and man, both for God and for man. It is a position of the highest honour, won through shame, life procured through death. If He achieved so much on the cross, what will He achieve now that He is crowned? It is a position of great authority; all power in heaven and on earth is given to Him. All the forces of good and evil are under His control. None can harm His blood-bought people. He is the advocate.

He is now uplifted *in the Gospel*. The enemies of the Lord are said to have remembered that He spoke of rising from the dead, and they consequently went to the rulers and asked to have the tomb sealed and watched, lest His disciples would remove the body and say that He rose. This was done, but no seal or watch was powerful enough to confine Jesus to the grave. This dead and buried Christ rose from the dead, and was seen alive by many infallible proofs. He is now presented in the Gospel as the living and exalted Saviour of sinners. All who experience the saving and transforming power of His grace testify with one unanimous voice that He is able to save and does save.

(2) *The Drawing Christ*
When men come to this Christ, it is voluntary. They come willingly, because they are drawn to Him. Men were drawn to Him on earth. There was an arresting power in His personality. There was a magnetism about Him which compelled the respect, fear and admiration of men of all classes. His people felt it, and so did His enemies. Lawyers, rulers, Pharisees, even

Pilate and the Roman centurion felt it. The Gospels present a picture of Christ as a man who could not be ignored.

But it is as uplifted on the cross that Christ is arresting. This cross which was intended to be the crown of His shame and defeat is in the view of Paul and all who understand its spiritual significance and worth, the power of God unto salvation. Thus the weakness of God is stronger than men. Christ on the cross has drawing power, through the clarifying influence of His Spirit. He draws the trust of men, by the satisfying value of His work to God. Here is all they need. He draws the hearts of men, by the impelling power of His love and self-sacrifice for them. He draws the life, devotion and the all of man. He who was a stone of stumbling to some is an attraction to others.

It is Christ Himself as the living and exalted One that draws. He is not dead but alive - living and exalted. As such He draws the hopes, aspirations and obedience of His people. It is to Himself He draws. This is their comfort, their confidence, their salvation. In experience, Christ draws His people to Himself and to others. He is the centre of their unity. They are one in Him. The uplifted Christ has an uplifted influence on His people so that they live in the world yet live above it.

Christ draws all men - men of every class, clime and colour. In Him there is an open way for all to come to God for forgiveness and mercy. He was to be, and is, the desire of all nations; 'unto Him shall the gathering of the people be'. People who live in hatred to each other are drawn to each other in Christ. The crucifiers of Christ thought that by crucifying Him they would drive all men from Him, and even divorce the affection of His followers from Him. But men and devils were outshot in their blow. They say 'Crucify Him and His influence is at an end.' He says, 'Crucify me and I will draw not a few but all men'. The world is gone after Him. Let Him have more time and the promise will be abundantly fulfilled.

In the Judgement day this will be literally true. All men will come and bow before Him who allowed Himself in weakness to be lifted up. Those who regarded His cross as His defeat and shame; it will be to their shame and confusion.

42. THE INDISPENSABLE CHRIST

'...without me ye can do nothing' (John 15:5).

It is generally assumed that this chapter constitutes part of the address given by our Lord at the last Supper, on the night in which He was betrayed. Some have ventured to suggest that it was spoken on the way to the Mount of Olives. There seems, however, to be fitting connection between it and His table talk. In the first two verses He speaks of His relation to the church in general, and in this verse of the vital union subsisting between Him and His people - they are in Him, and He is in them. That is the secret of fruit-bearing, in contrast to the fruitless, lifeless branches that wither and are cut off. He is not in such, though they stand in a certain relationship to Him in respect of outward privileges. Here He emphasises the supreme need of union and communion with Him as indispensable to fruit-bearing, and He enforces the truth by these words - 'without me ye can do nothing'. Here we have a most significant statement from which we may learn profitable lessons.

(1) *Christ is Indispensable*

'Without me ye can do nothing'. Such language would be presumption on the lips of a mere man. No sane person would say this to a company of sensible men. In this world, no man is necessary. There are many men who, if taken from us, would be sadly missed. Yet no man, however useful and prominent his place in life, is of such that we could not do without him. Among the virtues that we associate with the best of men, we invariably reckon modesty. It is freely admitted that Jesus was the most modest of men, and yet from Him the words are wonderfully significant.

Jesus regarded Himself as indispensable. This is not a bold, presumptuous claim, but one which places Him in His true position. That is the light in which He places Himself, and that is the light in which Scripture presents Him. This is true with regard to His natural and official relation to the Church. Of His natural relation it is said 'In Him we live and move and have our being' - in this sense He is indispensable to our very existence. But here He speaks particularly of His official place. Indeed, the words are inexplicable except in the light of this vital relation which He holds to His people. This, then, is a legitimate claim, and one which is worthy of Him. He cannot be understood or explained in any other light. Apart from this view of Him, He remains the mystery and puzzle of the ages.

He is regarded as indispensable by His people. He is their only hope of salvation. They have seen themselves answerable to God on the basis of law, in relation to which they are wanting and incapable of rendering the required satisfaction. On their own confession, they are guilty and helpless in their guilt. They need salvation but cannot effect it. In Christ, they see One who identified Himself with their case, and who by His self-offering rendered adequate satisfaction on their behalf. In Him they have the provision of mercy to meet their case, without whom they would be eternally lost. He is indispensable to them for salvation and their acceptance before God.

(2) *Christ is Adequate*

This is clearly implied in His claim. He is the one and only answer to our need. If without Him, we can do nothing, then in Him we have all we need.

He is adequate to salvation. We need a Saviour. Here is one equal to, and greater than, our need. He is so because by His self-offering He offered an adequate ransom for our salvation, and thus secured our discharge from liability to punishment. In Him God is just in justifying the ungodly. God is well-pleased with Him, and His work, as a basis for acceptation and forgiveness. The believer is well-pleased with Him, and rests satisfied with God's satisfaction in Him on their behalf. In Him they find rest of soul, peace of conscience and joy of heart. Here then is a God-provided, God-approved and God-commended Saviour. He is all we need and all we want. As the hymn-writer put it, 'Tha agam ann an Criosd na tha m'anam bochd ag iarraidh'. He is the complete answer to their need - in Him they find righteousness to meet their unrighteousness, liberty instead of bondage, pardon instead of guilt. Their soul rests in Him with superb satisfaction.

He ensures our spiritual development and growth in grace. He is not only our salvation: He is our life. He combines the two as necessary to fruit-bearing: 'He that abideth in me and I in him - the same bringeth forth fruit'. Thus, Christ's indwelling in us is as necessary to our spiritual growth as the sap of the tree is to the fruitbearing capacity of the branch. Here we learn the lesson of complete dependence upon Him - He is our life. He indwells His people by the Spirt, by whom He produces in us such fruits as constitutes evidences of saving grace.

And what fruit is this? Of these fruits we have a catalogue in Matthew 5 and Galatians 5. But with regard to the conscious experience of the believer, we speak of repentance, faith, love, hope, joy in the Lord as evidences of grace. Another is this very thing - complete dependence on Christ, not only for salvation, but also for growth in grace. These are the roots and fruits of Christian life, without which we have no reason to assume that Christ is in us.

This implies the needed discipline for our spiritual advancement. If Christ is in us, then we shall experience the pruning knife and the cleansing process. Only the fruitbearing branch is pruned so that it will bear more fruit. Thus believers are the subjects of painful and distressing experiences which are calculated to increase their capacity for bearing fruit. But He mixes the cup of discipline with the sweet consolation of His presence and His promise - 'Lo, I am with you...'

As He is adequate to our case in time, He shall remain so for ever. However pleasing the pleasures of life, they weary and cloy, but here is something of which the soul never wearies. In Christ we have a boundless fulness, unsearchable riches which never lose their effect. Here we have only a foretaste, the appropriate allowance, but with the coming of age, there will come the full possession. Here we see through a glass darkly, but then face to face. Here we cannot conceive what we shall be when we shall be like Him and with Him. There will then be a complete discharge from all the encumbrances of earth, and deliverance from all that bondaged and enslaved the spirit. Oh what a prospect of ineffable brightness awaits the child of God - no more hiding of His face, seasons of suspension that caused such soul sickness here. His people will be made perfectly blessed in the full enjoying of God to all Eternity.

(3) *Christ is Apart and Unique*

Without Him we have nothing. All that men deem to be of value in life, on which they devote time, health and strength, and which they regard as indispensable to their happiness is nothing without Christ. Everything will slip out of our hands but what we have in Christ. We came into the world naked and empty-handed, and we shall carry nothing out with us. Without Christ we have nothing of permanent value. We have no merit for acceptance with God, no experience of transforming grace, no sustaining comfort in the prospect of death, but a fearful anticipation of judgement, in which the Christless have no standing. But with Christ we have everything.

We can do nothing. It is true that the Christless man may render much valued service to the state, to good causes, even to the church. Many have left behind them memorials of good service to men. But with regard to spiritual service, there is nothing we can render apart from Christ. However sincere we may be, however correct our learning may be - through the works of the law no flesh can be justified.

Nor can we grow spiritually apart from Him. There is no spiritual progress apart from Christ. His indwelling is vital to the healthy exercises of our soul. Apart from Him we could not overcome sin and temptation. Nor can we do good to others. This ought to be a question of supreme importance to us - what influence do we have on our fellows, either for good or ill? It is only by grace we can be the light of the world and the salt of the earth. It is said of McCheyne that the holiness of his life and heart had greater weight than his words. Through Christ we can do all things.

Without Christ we are miserable creatures. We are miserable in life, and miserable in view of the prospect of death. Soon the pleasant ceases to please, and men are left restless, dissatisfied, unhappy, not realising they have deeper needs than can be met by worldly interests. The Christless are miserable indeed. And the believer, when his vision of Christ is cloudy, will be miserable too. Where do we stand?

43. THE MAN BEHELD

'Behold the Man!' (John 19:5).

These are the words of Pilate the Roman Governor, who may be rightly called an unrighteous judge. Jesus had been tried by the Sanhedrin, or Jewish Court, pronounced guilty of blasphemy (because He claimed to be the Son of God), and delivered to Pilate to undergo the punishment of death. Pilate was fully convinced of His innocence, and he strove with as much earnestness and concern as was consistent with the weakness and vices of his character to secure the acquittal and release of Jesus. But the policy that he adopted was unworthy of a man of his standing and position. He scourged Jesus as if He had been a malefactor. He suffered his soldiers to mock and make sport of Him. They plaited a crown of thorns and put it on His head; they put on Him a purple robe and hailed him King of the Jews. Having thus debased Him, Pilate brought Him out to the multitude probably thinking that this would persuade the Jews that their fears were unfounded and their hostility unnecessary. So he said to them 'Behold the Man'.

(1) *The Man*
Pilate at the instigation of the enemies of Jesus attempted to make Him an object of derision, whose fancied claims and present plight called only for contempt and scorn. But the words that he used - 'Behold the Man' - direct our attention to a view of Christ which is often either abused or forgotten.

There are (and were) some who take the words at their face value, and assume that Christ was purely and simply a man, though they freely and frankly admit He was one of the greatest of men. There are others who seem to lose sight of the fact of His humanity altogether and think of Him only as God. Now both views apart are unfair, unscriptural, and therefore false; and they render a great injustice to the Person of Christ. Christ was certainly a man, but He was more - He was God, but more than this, He was the God-man. He was not a man who somehow developed the consciousness of God, but was Himself God. He possessed two distinct natures in His one person. Here He is presented to us as a Man, and in thinking of Him as such there are certain doctrines revealed concerning Him which we must always remember.

First, *His coming and mission among men were foretold.* This is a very significant fact, especially when we remember that the events of His life as they unfolded themselves were foretold with amazing detail. Not a single word of what was foretold about Him was ever found to be inaccurate or unfulfilled in Him or by Him. The secret of this was that He came to fulfil the law and the prophets.

The promise of His coming was given immediately after the fall of man, and that promise was illustrated in type down through the ages till He came. Moses, David, Isaiah and all the other prophets - they all foretold His coming. The angel came to Mary and Joseph to announce the manner and time of His coming, and even the name that was to be given Him. Shepherds attending their flocks were informed of His advent by heavenly messengers. Such was the faith of the church in the promise of His coming that the faithful longed and looked for its fulfilment. Some recognised Him even when He was yet a child - Simeon, Anna and many more.

Secondly, *He was a faultless man.* He did no sin, neither was guile found in His mouth. His enemies tried in vain to discover flaws in His words and actions. They could bring no valid charge against Him. Indeed, He challenged them to charge Him with sin. He placed His life, words and actions, before them, and asked for their inspection. That is the very last thing a sinful man would do. Pilate found no fault in Him. He alone of all men is admitted to have been free from sin. Age after age tried to measure Him, and His foes as well as His friends are unanimous in their verdict that He was sinless.

Thirdly, *He was a self-sacrificing man.* He came not to be ministered unto, but to minister, and give His life a ransom for many. That was His testimony of Himself. He lived and died for others. For that purpose He became man; to be the surety and substitute for men. Thus He entered into the legal standing and obligations of His people, or sinners, and answered for them in things pertaining to God. God dealt with Him in their place or stead, and inflicted on Him all that they deserved. And He, by reason of the Glory of His Person, and the immense value of His sufferings and offering of Himself, rendered complete satisfaction to God for them.

It is true that He was crucified by men, that He seemed weak and helpless, and that Calvary seemed the crowning scene of His defeat and shame, but in reality His sufferings and death were voluntary, that He might effect this merciful purpose. Calvary then, instead of being the scene of His defeat and shame, is the scene of His greatest and most glorious triumph.

Fourthly, *He is Mediator between God and man.* He answered, suffered and died for men, and through these, effected reconciliation between them and God. He secured their salvation, and He lives to ensure the application of His benefits to His people. He is the divinely appointed and acknowledged Saviour of men. There is no other Saviour among men. This man who was laughed to scorn, who suffered and was crucified by wicked men, is the Saviour of the church , and one day the world shall crown Him Lord of all.

(2) *How should we behold Him?*
There were and are some who behold Him with pity. There were some in the procession to Calvary who wept for Him; but He, looking upon them rebuked them and said 'Weep not for me; weep for yourselves and your children'. There is something in the sufferings of Christ which causes tears; but our tears ought not to be of pity, but of penitence and shame. Peter wept, but his tears were tears of repentance for his own conduct. The person who weeps out of pity alone has not yet understood the meaning of Christ's sufferings and death. He requires not that we behold Him with pity, but with penitence, faith and love.

We should behold Him with a sincere interest and a desire to know and understand the secret behind the sufferings of the sinless one, the cause behind the fact. We should behold Him with admiration, reverence and worship, with gratitude, love and praise, with trust, obedience and dedication. Others reject Him. Let us receive Him and believe on Him to the saving of our souls.

44. THE EXALTED PRINCE

Him hath God exalted with his right hand to be a Prince and a Saviour, for to give repentance to Israel, and forgiveness of sins (Acts 5:31).

In the context we see the disciples imprisoned for speaking in the name of Christ, and delivered by an angel who commanded them to go and preach in the Temple. This created confusion and concern to the authorities, especially when they heard that the speakers were once again preaching in public. They were instantly apprehended and brought before the high priest, who addressed them, reminding them that they had been forbidden to preach. Their reply was that they must obey God rather than men, and they took the opportunity to preach to them about the God of their Fathers and His Son the Lord Jesus Christ. They had crucified Him but He had risen, bringing Gospel blessings to men. They had to listen to a very solemn sermon, which made its mark. Let us consider what the apostles declared about Christ.

(1) *The Exaltation of Christ*

Peter, who was probably the chief speaker, charged them with the crucifixion of Jesus. They had shown their hatred of Christ, although nothing worthy of death had been proved against Him, and although the judgement of Pilate declared Him to be innocent of all charges. Yet they demanded His death on the ground of blasphemy, for claiming that He was the Son of God, and thereby making Himself equal with God. This indeed was true, and His claim was sustained in His life and by His miracles. They could not disprove it though they would discredit it. So He was put to death - that was a fact; He was buried (in a sealed tomb, at their request), but something happened which confounded them.

God had raised Him from the dead. They killed the Prince of Life, but God raised Him up. This includes the resurrection, which was the first step in His exaltation. Why did the apostle lay such stress on the resurrection? Because it proved and declared the nature and value of the death He had died. It had fully served its purpose, for it was a purposeful and therefore a significant death. He came on purpose to die this death, and the ransom price of our redemption was paid by Him. It was of sufficient efficacy to secure the redemption of His people. Death could not hold Him; the reason was that by dying He had robbed death of its authority.

The resurrection also proves Him to be a Saviour. He is the Son of God with power to save. But He is the exalted Prince - exalted to God's right hand and by God's right hand. Now He occupies not the tomb of Joseph of Arimathaea, but the Throne of Glory. He is there in human nature as a Prince. The Kingship of Jesus is vested in and operates through His priesthood. It is true that He is King of Kings, and His authority extends over all. Yet as a Saviour, He is exalted as King over all things for His church.

Of this they were witnesses. They had seen Him alive after His passion, and were witnesses of the resurrection, but they were also witnesses of His exalted life. They had evidence of this, and were themselves the evidence of it. Nothing was more objectionable to the high priest and the council than this, yet they must hear it and were made to hear it. The resurrection was a fact; His exalted life was a fact. The apostles were the result of it. It changed them and inspired them. They bore incontrovertible witness to it.

(2) *The Fruit of Christ's Exaltation*

This is twofold. First, He gives repentance. The apostles were clearly guided in their use of terms; when they speak of repentance they use a term which is basic in the application of redemption, that is, the benefits secured by the death of Christ and put into circulation by His resurrection.

Repentance is a significant word. It is not a legal word as is often supposed, but an evangelical word, a gospel word, the coinage of Heaven itself. Repentance is not remorse. It differs from remorse, which is something from which men seek relief by self-improvement and good resolutions, which are no sooner made than they are broken again. It is not merely to be sorry for doing wrong, or to indulge in self-rebuke; it is to be changed in ourselves, to be against sin, to take God's side against it. It means a changed heart, resulting in a changed mind and life. Those who have learnt this repentance have no desire to get rid of it - they only want more of it.

The second fruit of Christ's exaltation is the gift of forgiveness. This is another heavenly word. And what a word! It extends to the greatest wrong. There are some crimes, for example treason against the state, which are said to be unpardonable. Such is the character of our sin - it is treason against God, and yet He is said to pardon sin. Man says 'I can forgive but not forget'. It is not so here. It is complete forgiveness - our sins are blotted out, so that no trace of them can be found, they can have no more existence. As when a debt is paid and the account erased because there is full compensation, so our sins can never be called forth again.

This we have through the exaltation of Christ. He has secured these blessings through His death, and He applies them to us through the power of His resurrection. As the exalted Prince and Saviour He is entrusted with all power in Heaven and earth with reference to the application of His purchased blessings and the discharge of His exalted duties. He is entrusted with the government of His church, and employs fit means to that end. He shall remain in this exalted position, and will return in glory to judge the world.

(3) *To whom does He grant these favours?*

'To Israel.' Why is Israel named here? There are several reasons. Peter, as a Jew, *was speaking to Jews.* It was among the Jews that Christ appeared, to whom He came and by whom He was rejected and crucified. They had been given promises about His advent. These truths He emphasised to bring conviction and repentance. It was among the Jews that these events had occurred, and among them the truth had to be proved and tested. Hence the command was given to the apostles 'Begin at Jerusalem'. There it must be proved that the scriptures were fulfilled in the coming of Christ to suffer. There the significance of that death must be shown in the truth of the resurrection and exaltation.

But as it was first to be proclaimed among Israel according to the flesh, it was also, and chiefly to Israel according to election and the spirit that the Gospel is effective. Thus it extends to the Gentiles. The promises of God were to Israel after the Spirit, to all who belong to the family of God, and are heirs of His salvation according to His promise.

45. THE SINLESS MADE SIN

For he hath made him to be sin for us, who knew no sin; that we might be made the righteousness of God in him (2 Corinthians 5:21).

It is a matter of paramount importance that a sinner, guilty before God, knows how he may be pardoned. Indifference to this matter is not worthy of rational creatures. The question of how a man can secure the favour of God is one which has occupied thoughtful and sincere minds in every age. Reason labours in vain to provide a solution. But God comes to our rescue by the provision of His mercy, recorded in the words of the text.

(1) *The Sinless One*
This refers to Christ - it cannot refer to any other. All have sinned. Adam sinned and all mankind fell in him. Sin has separated us from God. It has brought man under the curse of God, so that man is helpless.

But this is not true of Christ. He knew no sin. He was God, and as such knew it not. He was not ignorant of sin, but was of purer eyes than to behold it. Its vileness was seen by Him, and He knew the depth of guilt and misery to which it brought mankind. In His human nature He did not know sin. He was holy. He did not share in original depravity which sinful men inherit from Adam. The body prepared for Him was kept pure.

Even although He was tempted by sin He was without sin. Before entering on His ministry He was put on a trial. He was carried to the wilderness to be tempted of the devil, and for forty days and nights He was assailed by him. But those wiles which proved successful against Adam were employed in vain against Christ. The enemy had the mortification to be trapped in all his artifices. Never once did Christ yield before temptation. He withstood the fury of the blast, bearing the fiercest onslaughts of hell.

Again, He lived His life in a sinful world, associating with sinful men. Yet He remained pure through it all. Of all men He alone had no taint of moral contamination. His heart was upright and His soul had no bias to evil. He was holy, harmless, undefiled, separate from sinners. In discharging His duties He was narrowly watched and strictly scrutinised. His enemies were determined to condemn Him, but in vain. The more they tried the more His innocency and integrity shone forth in splendour. Such was their spite that they resorted to downright lying. But He could challenge them to convince Him of sin. So perfect was He that no one virtue stands out above the rest. He possessed them all in sublime and heavenly harmony.

That He should be so was essential if salvation was to be accomplished. No mere man was capable of undertaking salvation for his fellows. If a man is to answer for others before God, he must be pure, otherwise he can only suffer for his own sins. Therefore none but a perfectly sinless man could answer for sinners. The law demanded perfect purity of nature and perfect obedience in action; none but Christ could offer this. Such a high priest became us. That He was sinless is proved by the testimony of God and men and devils. What a blessed fact this is.

(2) *The Sinless Made Sin*

This is the most wonderful event in the whole history of the world. The words suggest that He was made sin by some one other than Himself. He willingly gave Himself and made Himself answerable for sin and sinners. But He did not make Himself sin. Nor was it by sinners He was made sin. It was God as Giver and Judge who laid on Him our iniquities. God was an active agent in the whole scheme of redemption. He was the author of it all. Here is the provision of God for the salvation of sinners. 'God so loved the world.' This suggests the covenant arrangement according to which Christ was appointed to bear sin. What a wonder this is - that the God against whom we sinned should love us and provide for our salvation.

And how was He made sin? It is not that He was made a sin-offering, although that is included. Nor was He made a sinner. To be made sin does not imply being made personally sinful either in act or inclination. He was not guilty of any sin that He committed Himself, nor was He guilty of our sins. He was made sin *only by the imputation of sin to Him*. He was by divine act made the sin bearer. From the assumption of our nature to His death on the cross He bore our sins and suffered for them. He was made sin, not in semblance but in reality. He stood in our place, and this rendered it necessary to visit Him with the punishment we deserved. And what punishment! The most fearful of deaths is exacted at His hand. And God has no pity on Him. Heaven is silent; all earth would give Him was vinegar.

And all this was for us. He suffered the equivalent of what we deserved to suffer, though not in duration. The sufferings of the wicked will be eternal in duration, but Christ exhausted the curse in time. It was not because He saw anything in them to merit His favour, attract His interest or appeal to His love that He did this. Nor was He under any obligation to Himself or to them to save them. Nor does it indicate that He takes a light view of sin, or that He will deal mildly with the wicked as some foolishly suppose. It only shows the contrary. His holy hatred to sin is displayed here. When God did not spare His son it is the purest folly to suppose that He will spare sinners if they persist in sin.

But again, here we see the punishment of sin, the death of sin, and the salvation of sinners made possible. What a glorious triumph is this. Sin is condemned and obliterated so that it cannot rise again to condemn the soul who takes refuge in Christ.

(3) *The Sinner made Righteousness*

This was the purpose God had in view in making our sins to rest on Christ, and making Him answerable for them. Now, notice that the righteousness referred to here is not the essential righteousness of God, for this cannot be transferred to any.

It denotes rather the righteousness which God required of us, and which Christ rendered by His obedience and death. It is thus a created righteousness wrought out by the God-man. It is the result of the concurrent action of both natures, and therefore is of infinite value and efficacy. It consists in action, not in the mere possession of a righteous nature. Adam had a pure nature, but failed in rendering the required righteousness. But neither is it a mere outward action, but a perfect nature approving itself to the lawgiver in the sphere of tried obedience. 'This is the righteousness which the righteousness of God required Him to require.' This righteousness belongs to Christ and consists in His obedience.

How does the sinner become the righteousness of God? Just in the same way as that in which Christ was made sin: by imputation, not by infusion. This imputation is the judicial act of God, not a change of nature, but of state, a change of standing with respect to our relation to law. God looks upon His people as concrete righteousness, not merely as righteous. Adam was righteous but not righteousness. This one differs in that it is everlasting and complete, and therefore more glorious. This is the righteousness which God imputes to believing sinners. On its account they stand acquitted at His bar, and they rejoice in the experience of a full and glorious reconciliation.

It is appropriated by faith. Faith is the eye that conceives it, and the hand that receives it. The result is the justification of the sinner's person, in consequence of which the sentence of condemnation is cancelled and reversed. Who then shall condemn? What a glorious fact is this! A poor sinner saved, sinful in himself, righteousness in Christ. This is a subject of great consolation to the believer, where we see the dreadful nature of sin, and the amazing love of the Saviour.

46. THE IMPOVERISHED CHRIST

For ye know the grace of our Lord Jesus Christ,
that, though he was rich, yet for your sakes he became poor,
that ye through his poverty might be rich (2 Corinthians 8:9).

One of the duties which the Gospel imposes on men, is to be kindly disposed towards others, especially those in need. That was true in Paul's day, and it still holds. It is not that all are so disposed - some are more so than others. So the apostle in writing to the Corinthian believers exhorts them to liberality towards the poor, not only among themselves but elsewhere also. He sustains his exhortation by the example of the Macedonian church, which he praises. But in this verse he goes to a higher example, to that of the Lord Jesus Christ, who gave of His goods to the poor. He speaks to them, as knowing this wonderful grace towards them, which in itself is the highest inducement to act similarly towards others. He also emphasises the fact that liberality for the sake of Christ is well-pleasing to God, and should be no burden to the sinner, but rather a privilege. Self-sacrifice is a real test of love. What is the Gospel worth to us? Let us note the high example of self-sacrifice brought before us here.

(1) *Christ in His Wealth*

Christ's riches are not specified, but are beyond specification, for they transcend our capacities of search. It is a great deep and a great height, yet so much is revealed as gives us an idea of their true greatness and glory, though they pass reckoning. The apostle speaks to these as 'knowing' this amazing grace, though it surpasses knowledge. God has revealed it by His Spirit. When we think of the person spoken of, we are not surprised that He is termed rich - He is the Lord Jesus Christ. What is surprising is not that He is rich, but that He became poor. It is clear that the Person spoken of existed in wealth and riches before He became poor. Here we have His pre-existence, which confronts us with the issue of His identity - who is He? The Lord from Heaven.

He was rich in Himself. He was apart from and independent of any externals. He was Himself God, having the fulness of Godhead in Himself, the coequal with the Father, in all the divine attributes. Thus He was rich in all sources of happiness which infinite moral perfection could furnish. He could not be enriched. He possessed all such perfection. He revealed such amazing and endearing qualities as makes Him the object of wonder to angels and men for ever.

He was rich in possession. Not merely in what He was and had in

Himself, but what He owned by right outwith Himself. Invariably we think of wealth in terms of possession, however it is obtained. Here is one who was rich as of right, and of whom alone it is true that 'The earth belongs unto the Lord and all that it contains'. This is clearly stated in Scripture. He owns all things, as Creator of all. His are all the riches of Heaven and earth.

Yes, He was rich, in possession of all things, so complete that they could neither be increased nor diminished. They were His essential and personal qualities and rights. In this He stood alone and apart. He had riches that were not capable of being given to any other; and He had riches that He could only give to others by becoming poor Himself.

(2) Christ in His Poverty

He became poor. What a startling thought! He did not lose any of His wealth, as happens to men. His personal fulness and rightful possessions are inseparable from His Being, so that it was true of Him that while He became poor, He was yet rich, for the fulness of the Godhead dwelt in Him bodily - He came to be what He was not, yet ceased not to be what He was. So how did He become poor?

His poverty was self-imposed. He was not made poor, He made Himself poor. He chose to become poor, purely by an act of free, sovereign grace, in which amazing grace and love are shown. Grace is a wonderful word, meaning undeserved and unmerited favour. That is what He showed by becoming poor. He came to this state by a voluntary, personal act. It is true that the Three-in-One God shared the grace and plan, yet here we have the personal act of the Son.

The poverty He chose was one of identification with His people. He became poor by assuming human nature, and so identifying Himself with us. This is clearly stated by Paul in Philippians 2: 'He took upon Him the form of a servant'. This was great humiliation for the Son of God to assume a created form. And again He is said to have 'emptied Himself', not having lost His glory, but having concealed it. The eternal glory which radiated from His Person He veiled by the garb of humanity, so that He appeared among men in the form of a man - God manifest in the flesh, yet not recognised. Think of it - the uncreated God in a created form and nature, on the level of the creatures of whom He required and deserved worship. He was in all respects a man, sin excepted. And all this in order that He might as kinsman act as the surety of His people.

He was made under the law, taking on Himself the legal obligation of His people, to render obedience as a servant in order to honour and exalt the law. Oh the wonder of the Lord, the lawgiver, in our nature the servant of law. What amazing condescension is this!

In this condition, He was subject to the sinless infirmities of our lot - He hungered, suffered, was weary, and lonely. He was misunderstood and maligned. He was poor in the esteem of man - the foxes had holes, but the Son of Man had no place to lay His head. He had no material wealth. He who owned all things valued the kindness of men to Him. He owned no house, boat or grave. He was poor in life and in death.

Why was this? 'For us.' The true nature of His poverty can only be estimated in the light of His relation to us and our poverty. It was our poverty He assumed. Our real poverty is spiritual rather than material. We were poor in ourselves, and without any rights or spiritual possessions. We were without God and without godliness. But Christ, in becoming our Surety, made Himself answerable for our poverty. We lost all, and were enslaved by sin. But He, in answering for us, was made to taste of the bitterness to which sin exposed us. He was made sin, and God laid on Him the penalty which justice required for our guilt. He became so poor that He was without a claim to Heaven or Earth.

(3) *The Reason for This*

It was that we might be enriched. See the price He paid in order to enrich us - it is through His poverty. This is what secured our enrichment. Oh what grace! He voluntarily became poor that He might thereby secure a right to enrich us by effecting a change in our state and case. He came down to our condition that He might raise us to the level of the children of God. He could not indeed sink to our level in every particular - to become a sinner - yet our sin was put to His account, and He was condemned for it.

We are rich in His riches. Not His personal riches, but His accomplished riches, the riches procured by His grace. We are so poor that nothing is ours save sin and wretchedness. But here are riches which flow out of poverty; hence it was poverty which contained value and secured riches for us. Thus we are enriched by riches earned, the riches of grace imparted - forgiveness, acceptance, justification, regeneration. We are enriched by the graces of the Spirit. The Spirit Himself is given us, with life and hope and all the necessary graces.

We are rich for all eternity. That is what matters. The treasures of Heaven belong to us if we have Christ. They have all that is necessary for time and eternity. Christ sanctifies His people and will glorify them. They will be blessed for ever. They will see His face, and His name will be in their foreheads. This is wealth worth seeking and finding.

47. THE CURSED ONE

Christ hath redeemed us from the curse of the law, being made a curse for
us: for it is written, Cursed is every one that hangeth on a tree
(Galatians 3:13).

The apostle was surprised that the Galatian church had so soon departed from the faith of the Gospel to become again enslaved to a system which could not save. He charges them with folly, and asks them pertinent questions to expose their folly. He points them to the benefits of the Gospel in contrast to the Law. By the Gospel they received the Spirit; they were justified and accepted before God. By the law no flesh can be justified. In our text we find illustrated God's way of salvation.

(1) *Our State by Nature*
We are under the curse of the law. This implies several things.

It implies that *man is under law to God.* We are answerable to Him alone as lawgiver and judge. When we were created, God, to whom alone it belonged to legislate for His creatures, gave man a rule of life, according to which he was obliged to bear himself and continue in favour and fellowship with his Creator. This law ensured life and standing on the condition of obedience, and death through disobedience. Man, as party to this transaction, or covenant, was fully capable of conformity, and the claims were in all aspects agreeable to man's nature. This expression of God's will is clearly demonstrated in the moral law, given to Moses in the form of the ten commandments, to show man, in his fallen condition, the duty God requires of him.

By sin *man failed in his required obedience.* He transgressed God's law, and became guilty of a breach of the covenant. He dishonoured God by an act of rebellion which instantly changed man's relation to his Maker. Sin constituted him a rebel, hostile to God, and this brought him at once under the curse of the law. That raises the question - what is the curse of the law?

This phrase embraces *all the consequences of man's disobedience.* Man and his offspring were exposed to the penal issues of a violated law. This act of disobedience brought man under guilt, and so condemned to endure all the consequences of guilt - the wrath of God revealed against all the ungodliness of men, set forth in the Bible under various aspects.

Sin, for example, separated man from God. Man lost all rights in God, and all claim to God's favour. Man lost his God; that is the essence of the curse. Nothing can make up that loss, and leaves man a dissatisfied sinner. He lost all that constituted blessedness and happiness. He lost his innocence, holiness, righteousness, and became dead in sin.

Again, sin left man unable to compensate his wrong, or merit divine favour, or even bring satisfaction to himself. He is now the subject of a defiled nature, incapable of good, given over to the miseries of life. But more - he is given over to the exposure and infliction of penal wrath, on some in time, but for all the godless in the eternal woe, when God as Judge will assign the full measure of deserts. There is such a place as hell. It is clearly described by Christ as a place of woe and anguish. There, all good is excluded. It is the misery of loss. Such is man's fallen condition. Few believe it, or are concerned about it. But there is no escaping it. Man is answerable to God.

(2) *Christ under the curse*

When Christ is under this curse, it is not for His own sake as in our case. On His part there was no personal deserving of curse. He was holy and undefiled. How then did He come to be under the curse? The text answers - it was 'for us'. He became identified with us.

His name 'Christ' implies this. It signifies the Anointed One, the Lord's anointed. Anointing signifies appointing to office, the discharging of duty which He assumed in terms of His charge. Thus His name implies official relation and action. He was anointed by God, who chose and appointed Him as alone fit for the work assigned Him.

The anointed Christ is the Lord from Heaven, who in order to save men from the curse became surety for them. He assumed their nature, entering into their legal obligations, answerable for everything that was required of them, in respect of obedience to the law and satisfaction to justice for their guilt. Thus, by His life on earth as under the law He exalted the law and honoured it; but as the surety of sinners it required full compensation and satisfaction in enduring the penalty of sin.

Thus He endured the curse of the law, and so tasted of it in all its aspects. By identifying Himself with us, although sinless Himself, He took the curse of the law upon Himself and endured it in human nature. There was no escape for Him. He must drink of the cup of wrath, or curse, to its dregs in His sufferings and death. He tasted the bitter drop of conscious isolation from God His Father. Men and devils inflicted as much agony as they could, but God laid on Him the full weight of the curse, until He exhausted the full measure of satisfaction required for its abolition.

And He endured it lovingly. Let us never lose sight of this loving embrace of the Father's will. The curse is inflicted upon Him. But there is also personal agency on His own part. This imparts infinite value to His sufferings, as a satisfaction to justice. The mode of His death was a symbol of the curse, for 'cursed is every one that hangeth on a tree', as if He was cut off from Heaven and earth. The land must not be soiled by leaving such a one hanging overnight; hence the Jews desired the bodies to be removed. It was a cursed death, and all in our room and stead.

(3) *The Redemption He effected*

He redeemed us. This is presented in Scripture under several aspects.

The redemption is a *legal* redemption. Having exhausted the curse He secured deliverance from liability to punishment. He paid the ransom price in full, and in law secured our discharge. Law has nothing more to exact. Therefore the Bible speaks as there being no more condemnation for God's redeemed. Their liberty consists in His merits and accomplishment.

The redemption is also *personal*. He imparts the purchased liberty to all His people, on whose behalf He acted. In this respect it is deliverance by power; in conversion, regeneration, justification and sanctification they are delivered from sin and its effects.

It is also a *conscious* redemption. It concerns their conscious experience. This is through knowledge of the truth. It liberates their mind, conscience and will. They are enabled to rejoice in His salvation. They are now God's free men. In Christ they are always free, though in themselves they are often in bondage, and fear they are still under the curse. They feel its effects; but soon in the glory there shall be no more curse. In Him believers are free.

48. THE SAVIOUR OF SINNERS

This is a faithful saying, and worthy of all acceptation, that Christ Jesus came into the world to save sinners, of whom I am chief (1 Timothy 1:15).

The apostle Paul, in writing to Timothy, his son in the faith, exhorts him to devote himself entirely to the proclamation of sound doctrine, and warns him lest he should be diverted from his high calling by giving heed to fables and vain jangling. In this arresting and pregnant passage we have the subject matter of the Gospel which Timothy was to preach, that Christ Jesus came into the world to save sinners. This was the Gospel which Paul preached, of which he had experience, and to which he testified. He was not ashamed of it, neither in Rome, nor in Athens nor in Corinth, because it was the power of God unto salvation. Let us consider several things about it.

(1) *The Fact Stated*

Christ Jesus came into the world to save sinners. This includes two things: the advent of Christ into the world, and His design in coming.

When Paul states concerning the advent of Christ that He came into the world, this suggests and points to an existence prior to His coming. He had an independent and underived existence, for He had life in Himself. As the Living Father had life in Himself, so He gave to the Son to have life in Himself. Hence it is said that 'His goings forth were from of old, from everlasting'. He was in the beginning with God, was God, all things were made by Him; without Him nothing was made that was made. Such is the Person who came - none other than the Second Person of the Trinity.

Sometimes He is spoken of as being sent into the world, and here He is said to have come. Both are true, for although in the economy of grace He was given and sent by the Father, this did not invalidate His own independency, voluntariness and action. It is true that the Father gave and sent His Son, but it is equally true that the Son came and gave Himself. Though rich, He became poor. This was His own action. And there was no compulsion or obligation in this. He acted freely, was willing of Himself. He and the Father are One, and were one in this. The Son willingly acquiesced in the Father's plan of saving sinners; hence He says 'To do thy will I take delight..'

So in the fulness of time the Word was made flesh. This was a new and unheard of thing in the earth. God became incarnate and appeared on earth in the form of man, truly man. Thus He came to be what He never was, and yet ceased not to be what He was. His coming involved great humiliation - the assumption of a finite and created nature. He was born of a woman made under the law - God, the author of law, becoming the servant of law, subject to the limitations and infirmities of that nature.

And why was this? What was the design, the purpose of this advent? The majestic purpose for which the Son of God came into the world was *to save sinners.*

That meant that there were sinners in need of salvation - for all have sinned and come short of the glory of God. Sin separated us from God, rendering us guilty, impure, unclean, and incapable of service to God and fellowship with Him. It exposed us to all miseries, to death and hell. Man has destroyed himself by his sin. We are beyond self-recovery, the children of wrath, enemies to God in our minds and our works. Man needs salvation, and that salvation must come from without. None in the vast universe of God was competent or suitable but Christ. His coming was necessary to our salvation.

And how did He accomplish His purpose? Did He succeed in it? Some said that He did not - in joyous derision and mockery they cried 'He saved others, Himself He cannot save'. But the truth is the opposite - He did succeed, by the giving of His life as the ransom price for their salvation. Sinners were condemned to death, and the Saviour too must die, did die, and died death outright. He was not deprived of His life, He offered it, but never lost it. Thus by the offering of Himself He secured our salvation.

And He lives to bestow it. He was given for our offences, and rose for our justification. He actually saves sinners, and will not fail in that purpose. 'None perish that him trust'. What salvation does He offer? Such a salvation as eye has not seen nor ear heard. It is applied powerfully, and saves by the working of the Spirit of God. It is full, free and complete. It is salvation from all that sinners deserve, from all the consequences of our guilt and the miseries of our lot. It is partly received and partly reserved.

(2) *The Character of the Gospel Message*

Paul states that the fact of the Gospel is a *faithful* or *true* saying. Most sayings that are current or sensational are wholly or partly false. Take a thrilling novel - or even a report in the press. While these things make you believe that black is white, you feel that most of it is all false.

Now, this is such a big saying that there never was a fact like it. And to many the truth of it requires to be clearly proved. In itself it is of an apparently incredible nature. The bigger a saying is the more difficult it is to credit it. There was never a bigger saying than that the Son of God came into the world to save sinners. Is this not too much to believe or hope that the High and Lofty One, who was eternally blessed in Himself, and in need of no additional glory, should occupy Himself for His enemies to save them? Does it not conflict with the grim events of life - trouble, death, disappointment, war - do these not argue against the proposition that God is love?

But glory to God that there never was a truth the evidence of which is so clearly demonstrated. The Gospel message is verified historically. The written records cannot be disproved, and indeed are accepted as containing historical data. It is also verified experimentally. The experience of grace in the lives of men proves its reality. This is not a cunningly devised fable. No doctrine can have higher authority than the testimony of God. And by His Spirit He brings His church into possession of this reality.

The Gospel message is also *worthy of all acceptation*. Some things are true, but are not worthy of acceptance. But what is worthy of acceptance must be true. Here is a truth worthy of acceptance because its subject matter transcends in value and worth all that deserves acceptance. The value and worth of a saying often depends on the author. Here is a message which has the authority of heaven. It declares truths about God and about man. It answers the greatest of questions - how can a man be saved? The truth and worth of it has been proved and attested by men in all ages. The redeemed are unanimous in commending it.

It is worthy of being received by all. Few sayings are so. Many are unworthy of attention - they are false or trifling and better not listened to. Other things are of limited interest. They deserve notice by some, but not by all. This saying concerns all, and is worthy of acceptance by all, because it concerns their highest good.

It deserves our most cordial acceptance. It is worthy of a place in your heart and mind. It is worthy of your confidence and trust, your constant study, regard and delight. It saves, comforts, inspires, cheers and satisfies. Receive it then, whatever your station, character or need. It is enough, suitable, efficient, eternal. Receive it as a sinner, for without it you perish.

(3) *Paul's testimony to the truth and power of the Gospel*
He calls himself the chief of sinners. This was his view of himself as he thought of his former opposition to Christ, and His persecution of the church. Constantly this was the estimate he had of himself - so he cries in Romans 7, 'Oh wretched man that I am'. This is the effect of the Gospel, bringing us to humility and the wonder that he ever looked on us.

But this shows too Paul's estimate of Christ, who is able to save to the uttermost. He saves the chief of sinners, and He saves now. He alone is Saviour. Salvation is in none other.

This is the Gospel for sinners. Come then. Why delay? You need it.

49. THE DESTROYER OF DEATH

...But is now made manifest by the appearing of our Saviour Jesus Christ, who hath abolished death and hath brought life and immortality to light through the gospel (2 Timothy 1:10).

It is evident that God was not taken unawares by the tragedy of man's sin and fall. He had formerly settled on a plan, which became immediately operative when the need arose. This plan was conceived by God in the mystery of His purpose and grace from everlasting. His Sovereign will in that purpose determined the form and certainty of it, and grace provided the cost of the salvation. This grace, known only to God Himself, was given us in Christ as our Covenant Head, who appeared in conformity with His eternal purpose to reveal it. He is the primary revelation of grace, and all the graces bestowed on the church flow from Him. He is the fountain from which all blessings flow. It is of this Saviour that our text speaks.

(1) *Christ - What He is*

He is here entitled 'Our Saviour Jesus Christ'. Each word of this designation is full of blessing.

He is called *Christ*. That means 'the Anointed One', the long promised and long expected Messiah. He was recognised as such by the shepherds and by the wise men. He was a heaven-sent Saviour, a God-appointed, God-sealed and God-anointed Saviour. He is competent to be such, because He is the only Saviour known to, appointed by and acknowledged by God. He undertook to save, and offered Himself a sacrifice to satisfy the justice of God, and reconcile His people to God. He offered an adequate satisfaction and God approved His offering.

He is called *Jesus*. This is a God-given name. He was so called by the angel when He was about to be conceived in the womb of the virgin. This is the name given to Him when He was born in Bethlehem. His name implies His official standing. In order to be the Saviour of men, it was necessary that He should be born of a woman, and thus have a true human nature. Only then could He answer for man. Our Saviour is divine and human.

Because of this He is called a *Saviour*. What a wonder this is! Never was a sweeter word conceived. If He is not your Saviour now, that fact that He is a Saviour should encourage you to seek that He may be yours. The word *Saviour* means one who rescues or delivers, and suggests the idea of saving from impending doom. From what does He save? You cannot have Christ as Saviour without an acknowledgement of sin and guilt. He is the Saviour of sinners, and He became so at great cost to Himself.

And He is called *Our* Saviour. The apostle, despite his trying circumstances, could place himself among those for whom Christ is a Saviour. He is not the Saviour of fallen angels, but of fallen human beings. The context bears out that He is not the Saviour of all men, but to those who are called with a holy calling. We have no claim on Him by nature to be our Saviour, because we belong to the sinful human race. Not until we experience this holy calling can we say that He is our Saviour.

Yes, Jesus Christ is the Saviour, and is so to all who experience the power of His risen life.

(2) *Christ - What He did*

His work is summarised in these words - 'He abolished death'. A destroyer of death He had to be, or else He could not be a Saviour to those who were exposed to death. In considering His wonderful achievements, let us think of this great victory in particular.

What did He abolish? He abolished death. This is a dreadful word! It strikes terror into the hearts of men. Those who view it merely as the natural conclusion of life think of it with awe. It causes men to disappear from among the living of the earth, and they shrink from it because the dead cease to be what and where they were. They care not to think of the prospect of it, or forecast what awaits them beyond it; they shut their eyes to the future and keep in the dark as far as eternity is concerned.

There are others into whose hearts it strikes terror because they feel they are not prepared for it. Beyond it they do see an after-life, they feel that they are not right with God, they are conscious of guilt and sin. They think of what they are in relation to God as lawgiver and Judge, and what death must mean to the unsaved. Death to such is something more awful than the cessation of earthly existence.

What does death mean? We meet with it first in the warning given by God to man in Eden when God entered into covenant with him: 'In the day that thou eatest thereof thou shalt surely die'. That was a direct warning and threat uttered by God in anticipation of man's sin. It stated that man could not sin without dying, nor die without sinning. Man sinned with full knowledge of the consequences. The threat indicated how sin, as the transgression of God's law, was regarded by God, and His determination according to His love of righteousness to award adequate punishment to the transgressors. Think of God arising in the glory of His justice against the transgression, and uttering these awful words 'The soul that sinneth it shall die'. Death is the penalty awarded by God in fulfilment of the sentence pronounced.

And what does death imply? It implies abandonment of the sinning soul by God, the loss of spiritual life, becoming liable to natural death. That is why God says 'Dust thou art, and unto dust thou shalt return'. But this does not exhaust the meaning of the awful word, because after this death there is the judgement, and then death eternal for the unsaved, when God will award the only adequate punishment to guilty sinners. Death shall usher the unsaved into darkness, into the woe, fire and torment of eternal hell. How awful is such a death! The death that Christ is said to have abolished involves all of this.

And how did He abolish it? By becoming their surety, and answering for them. Their sins were imputed to Him, and He was held accountable for them and punished for them. He tasted death in its threefold aspect. The sentence of death was passed on Him, and was fully executed in His death. But when He was apparently mastered by death and crushed by the curse,

He exhausted the curse by an adequate satisfaction to law and justice. Having done this He abolished death. It now has no further existence for Him, so He rose from the dead, having deprived it of its sting and power.

(3) *Christ - What He does*

Having come as Saviour, to abolish death, He now acts as a Revealer, bringing life and immortality to light through the Gospel. The law could only condemn; but the Gospel brings the message of life. The risen and exalted life of Christ is the good news of the Gospel. Christ has shown us another world more clearly than it had ever been known before.

The life which Christ brought to light consists in the satisfaction and efficacy of what He offered. By His resurrection He showed that He had procured it. The life He died to win He lives to bestow. This life means complete restoration to God's favour. It means the bestowal of the grace of His Spirit, a well of life, so that the soul is made capable of enjoying God and of living to Him. We are now debtors to grace.

Immortality is associated with this life, which means that there can be no corruption of the principle of life bestowed on them. This is life eternal, which cannot be lost, as Adam lost the spiritual life he had. Those who possess this life are now in the family of God, and there they will remain. Here this life is theirs in its initial stages in their experience. At death they will enter it in its full possession. Then all corruption shall be finally banished forever from them, all earthly sorrows shall pass away, every sin removed, every tear wiped away.

How has this been revealed? In the Gospel. The Gospel itself is a revelation of Christ, who alone reveals Himself. He is His own interpreter; as He revealed the Father, He reveals Himself in the Gospel, and the Gospel is the means by which He does it. He is the revealer and the revealed. Thus the Gospel is our life when we appreciate and appropriate Christ, and rest upon Him. Hence Paul says in Romans that we have the word of faith in our hearts - the Gospel. This declares and holds forth the blessings which He secured by His death, and which He now lives to bestow. Can we claim Christ as our Saviour? If so, the Gospel will comfort us in the prospect of death, and will lift our soul heavenward.

50. THE PERFECTED CAPTAIN

For it became him, for whom are all things, and by whom are all things, in bringing many sons unto glory, to make the captain of their salvation perfect through sufferings (Hebrews 2:10).

In the preceding verse the apostle assigns the reason why Christ was made lower than the angels, namely, that by the grace of God He should taste death for every man. He here shows that this method of salvation was in every way worthy of God, and was adapted to the end in view, the bringing of many sons to glory. We may consider:

(1) *What is said of God*

Scripture assigns the work of salvation to the Three in One God, and shows the part which belonged to each Person in this amazing work. Here, attention is focused on the Father and His purpose of mercy.

We are reminded that the Father is the first and final cause of all things. He is the one 'By whom' all things are. He is the origin and cause of all things in the universe, as the Creator of all. By the fiat of His will He called what is seen into existence out of nothing. That was a work in keeping with His greatness and worthy of Him.

He is also the end of all things. He created all things for Himself, as a means of His self-disclosure. All things were designed for His glory, else He should have remained unknown. He was to reveal Himself by the works of His hands. Creation, Providence, Redemption, were all designed to exhibit the greatness and glory of God. Thus He made all things for Himself and for disclosing Himself.

But here a special act of grace is ascribed to Him. It became Him to do a certain work which in all respects was worthy of Him. This becomingness concerned the revelation and execution of His purpose of mercy. It differed from all His other works. Herein His glorious attributes appear in glorious harmony in contriving and perfecting the means of bringing sons to glory. God did nothing more becoming to Himself, illustrating His perfections, highly becoming His wisdom, holiness, justice and goodness. He not only purposed to save a specific people, but the method employed to accomplish it was of all things the most consistent with His moral perfections. It was the best adapted to secure the end in view. He was under no obligation to save any, but having purposed to do so, He was obliged to do it in a manner consistent with His honour, and so worthy of Him.

(2) *What is said of Christ*

In order to execute the purpose of salvation, Christ was constituted the captain of the salvation of His people. God could not deal savingly with sinful men except through a Mediator, so it pleased Him to appoint His own Son to discharge the terms of the covenant. Christ engaged to act as the surety for them. The plan of Redemption was entrusted to Christ, and He is called the Captain, or Author, of salvation. This is to show that our salvation is wholly vested in Him, and His satisfying the obedience required of Him.

Here He is said to be made perfect, which might imply imperfection. How was this? There was no personal imperfection, because in His two natures He was perfect, holy, harmless and undefiled. In what sense, then, had He need of being made perfect? With respect to His office. Though the Captain of Salvation was divine, He had to become man, while not ceasing to be God. Only in this way could He be fit for the official relation and action required of Him. His two natures fitted Him for His engagement as Mediator, and a work was assigned Him which He had to discharge before He could be a perfect Mediator.

This could only be attained by suffering. He was made perfect through suffering. It became God to assign and inflict suffering on Him, since, as surety, He engaged to answer for the sin and guilt of men. Hence God laid on Him the iniquities of us all. He spared not His own Son. He must learn obedience by what He suffered. While His sufferings were for others, yet they were personal to Him. He endured them in body and soul, and having learnt obedience in suffering He is qualified to sympathise with His people in their affliction. Thus He is a perfect High Priest regarding His office and action.

These sufferings were penal. The Sinless one suffered in the room of the unjust. The penalty they deserved was carried by Him. He exhausted it and endured it. He gave infinite satisfaction for it.

Here then is Christ, the perfect Saviour towards God. He is nothing less than a perfect Saviour because He is God. He was perfectly adapted to the work assigned Him. By His action and endurance He fully discharged the work. He left nothing undone. And He is a perfect Saviour towards us. Having discharged our guilt He has the power and the right to save, and lives to grant and bestow it. He can sympathise with us, having suffered Himself. He has taken our case with Him, and He intercedes for us. He has all the resources answerable to our need.

(3) *The End in View*

Why was all this done? 'To bring many sons to glory.' Obviously this could not be done except by a Saviour qualified by suffering. Hence God sent

Him, appointed Him, proved Him and declares Him able to save to the uttermost all who come unto God by Him.

Let us remember that those designed for glory were not fit for glory. They were afar off, the enemies of God in their minds by wicked works, a rebel race. But God purposed to save them by a suffering Saviour. In Him God laid the ground of their salvation and glorification in a manner becoming of Him and worthy of Him.

Having done so, He then makes them His sons. This is an act of grace, making children of wrath to become the children of God. There are two aspects of this - legal and spiritual. The legal aspect applies to their adoption in Christ and their reception into the favours of God's family. The spiritual aspect relates to the application of spiritual life to them, quickening them by the Spirit, regenerating them, giving them a new nature.

Thus changed, they are being sanctified. This is a process in which the Spirit operates in them, to cause grace in principle to surface and reign in them to mould them inwardly and outwardly to His pattern. Thus He causes them to love God, His people and His cause, and gives evidences of the change to them. They hate the sin which once they loved. Now it is a burden to them.

And He is working to bring these sons to glory, that is Heaven. This is the inheritance of saints in light, a place prepared for them, where perfected in Christ's likeness they shall shine as the sun in the kingdom of their Father. It is a glorious place in which God's glory shines in Christ and in them.

And He will bring many sons there. It was for God to determine how many, as it was for Him to employ the means of bringing them there. They shall be many of all ages, classes, races and nations - Jews and Gentiles. They may be few as seen by us, but in reality they are a multitude which no man can number. We believe Christ will have more than Satan. We cannot conceive of Him considering otherwise. His triumph will secure it. But they are all known to Him, and will be saved to His glory.

51. THE OFFERER AND THE OFFERING

For such an high priest became us...who needeth not daily, as those high priests, to offer up sacrifice, first for his own sins, and then for the people's; for this he did once, when he offered up himself (Hebrews 7:26-27).

The apostle is here speaking of Christ, of whom He says 'Such a high priest became us'. He speaks of His special qualities for that office, in which He eclipsed all other priests by completing the order and rendering all other priesthood and service unnecessary because He ever liveth. This glorious aspect of truth is often overlooked because it is considered too deep and difficult to understand, but that is no valid reason for neglecting it. But clear views of Christ's priesthood are indispensable to an intelligent appreciation of Christ's mediatorial action. This is like the X-ray - it goes right through you. There is no more solemn or affecting view of Christ as Saviour in Scripture. In the depth of His sufferings we see Him active, while acted upon.

(1) *The Offerer*

Here Christ is set before us as a priest engaged in offering. Under the old order it was the priest's function to offer, or minister at the altar. Christ was appointed for this, from among the people. His calling was official; it was on behalf of the people, and He, as their representative, appeared and acted for them in things pertaining to God. Thus the priest's office was a sacred one, and was in charge of approved and consecrated men - Aaron and his sons. These priests, however, were imperfect and were prevented from continuing in office by reason of death; consequently they were numerous and so were their sacrifices, necessarily so because they were imperfect.

But Christ is not a priest after the law of a carnal commandment as these were. He was appointed by the oath of God and set apart for His office. This implied a special divine arrangement, a special or miraculous conception, yet a legal entering into office. He came of another tribe of whom none ministered at the altar. Here we see the supreme wisdom and mercy of God. Though not of the Aaronic line, He was nonetheless of our race, bone of our bone and flesh of our flesh. He is qualified for the task, as verse 26 says, because He is holy, harmless, undefiled and separate from sinners.

Such a priest, says Paul, became us. The old priesthood was imperfect, and we stood in need of a perfect order. In Christ we have all that we needed and desired, one who is holy. We stood in need of a priest who could deal with God for us, and in Christ we have the one we need, one who is both God and Man in one Person. As priest, his business is to answer on behalf of the guilty, and make reconciliation for us. He did this because He had an offering.

(2) *The Offering*

What did He offer? He offered Himself. This was never true of a priest before Him. None ever did it, or could do it. Priests under the law offered costly and numerous sacrifices, which they received at the hands of the people. They did not even offer their own property, much less themselves. Then the priest and the offering were apart and distinct.

But the glorious high priest of our profession offers Himself. In Him the offering and offerer are combined. In Hebrews 10 we read of Him once offering His body. In Hebrews 4 we read of Him as priest. He is the offerer who gave Himself. Elsewhere it is said that He was given by the Father, and so He was; but it is no less true that He gave Himself. He was the offering, that is, His human nature, not the divine nature. He was Priest, that is, in His Person He was the active priest. Thus He could say that He laid down His life of Himself. No-one took it from Him.

To whom did He offer? He offered to God, for the sins of His people. He was offering and making expiation for guilty, sinful men. The Old Testament order illustrates this thought. These offerings were of two distinct kinds. Some were offered as a sweet savour, of which the burnt offering was the most prominent; others were offered for expiation, of which the sin offering was the chief. The burnt offering was a sweet savour offered for acceptance; it was completely burnt on the altar of brass in the court of the tabernacle. In it we see Christ's perfect obedience to do the Father's will, as the supreme object of His delight. In this respect Christ offered and appeared for us, not as sinbearer but as offering to God a life of complete and unreserved surrender. This represented the fulfilment of man's duty of obedience to God.

The sin offering was different in that it was offered in atonement for sin. The fat was consumed on the brazen altar to show that it was accepted, but all the rest was burnt outside the camp to show the sinfulness of sin. So Christ suffered outside the camp. In this way He put away sin by the sacrifice of Himself. He was made sin. In this respect He was not merely active in offering, but acted on while thus engaged. He was active in offering while enduring suffering and death. Death did not put Him out of office or render Him inactive, as it did the Old Testament priests. There was never a moment when He was rendered inactive. He was active even when under the power of death.

(3) *The Value of His Offering*
This is implied in the words 'this he did once'. All priests before Him offered often, which showed the imperfection of the old order. He offered once, because by that one offering He exhausted the curse and earned eternal redemption for us. The evidence of this is seen in the resurrection and ascension. This was Christ's own testimony in Luke 24 - He had to suffer these things, then enter into the glory. It was Paul's reasoning too.

As the high priest of our profession He entered the holiest of all with His own blood and His blood-bought church on His breastplate. Of old, when the high priest entered the holy place the clatter of the bells on his garment was to the congregation the token of acceptance - the priest was still alive. So there are evidences of Christ's exalted life. What are they? The supply of His grace and the glorious ministry of the Spirit in the church.

52. THE GUEST OUTSIDE

Behold I stand at the door, and knock; if any man hear my voice and open the door, I will come in to him, and will sup with him, and he with me (Revelation 3:20).

The word of God is profitable for instruction, rebuke and correction. It tells us plainly what we are, and what we need. It employs arresting metaphors to enforce its lessons, such as we have here in our text. This is a message to the church in Laodicea. Now a church is composed of good and bad, of regenerate and unregenerate, the sinner in his carelessness and the believer in his slothfulness. To all there comes a message from the Throne of Majesty to a church in her imperfections in all ages. And it becomes us to examine ourselves honestly as to where we stand in the light of it. Let us consider:

(1) *The Speaker*
We cannot ignore Him, because the weight of the text rests in His character and authority. It is important to have clear views of Him, to grasp the importance of what He says. He cannot be placed on an ordinary plain, for never man spake like this man, in authority, power and faithfulness.

He speaks of Himself as the faithful and true witness, the beginning of the creation of God. He is similarly described in Proverbs 8 and John 1. Here then is the Lord of Glory, speaking to sinners on the earth from His exalted throne, where He is vested with all power and authority. To Him every knee must bow and every tongue confess that He is Lord over all. Surely He is entitled to a hearing.

Here He addresses the church of Laodicea, diagnosing the weaknesses and exposing the spiritual state of the church there, that He might bring her to a fitting frame of mind, to love and repentance. It was a most unhealthy and unfavourable condition that she had - she was lukewarm. He exposes the rot and prescribes the remedy.

What He said to them He says still to all those in a similar condition. The faithful and true witness speaks to rebuke the present day lukewarmness, to warn, counsel and correct. We must examine ourselves to ascertain our condition. This is a duty we owe to Him and to ourselves, lest He spue us out of His mouth and leave us to perish in our self-delusion. Better the pestilence than be cast off from God.

(2) *His Attitude*

He is standing at the door. What door? He is at the door of your life. Your heart-door is the entrance to your life. The heart is the most important member of the body, spiritually as well as physically. As the heart is, so the man is. That which occupies the heart possesses the man. It signifies man's mind, affections and will. The heart of man is naturally shut against Christ, and is occupied by a foreign tribe of rebels, robbers and destroyers, the lust of the flesh and of the eye, along with the pride of life. These embrace all evils, and exclude Christ from His rightful place, for He alone has full claim on man's heart. But the door is barred against Him by the monster of unbelief, furnished with the equipment of darkness which bars the door - ignorance, indifference, love for the world, formality in religion.

Yet He condescends to seek admission. He comes seeking to establish a better and healthier relationship. The wonder of it; that He seeks to enter such a vile heart and a sin-stained life. By the operation of His grace He can transform that filthy, barren region into a fruitful garden, where flowers of rare gem can bloom. He puts great value on the heart. He must have it or nothing. Everything depends on its surrender to Him.

Note too His posture - He stands, as if ready to enter, or ready to go away. He has been standing there for long - perhaps even from your childhood. Why keep him waiting? If He departs He may never return. His Spirit will not always strive with man.

(3) *His Action*

He knocks, announcing His presence and seeking to enter. This means there is a desire on His part to do us good. Thus He comes offering Himself, seeking habitation though He has often been repelled. He offered Himself for you in death to redeem you from the death you deserved, and now as the risen and exalted Lord He offers Himself to you for your salvation and eternal benefit by knocking at your door. This He does in various ways.

He knocks by His word. 'If any man hear my voice..' He says. By His word He entreats you, calling on the wicked to forsake his way and turn to Christ. By His word He warns you; tells you that the soul that sins will die. How shall we escape if we neglect this salvation?

He knocks by His Spirit, who operates secretly on your mind and conscience, convincing you of sin, giving you remorse, self-accusation, inclination to reform. Why not heed His counsel and yield to His teaching?

Otherwise you harden your heart again and again.

He knocks in His Providence. In adversity, sickness, chastisement, death - all these are ways in which He knocks. What is the meaning of that sick-bed of young or old? It is a warning to you to set your house in order, because you will die. There are evidences of God's displeasure in the removing of His Spirit and presence; let us retrace our steps and seek love and repentance.

In knocking, Christ emphasises our right to open. He seeks your consent. He instituted and acknowledges free agency. Men are accountable to Him for their exercise of it. He does not force an entrance. He seeks a willing people to receive Him, and they open, invite and receive Him.

Many disregard His voice, and will not have Him. But think of the consequences of refusing Him. He may depart, never to return. Death awaits and beyond it the judgement. Then there shall be no refusals. You will not be consulted. Now He comes to bless; then He comes to judge. Your destiny hinges on how death finds you. If you are in Christ you are blessed, if not you are cursed. Do not dishonour the Saviour and deprive your soul of blessing! A patriarch of old received angels unawares. Will you not receive the King of Kings?

(4) *His Aim*

That is to come in and sup with you. He asks nothing but what He will enable you to do. He only wants your consent, which by His word and dispensations of grace He seeks. He requires us to seek Him, to work out our salvation.

He desires to be our guest. 'I will sup with you'. He is hungry and deserves to dine. But what have you on which Christ may sup? You would like to put yourself in order, make a spread and show of good things. But such effort only excludes Him - He will have none of my righteous washing. He brings and makes the feast Himself. He has meat to eat, and He would eat it with the poor and needy. What meat? The unfolding of the Father's will in its bearing on your salvation. To reveal Himself as Saviour to your soul - that is His meat and drink. And does He want anything from you? Yes, He wants your sin-stained soul to save. He wants your confidence, faith, love and obedient service.

And when He comes in there is an exchange of places. He becomes host - 'you will sup with me'. He gives a feast of fat things - pardon, reconciliation, justification, adoption, fellowship, refreshment, peace, joy. And at the end you will sit with Him in His throne. There the Lamb will lead His people to living fountains of waters. Let us consider our relationship to Him. He desires our heart now.

JOHN MACIVER

on

THE WALK AND WELFARE
OF THE CHRISTIAN

53. JOY GREATER THAN WINE

Thou hast put gladness in my heart, more than in the time
that their corn and wine increased (Psalm 4:7).

Joy is natural to piety. God Himself is said to rejoice in all His works. Christ rejoiced in what was to be inhabited of the world, and His delight was with the sons of men. His word to His own was 'Rejoice and be exceeding glad, for great is your reward in Heaven'. Again He said to His disciples 'I shall see you again and your heart shall rejoice'. Paul gives the counsel 'Rejoice in the Lord alway'. Joy is natural to man. Sorrow and grief are the legacies of sin. Where there is no sin there is no sorrow. But there must be sorrow where there is sin.

Man is naturally endowed with a constitution adapted for joy. How often we see children in a joyous mood. They sometimes even laugh in their sleep. There would be nothing else in the history of man but joy were it not for sin. Sin is the source of all pain and unhappiness, all misery and sorrow. Man is naturally joyous. There may be exceptions, but they are few.

Man's natural joy, however, is misdirected. Joy only flows through its proper channel when man obtains a saving knowledge of God. There we meet with everything which inspires joy. In God there is perfect love, perfect goodness, perfect holiness. In Him we are given the assurance of an eternal home, which we are sure to enjoy. We know that we shall never leave that home, nor wish to leave it. This is not the case in every home in which a person may be dwelling.

The death of Christ is the instrumental cause of joy to the believer. He sees that Christ has not merely declared His love to him, but has proved it beyond any possibility of doubt by dying for him. Thus He has delivered him from eternal condemnation. People love naturally; love issues in the union of marriage. Why? Perhaps it is right to say because they cannot help it. Such love is beautiful and very strong. But it does not happen often, if at all, that the one party has been the means of saving the other party's life from danger or from death, and placing himself (or herself) in danger by doing so. But if it were so it would naturally intensify the rescued party's love to the rescuer, and probably also the love of the rescuer himself, because people generally care a lot for what costs them dear.

It is possible that that would have intensified Jacob's love for Rachel - she cost him dear. It probably intensified Rachel's love towards him to note how determined he was to win her, however much it would cost him. But it is natural that it would have influenced her love more for him had he saved her from danger or from death. He certainly would have done that had the occasion arisen, and had there been need of it. The signal proof of Christ's love is that He married the church after having loved her and given Himself for her, having died for His people. This was love for an unworthy wretch. What wonderful occasion for joy that is! The cross of Christ is a never-failing fount of joy. Christ has a special interest in His people because He suffered so much for them.

The teaching of Christ is an occasion for support and joy. It gives us a revelation of the Father's loving heart, and God's merciful nature. It is a revelation of God's grace, and that sustains our soul in assurance and peace, even though we are subject more or less at all times to spiritual darkness and spiritual anxiety. Notwithstanding, that revelation props us and supports us at every time. At that very time of darkness, our souls are inhaling the air of God's revelation in Christ, and our souls are breathing in that air and drawing spiritual sustenance therefrom in our darkness and spiritual concern. That air helps us more than we realise. We know that the Lord is, and what the Lord is. That is an unchanging comfort.

Suppose a man were to come home very hungry, and found no food prepared for him. While hoping strongly that it would be prepared for him, he feels very miserable because he feels himself on the verge of losing all strength with hunger. At the same time, he has the knowledge that there is plenty food in the house. How much he is supported by that knowledge! How desperate he would be if he knew there were no food there at all. So it is with us; the consciousness that God's preparation is ever there is an inestimable comfort and strength to us in a greater manner than we can possibly realise.

This joy may not be seen visibly in the conduct of those who have it. At times it may appear to be the reverse - that they do not have it at all. The occasion for it is so solemn and so glorious. The occasion of it really is a pierced Christ. And it is accompanied by mourning because those who have it see the indignity and suffering which their sins heaped upon Him. Their joy has that sense of sorrow for sin accompanying it. That does not reduce their joy; it only increases it.

There is, though, a sorrow without conscious joy which is the portion only of those who have had this joy. We suffer the greatest pain and sorrow over the parties we love best in this world. Our greatest affections are our greatest afflictions. People suffer most within the confines of their own loved relations in their families. When, for instance, death parts us, how painful is the separation. This holds good in a sense with regard to our relation to Christ. Our regard for Him makes our feeling of his face being hidden from us painful to us. There are yet the mountains of division. It makes our sin most painful to us because it is the cause of the interruption of our communion with Christ. In darkness of soul the essence of our pain is that we are deprived of a sense of joy through the enjoyment of communion with Christ.

Then there is the lack of a joyous feeling through our interest in Christ produced by trials and afflictions of various kinds. That sorrow is not designed to extinguish your joy at all, but will provide occasion for it bursting forth with greater strength through time. Consider, for instance, when you put peats on the fire, they partially extinguish the light and reduce the heat. The peats might well say to the fire, 'Haven't I brought you low in respect of your light and heat?' The fire might well answer, 'Yes, but you haven't extinguished me altogether. Wait a little, and I'll put yourself on fire as I have done many before you. You don't seem to realise it, but you are only food to me.' So the Christian can say to his trials 'You are only food to me, to cause my joy to burst in an ever stronger flame'. 'Unto thy people thou hard things hast shew'd, and on them sent; And thou hast caused us to drink wine of astonishment' (Psalm 60:3). Christ promised that His disciples would weep and lament, but that their sorrow would be turned into joy. That is the final result of trial, however much we feel that our joy is being extinguished by it. The believer's trials only tune his soul to produce a melody which shall never end throughout all eternity.

This is the greatest of all joys. The cause of it is greater than all causes. The duration of it is longer than anything else. This is the kind of joy we need. We do not get it at the concert, or the wedding, or the dance. We get it in Christ. And when it comes it sanctifies the joy we get from natural things. The love of Christ is the fount of the believer's joy, and it is eternal.

54. KNOWING AND TRUSTING

And they that know thy name will put their trust in thee: for thou, Lord,
hast not forsaken them that seek thee
(Psalm 9:10).

Adam, our first covenant head, had knowledge of God. He had knowledge of fellowship with God, and he had a knowledge of the goodness of God. That goodness met the needs of his body and his soul. He knew God with respect to His wisdom and His power. He knew Him too in connection with the covenant God had made with him. It was that knowledge that struck his conscience when he had broken covenant with God, and he hid himself amid the trees of the garden. He had no other knowledge of God apart from that first covenant.

Having broken that covenant, he became acquainted with death. He grew ignorant of God. It was on account of that ignorance that he began to make excuses for his sin, to try to justify himself by blaming Eve and by blaming God Himself. But he could not know that God had anything for Him but the fulfilment of His curse. He had never heard anything about the mercy of God. That side of God he did not know, for God had not revealed it. God had never said to him, 'Though you might fail, there is a way by which I can accept you again and forgive your sin'. How then could he entertain any hope, unless his hope was a false one? Indeed, his excuse was built on his entertaining a false hope. If he could put the blame on God or on Eve, he might expect that God would not regard it fitting or proper to meet out his threat, as if he was saying to God, 'Is it right for you to carry out your threat against me, when in fact it was the wife you yourself gave me that made me eat the forbidden fruit?' So people still try to divide the guilt of their sins between themselves and God.

As God dealt with Him, He revealed a way of escape before banishing Him out of the Garden. God said to the Serpent, 'I will put enmity between thee and the woman, and between thy seed and her seed; it shall bruise thy head, and thou shalt bruise his heel'. This was a treasure-house of mercy coming man's way, in which Christ was given to a fallen race.

Men can have knowledge of these things without having the knowledge that will lead them to trust in the Lord. That was the kind of knowledge the Jews had through the revelation of the Old Testament; but the light they had through that knowledge was the light which made them reject Christ, and at last crucify Him. Only by a personal knowledge of Him can we obtain mercy. In the Old Testament God revealed Himself by His names: Immanuel, Jehovah our Righteousness, The Branch of Jesse. The angel said that he would be called 'Jesus', for He would save His people from their sins.

When a person knows God personally through Christ, he trusts in Him. He made atonement for them. This he knows through the revelation of Scripture. That knowledge of what the Bible says is the foundation of spiritual knowledge, a personal knowledge of Christ. At the same time, no-one can truly know what the Bible says apart from that spiritual knowledge of Christ.

55. THE GREAT HOPE

As for me, I will behold thy face in righteousness; I shall be satisfied when I awake, with thy likeness (Psalm 17:15).

In this psalm the psalmist speaks of men who were looking to the world to satisfy them. Their hearts were not fixed on anything higher than this. But he himself was completely unlike them, because he says 'As for me...'. Despite what they are like, and despite their hatred for me, 'I will behold thy face in righteousness'.

The heart of the psalmist did not rest satisfied with the things of the world, but in something else, something quite different. And his attitude to the things of the world was coloured and affected by the hope that he had in God. That hope affected the way he looked at this world, and coloured his attitude to the next.

He says 'I will behold thy face in righteousness.' He was to find righteousness by looking into the face of the Lord. 'I have preached righteousness in the great congregation...I have not hid thy righteousness within my heart; I have declared thy faithfulness and thy salvation; I have not concealed thy lovingkindness and thy truth from the great congregation' (Psalm 40:9-10). These words tell us that righteousness, lovingkindness and salvation come together to mean the same thing. God's kindness is according to righteousness. The goodness of God to sinners accords with the holiness and justice of God.

The psalmist talks of a spiritual eyesight, a spiritual looking. Others saw Him, but they looked at Him with worldly eyes. But the psalmist talks of seeing Him, beholding Him, in a way that means he must have Him. To look on the face of God in this way is a source of great joy. The great mark of his faith is his assurance that he and God are reconciled. He had no fear of looking at the face of God, or meeting with God; his whole expectation was that he would see God's face. He could see the face of God in the types of the Ark of the Covenant. Did he not express a desire to dwell in the house of the Lord all the days of his life, 'to behold the beauty of the Lord' (Psalm 27:4)? It is in a person's face that you can see beauty. In God's face he could see the beauty of love, mercy and holiness combined. That is the righteousness he could see in the face of God.

In the salvation of sinners, God exalts the law and makes it honourable. This is righteousness, and it is righteousness that makes God's face so glorious to him. The face of Christ was fair, His countenance was 'white and ruddy' on account of this righteousness. This is what made it so attractive and wonderful to the psalmist - the holiness or personal righteousness of the Son of God, of God Himself. That righteousness, the 'whiteness' of God's countenance is what condemned the psalmist as a sinner, under the curse and penalty of the law.

If the only righteousness God had was the righteousness that makes Him condemn sinners and law-breakers, the psalmist could have no reason for rejoicing that He was going to see God's face; this would be a cause only for concern and pain. But the countenance of God is also 'ruddy', and David is looking away to the One who was anticipated and expected to come in the fulness of time, the promised Saviour. David was seeing the face of Christ, mixing whiteness and redness, the holy God and the promised Messiah. He is looking into the face of the Lord Jesus Christ, where he finds righteousness revealed in holiness and in mercy.

'In righteousness' - that righteousness was also covering the psalmist himself, like a garment. To behold Christ in righteousness means to have Him, to be clothed with Him. That is what gives us holy boldness before God. Covered in His righteousness we shall see His face. In any other way, seeing His face could only mean death for the sinner.

I can behold his face in this world by faith. Then I will be satisfied with him. But I will not have complete satisfaction. But I will have true, precious, clean, blessed satisfaction for all that. Today I see through a glass, darkly. That is how He reveals His face to me. I cannot see Him perfectly, because I myself am not perfect.

I will see Him in eternity. And I will rejoice to see Him there. I will awake with His likeness. The first 'awakening' the saints have is when they go in to inherit their eternal rest. They sleep here in death, but the Spirit wakens them in rest and happiness and glory. Some maintain that the saints sleep in an unconscious state until they waken in the resurrection. But Paul says that 'to be with Christ is far better', and that shows that he expected to go to be with Him immediately on death. At that moment they 'wake in His likeness', they are made altogether like Him. Were they like Him before this? Indeed they were, but there were many 'unlikenesses' there too; so many that at times they despaired of ever being like Him at all.

They were God's sons in the world, and God put the Spirit of His sons in their hearts. But it was not apparent to them then what they would be. But with the fulfilment of their hope, having been made altogether like Christ, they see Him as never before, and they are perfectly blessed and perfectly happy.

Again, they will awaken in His likeness at the resurrection day. They will waken with a body like His glorious body. The last sleep from which they will awaken is the sleep of death. They will then see Him and enjoy Him for all eternity.

56. LOVE AND STRENGTH

I will love thee, O Lord, My strength (Psalm 18:1).

The words in this verse are expressed in the future tense: I *will* love thee. But this future purpose is one which is prompted by the experience of the present. In a sense the declaration might appear to be presumptuous, because it might in a sense be manifesting undue self-reliance, as if he arrogated to himself the power and ability to act without aid from any other source. But he could not do this in the future without God's aid. It was also God's aid that made it possible to do it at the present.

But the experience of the present involved a knowledge and discovery of the Lord which in an incontrovertible way convinced him of God's loveableness and inexpressible beauty. Along with this was an unshakable conviction that that beauty and loveableness were eternally unchanging. That is a conviction directly communicated by an experience of communion with God. A man's view of God is firmly stabilised as a result of that communion because the Lord manifests His own character and attributes in that mysterious communion with the soul. The Lord does that by the medium of the truth reflecting the glory of God in His attributes through the effectual power of the Holy Spirit, which regenerates the soul and makes it possible for the soul to see that wonderful and ineffable excellency in the truth.

Not only this, but the light given to perceive these things is given by God Himself. This is recognized and is accompanied with the conviction that it is the gracious work of God to make it possible for the soul to perceive them, and that it is in accordance with His purpose not to withhold that light. It is a gift that He has communicated to be theirs in time and for eternity, to be increased by Him in this world as long as they live in it. Hence the assurance with which the psalmist says 'I will love thee.'

Because of the love of God poured into his heart by the Holy Ghost, David could say that God was his strength. It was a glorious and happy experience for David to know that the Lord was his strength in many different ways in Providence, for example, in overcoming Saul and his evil purposes to do him injury. Yet I am sure that it was a much more glorious and happy experience for David to know that God had put His own love into his heart. Whatever injury Saul could do him in his worldly interests and prospects, and even in respect of injury to his person, none of these things, though they were to occur, could deprive him of God's loving favour in regard to the change of nature God had conferred upon him, in his conversion, for in this was involved an everlasting covenant. God's strength in respect of this matter was more precious to David than in regard to any other relief that he had from Him. The personal protection from bodily injury or natural death which the Lord would afford him was not light in David's estimation by any means, for it was for such things that he was in this very psalm praising God.

David makes this declaration with the happy confidence that it was to God's liking that he should continue to love Him, that is, that he should love God and continue to love him after this. He knew that the Lord would not rebuke him or be displeased with him or discourage him from so purposing. He knew definitely that he was welcomed by God to love God.

Some people would not thank others for declaring to themselves or to others about them that they loved them, and that they purposed to continue doing so. It might only provoke from them a look of scorn and contempt to be informed by some people of that fact. Knowledge that God does welcome it is conducive to our loving Him. He has taken pains to overcome our natural enmity towards Him. He has regarded our persons with pleasure from all eternity, and this made Him purpose to break down that enmity. And that itself is now a means of provoking us to love Him, that He fought against our enmity and overcame it. In conquering our hearts thus and winning our love, it was done in a way which made irresistible appeal both to our conscience and to our reason, so that our reason and our conscience now prompt us to love God.

It is a glorious thing in prospect. No other person can look forward to any other prospect as pleasing as this, that is, the assurance that one is to love God through time and eternity. This is the greatest of all prospects. It does not diminish our right to look forward with appropriate gladness to other prospects of God's will, but this is the greatest of all prospects to rejoice in. It is legitimate to have gladness in connection with other prospects. But there is an ever-existing element of uncertainty connected with the realisation or fulfilment of all other prospects. And for those who have no other happy prospect but this particular one, there is a sufficiency for their happiness in it, though they may have nothing else. And this is the greatest that any child of God can indulge in, and he does not indulge in it as he should, nor does he praise and glorify God for it as he should.

The psalmist goes on to call the Lord 'my strength'. In the knowledge of the eternal covenant thou hast made with me, in the knowledge of the promises thou hast given me, the courage of heart and soul with which thy blessings inspire me, thou art my strength. It was David's confidence that these blessings would continue, and that they would continue to inspire him and strengthen his soul that inspired him to say 'I will love thee, O Lord my strength'.

What does it mean to love God? It means to have a delight and complacency in God because of His attributes and nature, and joined to that and inseparable from it is a delight in His condescending graciousness and His saving mercy to ourselves. He showed us this in giving His Son to atone for our sins and deliver us from our consequent guilt. Suppose a young man and a young woman were to be on board ship, and the young lady fell overboard. The young man would jump in after her and hold her, if he could, until they were rescued. She would love him for what he was in himself, and also for what he had done for her. You could say that she would love him with a double love. It might even be that she did not love him until her heart was conquered by his brave and self denying deed which his great love to her prompted. So God has conquered the hearts of His people - they love Him for what He is and for what He has done for them.

57. THIRSTING FOR GOD

As the hart panteth after the water brooks,
so panteth my soul after thee, O God (Psalm 42:1).

The psalmist is here separated from God's house, where he was accustomed to enjoy the presence of God. He had a great thirst for God. His situation is comparable to that of many souls in every age and generation. That itself is enough to prove that God and conversion do actually exist. This exercise of soul belongs to all those whom the Holy Spirit has brought to life. Many things, speaking naturally, can relieve a man's thirst. If a man were choking through thirst, he would rejoice at the sight of water, and milk would give him relief. But nothing can satisfy this thirst unless the soul finds God.

Many people can have similar symptoms to this thirst, without truly thirsting for God. Many people seek for God when the fear of death sets them in turmoil. When they are in trouble they want God then too. When things look dangerous or hopeless, they want God. And when relief comes, they can in a measure appear very thankful to God. But perhaps after that they show that their thankfulness was like the morning cloud and like the early dew that soon disappears. In sickness or in trouble the souls of believers themselves are made to thirst for God all the more. However, that can leave the believer in a state of perplexity; when slavish fear of circumstances mixes with the true thirst of his soul for God, the believer may wonder whether it was in fact a true longing for God he had. In this way, fear of death can weary a soul, and does many times - even on the deathbed. God permits some to be wearied with this fear even on their deathbed. But this fear can affect a person without him being on his deathbed at all; and he is afraid that all he wanted was to be relieved from his trouble.

This is not the thirst of the soul of the unbeliever in trouble. The believer thirsts for the help and fellowship of God, a thirst in which there is a strong longing after God. In this case the mind is filled with a longing for God which he does not have for anything else in the world. It is a thirst that grows out of love, but perhaps sometimes the soul that possesses it cannot even say this with certainty. But this thirst is a holy love - love for God. God alone can meet its desire and taste. Beforehand the sinner saw much in God that he thought was wrong, and did not like. But now there is nothing about God he does not like. This is the God that condemns and hates sin, but now the sinner loves this God, although these were the very things which formerly he did not like about God. He is now thirsting after the God who hates sin, and the God who forgives sinners. He thirsts for reconciliation, for loving, close friendship between his soul and God.

What leaves a man naturally thirsty? Nothing but *life*. And it is only the soul that is alive in Christ that can thirst for God. A child is thirsty as soon as it is born. That thirst is linked to the fact that the child is alive. There is no thirst for God anywhere but where there is spiritual life in the soul.

Thirst in a sense gives a person a taste for the thing he desires. Is this not true, for example, of a man who is very hungry? The prospect of satisfying his hunger delights him. When a man eats food that satisfies his hunger, he will not want anything but to be hungry. But if he does not expect to get food, he will prefer not to be hungry. So it is with the soul that has tasted of the sweetness of God - he wants nothing but to thirst after Him.

No-one will die of this thirst. God is in this thirst. The other day I looked for my scarf, and found it round my neck! In the same way God is in the very thirst itself; the soul that thirsts wants to experience Him and feel Him. That soul has a taste for the water of life in the mouth of his soul. And the soul that thirsts in this way thirsts for the God who gave Christ to be the Saviour of sinners.

58. BROKEN-HEART   SACRIFICES

The sacrifices of God are a broken spirit; a broken and a contrite heart, O God, thou wilt not despise (Psalm 51:17).

David wishes to offer to the Lord the sacrifice that would satisfy and please the Lord, and which would make God's favour sure to him. A broken spirit is the sacrifice that God requires. The offering of animal sacrifices would not atone for his sin. He knew that. If that would do, he would give them. But he realised that such sacrifices would never make atonement for sin. These sacrifices had a purpose as a trial of obedience, but did not effect in themselves a propitiation. They had an illustrative significance; they were the shadow of things to come. They prefigured Christ.

What is a broken spirit? A spirit that is wounded; a spirit that has been hurt. One who has such a spirit sees himself as a creature accountable to God. He is aware of the boldness and impudence of sin on his part as a creature against God. How terrible is that realisation when it is brought home to him! How shameful it makes him feel! Formerly, God was so far away from his thoughts that these things never entered his mind. It was as if God did not exist at all. That itself is a great sin to him now, that beforehand he was living as if there were no God. As the prophet said, 'he was despised, and we esteemed him not'.

There are some sins that fill a man's heart with shame, and in a sense break his heart at the thought of them, without this brokenness of heart being spiritual. Even natural men themselves can have great concern over some sins that they have committed, without that concern leading to godly sorrow. But the broken-heartedness of which the text speaks is spiritual, it is a godly brokenness. It comes from the effectual work of the Spirit in the heart. The person who has it has been awakened to a knowledge of his guilt in respect of how shamefully he treated God formerly. That thought continues to wound his heart.

Think of a man who has received news of his mother's death. He begins weeping because he had done nothing for her, he had never shown her any kindness. He understood things then, as it were, as in a flash - it hit him immediately - as it had never done before. That is how the soul feels through the work of the Spirit - suddenly seeing things as never before.

Again, this is not a hopeless broken-heartedness. The psalmist had a broken spirit, and he had hope: the hope that God would not despise his broken heart. How could he entertain this hope? Because his trust was in God. There was something in that broken heart where he could find love for God. There is sorrow there, sorrow for God - 'they shall look on him whom they have pierced, and they shall mourn for him'. They sorrow for how unrighteously they have treated Him.

And this kind of heart is one that has been broken by God Himself. And He has broken it in order to break the love of sin in the heart, the carelessness about God. God breaks the heart in order to break its love for sin.

59. HOPE AND PRAISE

But I will hope continually, and will yet praise thee more and more
(Psalm 71:14).

This psalm makes it clear that the psalmist was conscious of weakness, and of a lack of strength when it came to standing his ground against his enemies. He was conscious of the weakness of his old age, and the way in which his enemies seemed to be so successfully arrayed against him. They were making much of the lowly condition into which he had come.

In this psalm he can only make his situation a cause of prayer to God. He cries 'O God be not far from me'. Having made this petition, he then sets before him the one thing that he can do - 'I will hope', and more than this, that he will do this continually. There is surely a principle here for every believer. The Lord is going to defend all those who trust in Him, and help them in their situation. We would all like to think that we are getting stronger and stronger, and we look forward to being rid of all our troubles and infirmity. But it is not to be; and we are proceeding towards weakness as surely as towards strength.

But despite this, the psalmist says that he is going to set his confidence in the Lord. Why? Simply because he had come to know the Lord as one who was in a special relation to him; as he puts it in verse 3 - 'thou hast given commandment to save me'. The soul concerning whom the Lord has given no such commandment has no grounds for trust in God. The Lord did not do this with the psalmist's coming to Him. He came to the Lord, and got knowledge of Him, and since then expected to keep coming to Him. And in all trials he was to trust in the Lord. In all kinds of experiences, whether the day be sunny or dark.

What does it mean to trust in the Lord? You cannot trust in a person without a warrant from him. In some cases you can trust, for example, that a man will not steal from you. But you cannot have confidence that the person has your best interests at heart without assurance from him in some form.

This is the kind of confidence the psalmist has in God - trust that the Lord would work out all his situations to a good end; trust that even the worst of them will have a favourable issue. Illustration - the cleaning of a house in preparation for a wedding. The soul is being prepared for the Lamb's wedding supper. It is in order to clean the soul of His people that God brings them through difficulties and trials. 'Tribulation worketh patience.'

Now, the angels trust God, and always will. There is no love without trust. The angels love God and exercise trust in Him, in His goodness, and in His justice, and the knowledge that in all His ways He is good and just.

Similarly Adam trusted in God in his state of innocence. But what God was to Adam in his innocence, and what He is to the angels, as an object of trust, is different to what He is to us. We are fallen creatures. And he has taken our nature, and taken the curse away from us. He now asks us to put our trust in Him as one who has dealt with our sins, and given assurance of this in His word.

60. ON PILGRIMAGE

*...Who passing through the valley of Baca make it a well;
the rain also filleth the pools* (Psalm 84:6).

These are words that apply to those whose strength is in the Lord, and who have His ways in their hearts. This is what they do with the strength they have in God - they make wells in the valley of Baca, and the rain is going to fill these wells with pools.

Let us look at the place through which they are passing - the Valley of Baca. This means 'the valley of troubles' or 'the valley of tears'. You could say that this is the world. This is how the world is to the people of God. Indeed, the world is a place of trouble to many people that are ignorant of God. 'Man that is born of woman is of few days and full of trouble.' And the people of God must go through these troubles in this world. The world is to be for them a vale of tears.

But the people of God have things that make the world for them more a place of troubles than it is for others, things that unconverted people do not have. What do they have? Their own sins, for one thing, which is a cause of great sorrow for the people of God in the world. And the ways through which they pass as God cleanse them from sin often cause them to shed tears in the world.

God in His kindness sees it fitting to make the world bitter to us, in order to lift our heart away from it. By receiving many afflictions, of many different kinds, we come to bid farewell to every desire we ever had for the world. Afflictions are the Lord's medicine for His people. When the Lord shows us the vanity of our minds, our desire for the approval of the world, our thirst for a great inheritance in the world, things that are in the world, we realise that these plagues are in the souls of the Lord's people. And this is the medicine with which the Lord comes to them - afflictions that will make the world like Baca's valley for them. The Lord makes the world a restless place for them. They are like a man walking barefoot over broken glass. There is no contentment there. Though there might be moments of relief, they do not last long.

You will say to me, I am sure, that your life in the world has become more troublesome since the Lord met with you, than it ever was before then. The Lord wants your heart to rest more on Him, and be fixed more on Him, than on the world. The way He does that is to make the world a bitter place for us.

He has another way too - he gives us to taste of heavenly things. But the Lord does not deem it sufficient for our souls to be lifted away from the world through a taste of the sweetness of heavenly things. When God grants people happy times on earth, times when they feel contented and at peace, they are in danger of making that spiritual experience their Heaven on earth. I mean spiritual blessings, which you could easily make your Heaven on earth. The Lord, therefore, in His wisdom, mixes the bitter with the sweet. Sometimes you get a bottle of medicine from the doctor, which has a mixture of bitterness and sweetness in its taste. That is how the Lord deals with those whom He is preparing for glory. God is looking to loose your heart from the world, and He will certainly make it as bitter for you as you need it to be.

Will you then be downhearted? Not at all. You will not be without happiness and joy. For if God spoils the world on you, He also gives you other prospects. Apparently the Valley of Baca was a valley through which the tribes would walk on their way to the feasts at Jerusalem. It was a dry, tiring, hot place; but those who were walking there, whose hearts were united to God, discovered that God would give them strength for that journey. They would not be weary in the journey through the valley. They were not journeying to the valley, though they had to journey through it. They are making for Jerusalem.

When they would stop in the valley, because they were becoming weary and thirsty, they would make wells, in order that they might find water. And sometimes, before they would find water in the ground, the heavens would open, the rain would fall, and their wells would be full.

So it is with the people of God going through the Baca's vale of this world. They make wells in it. How do they do this? By their prayers. By their meditation on the Lord in the hot, tiring, dry valley of this world. By resting more completely and wholly on the Lord. They dig their wells by using the means of grace which He has ordained.

Again, they would help each other in the making of these wells. All of them had a part in the same work. It was not a case of some standing idle with their hands in their pockets, while others sweated to complete the work. Not at all. And God's house ought to be a well for us. There we work for ourselves and for others. It is not for one person to work there on their own.

The minister ought not to be working alone digging the well. Ought not God's people to be praying for the preacher and for one another?

The rain will fill the pools. They were using the means, and the Lord was making sure that their labour was not in vain. There is reward to be obtained from casting off the foolish yearning we have for the vanities of the world. You will gain submission to Christ. You will gain patience. You will come to see more preciousness in God and in Christ. You will see the fittingness and suitableness of working for the glory of Christ on earth, by giving your heart completely over to Him.

61. A WILLING PEOPLE

Thy people shall be willing in a day of thy power...
(Psalm 110:3).

The Lord's people are a willing people. Which implies that they were otherwise formerly. Once upon a time they were unwilling to turn from sin to God. That was on account of their enmity towards God. What has turned man to sin has turned man away from God. It is natural to man to be an enemy of God and to hate God, as natural as for the river to pour downwards into the ocean. It is futile for any other power than God's to endeavour to change the course of the sinner's heart in relation to God. There is just as little efficacy in this as there would be in a man's attempt to stand in the path of the river and try to persuade it to run somewhere other than to the sea.

Why then are men asked to do something in connection with their salvation? Because man is a rational and accountable creature. And in many instances this has been accompanied by the Lord's power and blessing. Man is asked to pray for mercy, and for God's power to convict Him, which God alone is able to give. The Word reminds man of God's rights over him as a creature, and of his guilt as a sinner, at enmity with God and disobedient to Him. Although man cannot change his own condition, God is able to change it for him, and is able to bless him. It is his duty to cry to God for it.

Again, it is through the preaching of the Gospel that the power of God comes to work in a sinner's heart and make him willing. God's word is made known through preaching, and is blessed to the souls of men so that they are made willing as the Spirit of God makes these matters known to the heart.

This divine power that makes a sinner willing does not leave the soul. It only takes hold of the heart thereafter. It continues to make him willing;

as the Lord gives and sustains natural life, so He sustains spiritual life where
He gives it. The soul of the believer thus grows in grace. And that implies
a soul becoming more and more willing to have Christ as Saviour.

Without a doubt there is such a thing as backsliding. And although a
sinner can put himself into a backslidden condition, he cannot get himself
out of it. He requires that his soul be delivered from the power of that
worldliness. And God does deliver him, by ministering to him through the
Holy Spirit, giving him spiritual food through the Word, feeding him on
Christ. The growth of that spiritual life, despite the backsliding, shows itself
in the soul by the soul's desire to have Christ alone as Saviour, and glorify Him.

The soul of the believer may be anxious often that although the spiritual
life has begun, it may not continue. And there are many believers in this
condition, who remain so for a long time before they can begin following
Christ in a public way. Only the power of God can keep them willing. And
while that anxiety lasts with them, they cannot fall away. The Lord will
sustain them. Many people have been anxious like this before they died, but
the Lord kept them, and did not suffer death to come upon them until that
worry had gone. And when death came, that anxiety had gone for ever.

This willingness occurs in a day of God's power. That power brings
souls to a view of the mercy of God in Christ. Mercy, and mercy alone, is
the cause of this willingness. Do you say that if God was as willing to have
you as you are to have Him, then your salvation would be sure? You are
mistaken; it was He and He alone who made you willing to have Him. Apart
from the Power of God, you would remain unwilling to have Him. It was
because of the exercise of His power in connection with your need that you
were made willing. He is the one who sought you, and so worked in you
that you came to run after Him. He remembered you, and purposed to go
after you, when you had no thought at all of Him.

62. LIGHT IN DARKNESS

Unto the upright there ariseth light in the darkness
(Psalm 112:4).

Who are the upright? They are those who have received light. They had been
sitting in darkness, until the sun shone on them, the sun of the glorious
Gospel of Christ. The Sun of Righteousness rose on them, with healing in
His wings. It was the Sun of *Righteousness* that made them *righteous*, or
upright. As the apostle says, 'Ye were sometime darkness, but now are ye

light in the Lord'. Are you light? Does the light of godliness shine in you, through you and around you? That is how the case ought to be, instead of the darkness of carelessness going through you. It is only by being a light in the world that the believer fulfils the purpose for which he was redeemed.

Even although they are light in the Lord, believers are sometimes in darkness. But it is a darkness in which light will arise for them. There is a big difference between the situation in which they once were, formerly in darkness, and in which they are now, when they are in darkness but light arises for them. That former darkness was one in which light could not rise for them at all. And they were content in it. But the darkness in which they find themselves now is one of which they are only too acutely aware.

In former times, the people of God found themselves in the darkness of ignorance and enslavement to sin. That was a terrible darkness. It is the darkness that every rational creature is in, for it affects all a man's powers of reasoning and intelligence. It affects a man's thoughts and opinions about God. Perhaps such a man thinks often about God, but these thoughts are dark thoughts - the thoughts of darkness. They have been begotten and are ruled by the darkness. They are worldly thoughts. Whoever loves the world does not have the love of the Father abiding in him. Such a person calls good, evil, and evil, good; he calls what is bitter, sweet, and what is sweet, bitter; he calls light, darkness, and darkness, light. Even as he thinks about God, the thoughts he has about Him are dark, and are not sufficient to give him knowledge of God.

The kind of God in whom the righteous man believes is denied by many natural men. These wicked men think that such a God is the figment of imagination. But the imagining belongs to them; it is they who are guilty of the very thing of which they accuse others. The wonderful thing is that it is such men and women who are now made righteous, or upright. When that happens it is because divine life is taking to do with them, that is, the light of the Holy Spirit.

What does that light do? It shows up the darkness for what it is, and shows up the horribleness of that situation. Before this, there was light, but 'the light that was in them was darkness'. How great is such darkness! Men in such a condition can find many good things in themselves - good principles and good standards of behaviour. The Pharisee in the Temple had light, but the light in him was darkness. He had very high and good opinions about himself and his lifestyle - things that he was prepared to show to God. He thought these things satisfied God. Such is the delusion of natural man.

But now the light has come, and it has shown us the darkness for what it is. When it comes, it does not do away with the darkness; it only shows us that darkness and what it is like. Before men possessed torches, if they wanted to go out on a dark night they would have to light a candle or a flaming torch of some kind. If it was a starry night, bright enough for you to make out the shape of the houses and the landscape, and you were carrying your light, do you know what the effect would be? With your light in your hand, the darkness around you would be scattered, and your light would blind you to the brightness of the stars and everything else. You would be able to see nothing. Perhaps then the dark night would feel more lonely than it had ever felt before.

And that is what happens when the grace of God begins to work in the soul. The light of God's Spirit extinguishes the brightness of many a star in the sky of the soul, which you thought yourself was so beautiful; now that the light has come in you see the darkness of your soul to be similar to the darkness that once covered the land of Egypt. But that is good. God has done that to take you to the one who said 'I am the light of the world', that is, to Christ Himself. It was for this reason that you came to see your darkness, the darkness of your own sin. And when you see your darkness in this way, you then understand that you deserve nothing but to be cast into outer and eternal darkness. This darkness of your soul is the cause of your condemnation. Your opinion of yourself in the night of your spiritual ignorance was deceptive. No-one will choose a suit-pattern at night, even in the light of the lamp, because although it might please him then, when the day comes and its light dawns, he might change his mind and then choose another one. You may choose the pattern of your self-righteousness as the suit that will clothe your soul in salvation, and choose it in the night of the ignorance of your soul; but when the light comes, when the day of God's grace comes, then you will want Christ to clothe you in a suit of righteousness which He Himself will make for you. Then your choice will be good, and you will be safe.

As I understand my darkness, I will see myself becoming worse and worse, and Christ becoming better and better for me. I become ashamed to see the darkness that there is in me; I ought to put less and less confidence in myself. I believe that the more I understand about my darkness, the more I understand about Christ; and the more I understand about Him, the more I see of my own darkness and my own corruption. For the believer, knowledge of Christ arises in his darkness.

The believer also faces the darkness of temptation. Light flees from his affections, and he loves the darkness. Our affections are so changing and changeable, light one moment, darkness the next. The word of the truth of the Gospel is unchanging. We must look to Him for light so that we will walk by faith, and not by sight.

63. PRECIOUS IN DEATH

Precious in the sight of the Lord is the death of his saints
(Psalm 116:15).

Who are the saints? Those who are effectually called by God to holiness, to be saints. They are called with a holy calling, and they have in them the true holiness of God. They are made partakers of holiness; their lifestyle in the world is holy. They are not perfect, but they are holy in a measure, and they are progressing towards complete holiness. Notwithstanding the kindness of God to them, they are to die as others, just as they suffer as others. It is not from suffering and death that we know that they are saints. They may suffer in their life and death even more than the unregenerate. They are not exempted from death; and in itself, death does not appear to be a great kindness to saints. But it is.

The saints are precious to the Lord in every condition of their lot. There is a sense in which they are precious to Him as they are born into the world; they have no preciousness in and of themselves, but they are precious to Him because of His gracious purposes of grace regarding them. Therefore they are precious to Him even in their unconverted condition, and he preserves them from death itself, so that no ill will befall them before they are converted. They are in His eternal purposes of salvation. John Bunyan tells us of how a soldier went on sentry duty instead of him when he was in the army, and was killed. There are many people who had narrow escapes of that kind, through sickness and in other ways, and God protected them and lifted them up, because He had purposed to save them afterwards, so that they would be His witnesses.

Have you been kept and preserved by God? Pray that it will be to your good; that God will bless you by giving you to see his salvation in all its glory in a way that will do your soul good, and not in a way that will ripen you for a lost eternity.

Again, the conversion of the saints is precious to God. Without a doubt! It is a precious time when by grace the heart and ways of a man are separated from Satan and his service.

But the text specifically says that the *death* of the saints is precious to the Lord. What makes it so? It is precious in view of the end that God has in view; He is bringing His saints to perfection, and death brings them nearer it. God's purpose of salvation in Christ is that His saints will come to inherit the rest prepared for them. So Christ prays, 'Father I will that they whom thou hast given me be with me where I am...' When they die, they come to be near God. The greater happiness to which they come at death is what makes the death of the saints precious in the sight of God.

It is precious to God that His people are free from sin, perfectly holy, to be in the situation where they do not need to submit to the disciplining rod any more. They need to suffer no longer. It is not willingly that God chastises the sons of men, and it is precious to God that death has brought His people to a situation where they no longer require to be brought through sufferings. In glory, they require to know the love of God, but they do not require to know the pity of God. Not only do the saints who have gone no longer require pity from men, from those they left after them; but they will not require pity from God throughout eternity. When the child is sick he needs the pity of his father or mother; but when the child is sound and healthy he does not need it. But all the time he has their love. Here we are sick; but in Glory there is no sickness.

There are other reasons why the death of the saints is precious to God. It is precious because now they are outside the possibility of falling into sin, or bringing shame on the Lord's cause in the world. It is precious because it is so great a portion of the death of Christ that His people die, and inherit perfection and happiness as a result.

It is also precious because when saints die, the minds of other believers are often lifted to consider the rest that they know their departed brothers are going to enjoy for all eternity. It is therefore a means of sanctification to them, and it binds their hearts to the glory that waits for them, and the one through whom this is possible.

The death of His saints is precious because the Lord has victory over death every time the soul of one of His people goes through death to Glory. Death that came to ruin man as a result of sin is now a door through which the saints are permitted to enter to arrive in Heaven, and to have victory over sin itself. Imagine two countries at war. One builds a railway, which, it is intended, will carry soldiers to the other country, so that they will destroy its power. But instead, the other country is so prepared, and so powerful, that it takes over the railway, and uses it as a means to destroy the country which possessed it formerly. That country had constructed it in order to defeat and have victory over the other, but instead, under the control of the other country, the railway is used to destroy the very people that made it.

So it is with death. Death entered the world as a result of sin, as a means of destroying man. But through the battle Christ fought at Calvary, death is now for the people of God a weapon of destruction against sin, and gives them liberty from the power of darkness, that very power that brought death in in the first place.

Death is also precious to the saints of God because of the confidence which grace gives them going into it. As Addison says, 'See how a Christian

can die'. What a heartbreak it is to see someone going into death who has
no such hope, and no glory or happiness awaiting him on the other side!

64. STRANGERS ON EARTH

I am a stranger in the earth: hide not thy commandments from me
(Psalm 119:19).

The reason the psalmist asks that God will not hide His commandments
from him is that he is a stranger on the earth. The request is based upon a
sound and valid reason. The request: 'Hide not thy commandments from
me'; the reason: 'I am a stranger on the earth'.

Let us look at the reason first. We can see that if the psalmist had become
careless or indifferent to the commandments of God, that would be a sign
of increased earthliness and worldliness. The more careless about these he
is, the more his heart is bound to the things of the world. But he has seen
the foolishness of this, because he knows that he will only be on the earth
for a short while.

David is a strange person. He had faults, falls and failings; but he is
nonetheless careful that the world will not take his true portion away from
him. In other words, he kept a careful eye on what is expressed in our text.
He shows truly that he is a watchful and careful man, because he has
discovered himself to be a stranger on the earth. He had worldly riches and
wealth in plenty. He had royal authority, which he could use whenever and
however he wished. He had power to withstand any assault made against
him. In the midst of such riches a man is inclined to forget that he is only
a stranger on earth. That forgetfulness is often tied to worldly wealth and
prosperity.

But I think that David's confession shows how easily he could be
persuaded to become worldly. It is as if he is saying 'Something in me likes
and wants to rest in the world, content with what the world can give. My
heart wants the world; but is that not foolish, when I am a stranger in it, and
here for such a short while? My heart wants to go after the world, its glory,
its respect, its wealth and prosperity, its peace and security; but what will
it profit me to give my heart to these things when after a little while I will
have to leave the world to go to another place? Lord, it will profit nothing.
I know it will profit nothing. You alone can tell me that. Therefore, Lord,
since this is the truth, that I am a stranger who must leave the world soon,
do not hide thy commandments from me.' David is telling the Lord what

the Lord told himself first; now he has taken it so much to heart because it has become so clear to him.

But for what reason does he mention the commandments in this context? Just because God's commandments were what mapped out the road for him, the road on which he ought to walk in preparation for the world to which he was going, that is, to eternity. It is God's commandments that taught him to take to heart truly that he was a stranger in the earth, that taught him that preparation was needed for eternity, and that taught him the kind of preparation which was required. Apart from the commandments, he would be in danger of losing sight of all these things, and his sight would be fixed no higher than on the earth itself.

He prays 'Do not hide them from me'. Were the commandments of God hidden from David at this point? Not as far as revelation was concerned; God had revealed them to His people. But they could be hidden from him for all that. A man can have God's revelation and still it be hidden from him. 'If our gospel be hid it is hid from them that are lost.' What are the commandments? There are the ten commandments, and the commandments of Scripture which say to us, 'Love Jehovah your God'. Are not these commandments beautiful? Why does David say 'Do not hide them?' Simply because he knows that God must open for him their loveliness and glory, so that they will take hold of his heart, and so that he will see and feel Heaven itself in them. Those who pray like David have heard the music of Heaven in the commandments. They can say that God's law is their song in their house of pilgrimage. This is the will of God, that we keep His commandments, and His commandments are not grievous.

Only the Holy Spirit could reveal the commandments to David in the way that he was wishing for. And the Spirit's revealing the commandments to him in this way is the only thing that will bind his heart to Heaven, and that will keep him from being bound to the world in a way forbidden by God, and in a way which will bring loss to his soul.

When the commandments are revealed to a person in this way, they bring heavenly life into the soul, drawing the soul more and more away from the world. The more the measure of heavenliness and spiritualness grows, so the worldliness decreases; and at the same time, with increased worldliness there comes diminished spiritualness. There are many ways of becoming worldly; but there is only one way of becoming heavenly, that is, to have God's commandments revealed to us so that we will perform them.

65. STRENGTH RENEWED

But they that wait upon the Lord shall renew their strength; they shall mount up with wings as eagles; they shall run, and not be weary, and they shall walk, and not faint (Isaiah 40:31).

What is implied in waiting upon the Lord?
It implies a consciousness of lack on the part of the person doing it. A sense of emptiness and insufficiency, and a desire that it should be met. It implies a knowledge that the party waited upon has a provision enabling Him to meet the needs of the party who waits upon Him. It implies an assurance that the party possessing that provision is disposed to bestow upon the waiting party the things which he requires. All these features are involved in waiting upon the Lord.

The soul has a sense of the need of righteousness to make him acceptable to God. He is conscious of not possessing it. This is a concern to him; indeed, it is the greatest of all concerns to him. This realisation is through the illumination of the Holy Spirit.

He sees that the righteousness he needs is in Christ. There is not only a righteousness, but one which is perfectly suited to all our needs. And he realises that the Lord has a disposition to bestow that righteousness upon him. All the vision involved in the soul's knowledge of need, and of the Lord's provision, and His disposition to communicate thereof to those who need it is *faith*, or waiting on the Lord. When you approach God's provision, you apprehend His gracious disposition to communicate His provision to those who are truly in need.

What is the result of waiting upon the Lord?
Those who do so will 'renew their strength'. There is in a sense strength in our very sense of need itself. Our being weakened in our own strength is the result of God's strength taking hold of us. It is God's power in us that deprives us of our belief that we have spiritual strength of our own. This is getting strong by being made weak. 'When I am weak then am I strong.'

This strength consists in loving God as well as believing in Christ. What great strength you require to believe and love. If you believe, you love. The one is the inevitable consequence of the other. What wonder it was to you to feel that you love God, that you can love God. You felt your nature so inimical, so hostile to God, and Oh! what joy it was for you to discover that you could love God now, that you would wish to love Him more than it is possible for you to do so. Strength to enable you to desire to be like God (not that God would be like you - that is the desire of unconverted people).

How is that strength manifested?

By its causing them to mount up on wings as eagles. This denotes heavenly-mindedness; having a more accurate conception than before of the world and the things that pertain to it. This is to have real vision. When you have it, you see heaven and earth. This strength enables you to see the heaven of Glory, as well as the world in which you dwell. You will get a true conception of both in the measure in which you are governed by this strength. You see the glory of Christ and the vanity of seen things. This is like a believer in his first experience of grace. He mounts up so high. But it may not be so continually.

The soul may be reduced to running, and then walking. Troubles, trials, corruptions - all these assail him. He is not to be in Heaven as soon as he expected. The Lord's face may be hidden from him. He is like a weaned child. How happy is a child when he is young! So is the believer. The child smiles in his sleep. The time of one's experience of grace is a time of smiles. The Lord has smiled on the Christian in love. But the weaned child goes to stronger food. The Lord raised his children as upon the wings of the eagle. He grows up after being weaned. If he were kept on the breast he would remain a dwarf. But it would be happier to be left on the breast. But what is happiest is not always best. The child as he grows becomes more conscious of the love of the parents and of what they did for him, and of his dependence upon them. So it is with the spiritual child also.

And those who are thus strengthened shall run and not be weary. They shall walk and not faint. They feel weary enough and faint enough at times. They are weary of trials, and weary of themselves. If this is your condition, then this text will suit you. You will not be weary of being weary of sin. You will not be weary of loving Christ. You will not be weary of wishing to be made like Christ. And you will be made like Him, and will not be weary through all Eternity.

66. SINS BLOTTED OUT

I have blotted out as a thick cloud thy transgressions, and as a cloud thy sins; return unto me, for I have redeemed thee (Isaiah 44:22).

There are two main thoughts in this text: the illustration the Lord uses for the sins and transgressions of His people, and the way in which He was going to deal with them and forgive them: 'I have blotted out as a thick cloud...'; and secondly, the way the Lord uses that forgiveness as an argument for constraining them to return to himself: 'I have redeemed thee'. That redemption was in the blotting out of their sins.

The sins and faults of the people of God are here compared to a thick cloud, and the forgiveness of sins is compared to the blotting out of these clouds.

Now, the clouds that we see in the sky grow out of the earth and the oceans naturally. The water in these places rises up under the influence of the sun's heat as clouds, and become clouds in the sky, often coming between the earth and the sun, and interrupting the light and heat of the sun for a while. It is because God is like a holy sun that He causes the sins of people to rise up like clouds of darkness between themselves and God. If God did not exist as a holy God, there would be no such thing as sin. Sin would lose its meaning, and would not draw to men its condemnation, curse and its liability to eternal punishment, if there were no God. It is because God is what He is that makes sin what it is.

Often the clouds are the reason men make forecasts about the weather, and the kind of weather they can expect. People can tell, by looking at the clouds when a storm or tempest is coming. The thick clouds that arise from the sins of men and which come between themselves and God, mean that a full and eternal storm is coming, that will fall on unconverted sinners at death and judgement.

Another meaning of 'cloud' is a 'multitude'. In Isaiah 60:8 we read 'Who are these that fly as a cloud?' The person who experiences forgiveness of sins cannot do so without being aware of himself, and aware of the fact that the kindnesses which God showed to him each day of his life were beyond number. He is aware that his transgressions were a great multitude - sins of thought, word and action, each one of them deserving the anger and curse of God. When there is a light shower, you see tiny droplets of water falling on your clothes, droplets which are far smaller than in an ordinary shower. But the droplets which constitute the cloud which sails through the sky are even smaller still. There is an amazing number of tiny drops of water in a cloud. The sins that God forgives can be compared to a cloud, made up of many, many droplets of water - our sins go beyond our ability to number them. But the forgiveness of God extends to each one.

Those whose sins have been forgiven certainly see their sins as a thick, dark cloud which was an unspeakable provocation to God; and they were afraid that these sins would be a means of turning God's mercy and favour away from them for ever. The reason was that they saw every one of these sins as deserving the wrath and curse of God, which rested on them until God's forgiveness reached them. Perhaps they reckoned the cloud so dark, so great, and so provocative of God that they came to fear that it would be very difficult, perhaps even impossible, for God to forgive their sins. Although not all feel like this, there have been some, and there always will be some, who saw their sins in such a way that they thought it might be impossible for God to forgive them at all. And that makes the cloud look even greater and darker for them.

But God has shown His willingness to forgive sins. He has shown that He is willing and determined to forgive them by giving Christ to die for them. For it is as a result of giving Christ over to death that it is possible for Him to forgive sins in a way that reveals His own glory and His greatness. He is more willing to forgive than to condemn, although condemnation is what they deserve.

Yet, although God is willing to forgive all these sins, it is impossible that the cloud of transgressions should appear greater to the sinner than it does to God. The sinner is not aware of the multitude of his sins, as God is aware of them. That is when they would be afraid God would not forgive their sins - when they saw them as He does. God alone knows the multitude of these sins and what they deserve; yet He could not be any more willing to forgive them than He is. And He has shown that by giving Christ for them, by means of which He is glorified. And to whom will He extend forgiveness but to those for whom Christ died as a perfect and willing Saviour?

It is possible that a sinner comes to understand the cloud of his sins in the same way that Elisha's servant saw the cloud, at first appearing no bigger than a man's hand, but which grew and grew until at last the whole sky was filled with that cloud. Perhaps the Spirit will begin His work on a man with solemn thoughts that will not trouble him too greatly, but that will so influence him at last that he will have no room to think of anything else from morning to night but that provocative cloud of sins that has arisen from his birth between himself and God. And in that way, God ripens him and prepares him to accept forgiveness, by making him dependent on Himself through experiences of the power of the Holy Spirit.

Again, naturally speaking, the clouds put a sad complexion and countenance on the face of the creation, affecting the sight both of the sea, the land and the sky. That is how a man is when his conscience has been awakened. God's frown is written on everything he sees. As he goes to sleep, he fears that God will call him to account before the morning comes. He is in the same bondage too when he wakes. That cloud meets with him in health and sickness, and he sees it as he anticipates death and judgement, which lie before him. Although I said that the sinner cannot see how terrible that cloud is as God did, yet he sees something in it that God Himself does not see in a sense - this terrible wrath against him for his sin. Perhaps he is afraid that the unforgivable sin is in that cloud, sin against the Holy Ghost.

And in this sense, the sinner looks at the cloud in a way that God cannot.

A cloud is different to a mountain or loch - it is not steadfast and unchanging. Clouds do not remain in the one place without moving. They come and go. God rules them. He rules them by His decree. No-one but He can move the clouds. Paul thought that he could keep the sky between himself and God clear through his own self-righteousness. He thought that he could prevent a cloud of sin from opposing him. But God could see the cloud of Paul's sins although Paul could not. And God showed it to Paul on the way to Damascus, and Paul then realised that instead of moving the cloud away, as he thought he was doing, he was only making it even greater. He saw that between himself and God the sky was completely black. But he also saw God moving the cloud and leaving a clear sky.

This is one way in which the illustration can be adjusted. When the clouds go, they leave the sky clear and blue. The goodness and love of God have cleared our sky, so that God sees no cloud there any more. 'I, even I, am he that blotteth out thy transgressions for mine own sake, and will not remember thy sins' (Isaiah 43:25). Many times they see the clouds there that He does not see, for he has blotted them out. How can they return when He has sent them away? The cloud of the sins of the people of God cannot come in between them and Him any more.

How did God find a way to blot out the cloud of their sins? By sending the cloud of their sins on to the Son of His love by sending Him to die for them. Christ hath redeemed them from the curse of the law by being made a curse for them. Because the Father poured our sins on Him, eternal blessing is given to us through Him.

The call to those who have been thus forgiven is 'Return to me'. Nothing puts them under a greater obligation - a greater debt - to return than the sufferings endured by Christ when He bore our sins in His own body to the tree. Apparently, although God had blotted out their sins as a cloud, they were lost themselves, far away from God. Is it not strange that things could be like this? Waywardness and unthankfulness are strange things in the heart of man! But the kindness and long-suffering of God are wonderful. And these are what will bring the backslider to return to God. To see the love and mercy of the One who redeemed us, and who calls us to return to Himself.

67. LOVED WITH EVERLASTING LOVE

The Lord hath appeared of old unto me, saying, Yea, I have loved thee with
an everlasting love: therefore with lovingkindness have I drawn thee
(Jeremiah 31:3).

At this time the church was in great affliction in captivity in Babylon. She
was remembering the many ways in which the Lord had freed Israel of old,
both in Egypt and in the wilderness, and now finding herself in a situation
where the power of God was not being displayed for her freedom at this
time. But the Lord appeared with this great word: 'I have loved thee with
an everlasting love'; His love for His people was not to be displayed or
exercised on her behalf in one moment of time, but for all time.

This is the nature of the love which God shows to His own sinful people,
love that is eternal, everlasting love. If a man loves another, he has delight
in that person. God does not deceive anyone when He says that He loves
them; God is so faithful and true that it is impossible for Him to lie about any
matter. Naturally speaking, a man who loves another person is concerned
for the good and happiness of the one he loves.

From one point of view, if there is anything that is impossible for men
to believe, it is that God loves sinful men. That is because as far as their
natures are concerned, God and man are completely different. God loves
righteousness; men love sin. God is purer than to behold sin; but man wants
to behold nothing else. Sin is man's pleasure and pastime; yet, although that
is so, no-one ever loved another in the way that God loves His people. The
apostle Paul says that God is love. The angels do not love each other in the
way that God loves hell-deserving sinners. God loves in a way that none
other can love, whether a man or an angel. Now, not only were the objects
of his love sinful; we must also inquire as to what that implies. It does not
only mean loving the very things that God hated, and that He had forbidden;
more than that, it means that they were His enemies. He was hated by them,
and obnoxious to them. They despised Him, and ignored all His warnings,
although it was in His power to condemn them. They were bold in their
opposition to Him.

A man chooses to marry a woman for the sake of the strong, healthy,
faithful bond of love between them. He loves her because she is lovely in
his sight, and he thinks much of her; he considers anything worthy of her,
because he loves her more than himself or anything else. But even this is
a poor illustration of the love of God. This love is so surpassingly
wonderful, because it is the love of an eternal God to man who is a corrupt
sinner. It is not a love that is going to let go, or a love that is only going to

last for a year or two, which so often happens naturally. Men and women promise to love one another until death separates them. Yet so often they break covenant with each other. But Christ says 'I have betrothed thee to myself for ever'.

Those whom Christ loves were at enmity with Him. This shows up how wonderful, and amazing Christ's love for them is. It is seen in its glory in the light of their sins, and in the light of Christ's dying for them. There are some people who appear obnoxious to us, who never did us any harm; but although they never hurt us in any way, we would not like them to be our friends or companions. But not only were we creatures who were abominable to God; we were committing sin against Him constantly. We were fighting against His will and His commandment, despising His authority and His greatness.

This verse shows us that we did not deserve or merit this love that He had for us. God had to draw us to Himself. '...therefore with lovingkindness I have drawn thee'. We ought to be ashamed that God had to draw us to Himself. If we were what we ought to be, God would never have had to draw us. We would have continued loving Him and obeying Him, as the unfallen angels did from their first estate.

But by drawing us, God showed His love to us. He drew us in order to acquaint us with His love, and He draws us in order that we will know it more and more, so that it will become more wonderful to us, and give us food for thought. Before He drew us, our mind and interest were in the world and its follies, its riches and its happiness. But He drew us away from perdition. He united us to Himself. He drew us away from the peace that sin gave us; by His own love He drew us away from the love of the world. What was that lovingkindness by which He drew us? Nothing but Christ - He said of Himself 'I, if I be lifted up from the earth, will draw all men unto me'. That is, all that the Father gave Him; they will come to Him, and those who come to Him He will in no wise cast out. This is the power that always draws. Christ draws by revealing to sinners the glory of His Person in chastisements and afflictions. They say 'We love Him because He first loved us'. The love of God sets their heart on fire. The disciplining of God will be of no spiritual or sanctifying benefit to anyone unless the love of God is on fire in the heart. That is what enables us to benefit from chastisements. There is filial love in the heart of the person bound in ties of blood to Christ; and it awakens the thought of having provoked God to wrath on account of sin. This moves them to repentance. No-one can repent without the influence of love. The love of God will bring a person to repentance.

Sometimes a child will come running to its mother for a kiss, because of the awareness of having done something wrong, something with which she will not be pleased. Perhaps this will occur after discipline or correction. What makes them do this? Is it not their love for their mother? The thought of having hurt mother draws their heart. The marrow of repentance is to be truly mournful for God, for having been an offence to God; and repentance is the weeping that a person weeps for God, more than for himself. God's love is what awakens repentance in him, so he comes, looking for the kiss of reconciliation with God. Perhaps, however, that will not come consciously to him ever in the way that he desires.

God draws His people by testing them. Testing turns to love in the heart of the believer. There is a 'spiritual factory' in the believer's heart, that can make love out of testing-times, just as a factory might make clothes out of tweed. That fire of the love of God turns even afflictions into new occasions of love.

God draws with the revelation of His power accompanying the preaching of the gospel. There will also be a drawing at last, beyond death, at the resurrection, when He will say 'Gather my saints unto me'.

This love with which He draws is eternal, without beginning or ending; therefore it will not be liable to change. Although man had a beginning, God did not. His love for His people is what it always was and will be.

68. CHOOSING THE GOOD PART

But one thing is needful: and Mary hath chosen that good part,
which shall not be taken away from her (Luke 10:42).

As you will see, Christ spoke these words by way of answer to Martha, who complained that her sister Mary was not helping her in serving Christ. Apparently she was annoyed with her sister; and she looked as if she was rather annoyed with Christ Himself for allowing her sister to sit there listening to Him; when, as Martha thought, she should have been helping her look after Christ.

There is reason to believe that Martha considered her complaint wholly reasonable, and therefore she would be even more amazed that Christ had paid no attention to this matter. But in fact, Christ was noticing everything; and if Martha thought that Christ would have considered her complaint a reasonable one after she uttered it, she was sadly mistaken and deceived. For Christ did not agree with her at all in her complaint; indeed, His words condemned her, and commended Mary her sister.

For it is very clear that Mary was giving greater glory to Christ at that moment by sitting at His feet, than Martha was by the work she was performing, even though she was doing it for Christ. I remember a very godly woman who died when I was young, long before I found any delight in the Gospel, saying that she would take it as a good token, when conversing with any of the Lord's people who came to see her, if they had such freedom in their conversation about spiritual things, that she would not get as much of her worldly work done as on other days. I heard that long before I began to follow the means of grace, but I never forgot it. Now, that woman was not speaking because of a spirit of laziness that was in her, for she was a diligent, working woman; when she spoke of not doing her work it was as a result of feeling such a glorious presence of the Lord with her. Nor was it a spirit of laziness that had come on Mary here; it was rather that her soul was spiritually hungry. Had she been making excuses, Christ would never have accepted them.

Mary considered it more important that Christ should serve her soul with spiritual food, by His words, than that she should serve Him with natural food. And this corresponds with what He Himself said, 'The Son of Man came not to be ministered unto, but to minister...' And there is a sense in which the dependence and the need she displayed to Him there was the stuff of His very life's work. See what Christ said to the disciples at the well of Samaria, where He had led that woman to see her own need of the Saviour; He told them, when they asked Him to eat, that He had meat to eat which they knew not of. His meat was to do the will of Him who had sent Him, and to finish His work. He had asked that woman for a drink, and although she had not given it to Him, before the conversation was over, He had given her a drink of that water of which He said that if anyone was to drink of it, they would never thirst. And Christ received a drink from her, in the thirst which she had in her soul for salvation. Christ said on the cross 'I thirst', and there is a sense, speaking reverently, in which His whole life said 'I thirst' - thirsting for the salvation of His people, to perform the work of salvation on their behalf. He thirsted to bear the cross for them; 'I have a baptism wherewith to be baptized, and how am I straitened until it is accomplished!'

Without a doubt, Martha's work was good and precious. The only thing that was wrong with it is that she considered it advantageous for herself with the kind of thinking she had. Had she said 'Mary, sister, stay as you are, since the Lord gave you the opportunity and the precious circumstance which you now have, drinking in His words', things would have been differed. Then her serving would have surely been a pleasing sacrifice, giving glory to God. But that is not how her situation was. Christ answered her, and rebuked her for the kind of mind that was in her. She was doing a good work, and I have no doubt that she was a believing woman; but her spirit was not what it ought to have been. That is why Christ said 'One thing is needful...'

What had Mary chosen? Nothing but Christ Himself. She had chosen to drink in the teaching of Christ. That indeed is the 'one thing needful' according to Christ's words here. Christ Himself said it, not someone else who knew less of the circumstances than Christ. There are many things needful in life: food and clothing, helping the hungry - all these things are good and needful, but Christ, who knows everything, says that above all else, one thing is needful, and that is to have Christ Himself.

69. AS A LITTLE CHILD

Verily, I say unto you, Whosoever shall not receive the kingdom of God as a little child, shall in no wise enter therein (Luke 18:17).

(1) A child's entry into the world is through birth. The entrance of a child into the kingdom of grace is by birth too. A child is the most helpless of creatures, even more helpless than other creatures that are born. So a child of God is reduced to a condition of absolute helplessness when born into the kingdom of grace. This might not have been his opinion of the situation originally. Man sets out to satisfy God's claims with a high conception of his own powers. Pride and self-sufficiency characterise his state of mind. He exalts himself, but lowers God at the same time by considering himself capable of satisfying God's claims. It is his low conception of the character of God's claims that causes him to consider himself capable of satisfying these claims. But when he receives the necessary light, which acquaints him with the character of these claims, he is reduced to a condition of conscious helplessness. Thus he becomes like a little child. The issue he rests with Christ. That is all a child can do.

(2) A child has life, notwithstanding his helplessness, so consequently he hungers. But he does not have the resources in himself to meet with that hunger. So it is with the child of God; he has life, but he is dependent on resources outwith himself for sustaining that life. Thus his sense of personal helplessness is accentuated by a realisation of his utter dependence on the resources contained in Christ, and Christ's will to communicate these needed blessings to his soul.

(3) The life of a little child is needy, solicitous and importunate. One thing a child can do is cry; and the more it is denied, the more it cries. A child's needs would keep it crying until its death. It could not help asking. It would inevitably be importunate by reason of its life. The child of God is perpetually solicitous.

(4) There is an instinct in the child which enables it to realise that it is welcome to its mother's breast. So the believer possesses a similar spirit. He knows there is enough - like the prodigal - and he has confidence that he is welcome. There is faith in the Father's love.

(5) A child's attention is concentrated primarily on the mother who feeds it. So a believer is weaned from the world and his heart is centred upon Christ.

(6) A child has love for the parent who feeds it and shows it kindness. The believer has love to God and Christ. It is little in comparison with the love the Lord bears to him.

(7) When chastised, a child draws closer to its mother. The chastisement as it were, seems to increase the child's love. So chastisement does not alienate the hearts of the children of God from Him, but knits their hearts the more to Him.

(8) There is timidity in the child. When frightened, it makes directly for its parent. There is a holy timidity in the children of God from sin and from the devil's schemes.

(9) A child is also characterised by teachableness. A child has an open ear. He does not argue, but takes things simply and credulously. A child does not differentiate between persons as far as position in the social scale is concerned. The tinker's child is to him like any other child. The king's child would play with a tinker's son as with a duke's or a lord's. So the believer looks at all people from the point of view of their having immortal souls which are infinitely valuable. The believer attaches an equal value to each person because he looks at them all from this solemn standpoint. Whatever makes one look down on his fellow men, he has not learnt that from Christ.

70. LOVE FOR THE SON

Jesus said unto them, If God were your Father, ye would love me:
for I proceeded forth and came from God; neither came I of myself,
but he sent me (John 8:42).

God is only Father to those who love Christ. He is not the Father of all men
at all. There is a sense in which one can speak of God being the Father of
all, that is as far as His creation of all men is concerned. But from the point
of view from which Christ speaks here, God is not the Father of any man
who hates God and Christ.

Christ makes it clear here (a) that God is the Father of some; and (b) that
there are those to whom He is not Father. God is not the Father of those who
are speaking to Christ at this point, and yet whose opinion about themselves
was that God was indeed their Father. Christ was denying this, and saying
that in no way could God be considered their Father. And the certain and
sure token of this was the fact that they hated Christ Himself. For He says
here that those who have God as their Father love the Son. In addition, he
tells them without any doubt who their father is - they are of their father the
devil.

It is apparent that there is a spiritual sense in which no-one is without a
father. God is the Father of some, but not of others. And those who have
no claim on God as their father have the devil as their father.

Further, the Scriptures make it clear that there are none of the children
of God, to whom God is their Father, who were not found originally in the
family of Satan. And what did God do for them? He adopted them into His
own family in order that He might be their Father, and they His sons. The
apostle says that they have received the spirit of adoption through which
they cry 'Abba, Father'. What does it mean to adopt? It means to take a child
into a family which is not his natural family, and raise that child as a child
of the new family. The child will now, ever after, be named by his new
family. He will still bear the image of his natural parents; though a man
might adopt a son, he cannot make that child bear his own image. He cannot
put his own nature in him.

But when God adopts His children, He imparts His own spiritual image
to their soul. The spiritual life that is in Him is bestowed upon them.
Without a doubt, the image of the old nature, the old man, can be recognised
in them while they are in the world; but they have the image of God
implanted in their souls, the image they lost through the Fall. The seed of
spiritual life, the seed of holiness - this is implanted when they are adopted
into the family of God, and that image will be striving for all time in this
world with the image of the old man.

And those who have God as their Father have new life in their souls, because they are the children of God; and that life manifests itself in particular ways. There is one way that it shows itself and which Christ emphasises here, and that is by love for Christ Himself. Why is this? That is easy to understand - it would be impossible for them, having received this new nature, this new life, the new principle which God has put in their hearts, being now ruled and governed by that new nature, not to love Christ, for He is the Son of God, the brightness of God's glory and the express image of His Person.

Why do they love Him? He came from the Father; the Father sent Him. That is the proof that the Father Himself loves Him; the Father commissioned Him. And the work the Father gave Him shows the measure of love He had for Him. 'This is my beloved Son, in whom I am well pleased.' The Father loved Him, and it is the Father's will that His people should love Him also. The Father loved Him because of His suitability for completing the work, through which salvation would extend to His people. And they will love Him too because of His having completed the work of salvation on their behalf as one who engaged in that work completely, but who did not undertake it apart from in obedience to the will of the Father.

They love Him because of His relation to the Father as the Eternal Son of God, that is, the only begotten Son, the one who revealed the Father to them. No man hath seen God at any time; the only-begotten Son, who is in the bosom of the Father, He has revealed Him. They love Him because of the loveliness of His Person and natures, His holiness, His mercy, His kindness, His love. No-one can love Christ without loving all of Christ.

The disciples who were with Him in the world loved Him. They recognised Him because they had been given a new nature by Him; but they loved Him with greater intensity when they came to understand in a proper way the reason for His dying. In a sense it is easier for believers today to love Christ than for the eleven disciples prior to the crucifixion, even though they were with Him; for it was when He was parted from them that they came to love Him in a way that they had not done while He was with them.

Do you love Christ? If so, you will love to hear about Him. If so, there is no name sweeter in your ears than His. If so, you will be sad on account of the ways you grieve Him, and the way you do Him despite by sinning against Him. If you love Him, you will desire nothing other than to be like Him.

If you love Christ, you will be afraid that you do not love Him, and you will mourn over how slight your love for Him is. If you love Him you will hate sin, and you will want to be holy, to be clothed with your house from Heaven.

If you love Christ, God is your Father. God loves you, despite how obnoxious you are in your own estimation. If you love Him, you will follow His example; Christ said that it was His meat and His drink to do the will of Him who had sent Him. Make sure that this is true of you, that it will be your pleasure at all times to do the will of God, to hate and flee from sin.

71. DESIRED BY CHRIST

Father, I will that they also whom thou hast given me be with me where I am, that they may behold my glory, which thou hast given me; for thou lovedst me before the foundation of the world (John 17:24).

The form in which this request is made of the Father intimates the Son's consciousness of equality with the Father. He addresses the Father as an equal, and the petition is based on a covenant entered into previously between the Father and the Son. That is the eternal covenant for the salvation of God's elect.

The request concerns certain parties, and its purpose is to secure a certain favour for them. The parties are designated in this way: 'they also whom thou hast given me...' They are further described in verse 6: 'thine they were, and thou gavest them me'. There is a similar description in verse 11: 'those whom thou hast given me', and in verse 12: 'those that thou gavest me'. These verses refer immediately to the disciples, and they also embrace the whole church of God.

The Father gave them to the Son, and the Son accepted them in covenant. It does not imply that the Father parted with them, and that He was not concerned with their interests any longer. This petition implies otherwise. The Father has still an interest in them, and it is His prerogative to dispose of them in accordance with the terms of that covenant. 'My Father, which gave them me, is greater than I, and none can pluck them out of my Father's hand.' So the Father has them in His own hand even when He has given them over in covenant to the Son. It is for the purpose of their redemption that He has given them to the Son, and He is actively interested Himself, with the Son, in the matter. The love of the Father is seen in giving them in covenant to the Son; and when he gave them to Christ He gave them to one who loved them as He loved them Himself. The love of the Father is seen in giving them to Christ in the Eternal Covenant to be redeemed by the Son; and the love of Christ is here seen in praying to the Father with the petition which we have in this verse.

The Son is here manifesting His desire for their companionship in Eternity. This is a request prompted by love for them. Christ will not be satisfied without them, without having them with Himself. His personal love for them is shown here, as is His interest in their blessedness. His thoughts are thoughts of goodwill towards them. He shows a desire for their fellowship. His heart wanted their companionship and love. Christ shows His interest in their eternal safety and happiness.

He prays on the one hand for what is in accordance with the Father's mind; He also prays for what they themselves would desire to attain to. This is the ultimate object of every soul who has enjoyed communion with the Lord in this world, namely eternal communion with Him in Heaven. To be with Christ is far better.

The particular reason why He wants them in Heaven is that they will see His glory. This is not strictly the glory of His divine nature as God, because it cannot be said that that glory was *given* to Him. But it is His glory as Mediator in human nature, which the Father gave to Him. In the exercise of His work as Redeemer, the glory of His divine nature is necessarily revealed, and will be seen by His people in Heaven throughout all Eternity. But what is particularly meant here is the glory of His mediatorial work.

This glory is to be seen through the glory of His love and mercy and His atonement. It is the glory of Christ as surety. Here it is apprehended in a measure; there it is seen in a more glorious form, in an infinitely greater measure. There we shall see face to face. We are the children of God, but it does not yet appear what we shall be. This was a glory given to the Son by the Father. It was a revelational glory, securing the redemption of sinners. It was a glory given to Christ through the eternal covenant of Redemption. It was seen by men and angels. The saints see it in this world. But they shall see it more fully in Heaven. It is a joy to Christ to have His people see His glory by faith in this world; but His purpose is to have them see it in His immediate presence eternally. And this will be the glory of the saints. May the Lord grant us to be of that number!

Notice the ground on which Christ bases His petition - the love which the Father had for Him before the foundation of the world. God loved Him, and He loved them in Him as their surety. In God's relation to His people, He loved them in Christ; and it was a reason for His loving Christ, that He was their surety. But He loved Christ in a way that we can never understand. He loved Christ as His only begotten Son, and He loved Him as the surety of His people. He loved the Son from all eternity in the merits of the atoning sacrifice which He was to bring for His loved ones.

72. THE OLD MAN

Knowing this, that our old man is crucified with him, that the body of sin might be destroyed, that henceforth we should not serve sin (Romans 6:6).

There are four thoughts here: 'The old man' - what the expression denotes; what happened to it - it was crucified with Him; the reason - that the body of sin might be destroyed; and the fruit of this - freedom from the service of sin.

'The old man' - this denotes our corrupt nature, something which is exactly the opposite of the new nature which God has given us. The word 'man' denotes a healthy man, a whole man, who has been crucified with every member that pertained to it. It is called an 'old' man because it is there from the beginning. It is the oldest thing in the history of a converted soul. And the designation 'old man' distinguishes this corrupt nature from the nature that is designated in a different way in Scripture, called 'the new man'.

Unconverted sinners have this old man. They have nothing else. It denotes the sinful heart, hating God with all its lusts and desires. This phrase denotes man from a spiritual point of view. And this is the situation of the unconverted; men and women born into the world are born the children of wrath. But converted sinners have this old man too; but they have more - they have a new man. And when this happens - when the soul is possessed of a new nature, they cease to be the children of wrath, although, without a doubt, the old man remains.

By the word 'man' we are reminded that this corruption of nature affects the whole of a man's being. It is present in the understanding, where there is darkness, in the will, where there is rebellion, and in the affections, where there is vanity, worldliness and carnality. That is true concerning natural man. But it is also true in the person who has a new nature by the working of God's grace. Although he has a new man born in his soul, yet the old man, the corrupt nature, is present in every part of his mind, will and affections.

For example, a man may have a wasting disease throughout his whole body; it is in his foot, his hand, his heart, his tongue; it is in all his powers. But he is still alive; even although his disease is the enemy of life. Similarly, the new man has its effects in the power of the soul. In this way, there are two men in the one converted man, who are as totally unlike one another as it is possible to be. Two men who can never be reconciled to one another.

Now, when the new man comes into the heart of the child of God, he ceases to be a child of wrath. But does he still have the old man? Yes indeed. And is anything done to that old man? Yes; he is crucified, that is, crucified along with Christ. Indeed, that was the reason that Christ Himself was crucified, that the old man in His people would be crucified with Him, and at length destroyed. The old man is the enemy of Christ, and it is as if Christ said to this enemy, 'You may rejoice that I am being crucified, but do you know why that is? It is that you will be crucified too, with your evil power in the hearts of my people, so that you will be plucked out of there.'

And how does this happen? Christ bore the sins of His people on Himself. They were with Him on the cross. He was suffering for these sins when He was crucified. It was because of them that He was there. Christ was there as a Mediator; and our sins with their deserts were carried there in order that these deserts might be forever parted from us. In this sense our old man was crucified with Him, in His bearing the deserts of those who were the children of wrath, having been once ruled by that old man.

Christ was crucified not only in order to bear the deserts of the sins of His people, but also in order that sin might be taken out of them for ever, and so that His power might break in to their hearts as He Himself enters their heart. Christ was at Calvary, crucified there for us, in order that thereafter He might come in and take up residence in our hearts. He died in order that He might open a way into our hearts, and when Christ came to dwell in us by faith in regeneration, that was when we possessed the new man. And when Christ comes in to our hearts in this way, He brings the glory of His death on the cross with Him, and the heart of the believer is captured by that glory in such a way that sins become yoked to his cross as the glory of a crucified saviour awakens in us an appetite away from sin to holiness. The authority and the sway once held by the old man over the soul is now lost, because he is yoked to Christ's cross, crucified. That cross draws out of the soul a love for Christ, a love for God.

When the Spirit of God presents the glory of the cross of Christ to the view of the believer, sin becomes bitter, and hated. Every thought of love that you have about Christ, every longing and desire you have to be rid of sin, every thought of hatred towards sin in your heart - all of this comes from the glory of a crucified Saviour entering your heart by the power of the Spirit.

Why does this happen? So that the body of sin might be destroyed. The power that Christ has now over sin in the soul, is a sign that for His people sin will soon be destroyed forever. But in this world that old man, that corrupt nature will be with the people of God, although the habits and impulses of that nature will be restrained. The old man will be like someone put in prison in order to restrain him from enjoying the liberty he once possessed, and he is to be kept in prison, so that he can never again use the liberty he once had to do his own will. The death of the old man is long and slow. It began when you saw the suitability of Christ for your need, and that began the destruction of the corrupt nature, the old man. Now that old man is condemned to death. Many days will pass before the sentence of death is finally carried out, but that is the end in view.

The fruit is that we will no longer serve sin, but serve righteousness. This is with the full agreement of our will, as our service to sin once was. The service and allegiance of former days is now broken, and will one day be gone for ever.

73. SEALED AND GIFTED

Who hath also sealed us, and given the earnest of the Spirit in our hearts
(2 Corinthians 1:22).

The apostle here speaks of a privilege which belongs to every believer: the Lord has sealed His people and given the earnest of the Spirit to them.

This seal is a token of the fact that they belong to the Lord, that they are the Lord's possession and inheritance. The letter to the Ephesians says that it is the Spirit who sealed them: 'you were sealed with, or by, that holy Spirit of promise.'

Seals are put onto inanimate objects: on letters, coins and many other things; but these objects are unaware of the seal that has been placed on them because they are dead objects without any consciousness. But those who are mentioned here are conscious of this act having been performed on them and of their having been sealed, because they are rational, conscious creatures. For that seal has been placed on the soul, and the soul is composed of rationality and consciousness.

I am not saying that the person who is so sealed is aware immediately, and with absolute certainty of this fact; but he does know that something extraordinary has taken place as far as his soul is concerned. This seal cannot be placed on the soul without an awareness of something strange happening; but it is possible that he is not very sure that it is God's seal that is being put on him when he is made aware of this. And he knows this, because God does not seal those who are spiritually dead, but those who are alive.

Naturally speaking, a seal is a sign which gives public intimation of the status of a thing or person. Of what is the seal which is placed on the people of God composed? What else but the effectual work of the Holy Spirit in the soul? The Holy Spirit calls effectually, and those whom he calls are regenerated, or born again. And it cannot be that that regeneration will occur in the soul of man without him being aware of something wonderful and new taking place within him. What does this imply? It means that the eternal power of God the Spirit is so operating on the soul that it makes a new creature of the man who is thus born again. And this is the seal. Perhaps the man born again does not realise that he has been born again, but he has new thoughts and an awareness of new things taking place, as a result of the power of God being in the matter. It is the Holy Spirit who places this seal on the soul, but He has an instrument, which He employs in connection with this. And what is that instrument? The Gospel.

On some seals, the King's image is stamped on the item when the seal is applied, for example, on coinage. It has the image of the monarch on it. And what shall we say about the seal which the Holy Spirit applies to the believer? The image of God, which was lost in the Fall, is carved anew upon the soul; or we might say the image of Christ, through whom God reveals Himself in His kindness and love to poor souls. The Holy Spirit, by the power of love and mercy, melts the sinner's heart, and takes the name of Christ in its fulness and all its substance and places it in that heart. Or perhaps it is more appropriate to say that the Holy Spirit melts the heart by bringing the glory and suitability of Christ effectually before it, and it is that image, the image of Christ, which is thereby engraved on the heart which now, forever more, loves and longs to do the will of God. The power that accompanies the sealing gives a person a mind now to live for the glory of God, which is the reason that God seals the sinner in this way.

This seal not only shows that the soul belongs to God; it also sets the soul aside in devotion to the Lord, that is, to serve God, for God's use in the world. Christ says that He ordained His people that they might bear fruit, and that their fruit might remain. The Lord says to them: 'You are mine. Your will, your heart, all your life is mine.' The soul is sealed so that it might exercise itself now for the glory of God alone. A soldier's uniform is a seal and sign that he belongs to the king. He wears the king's uniform which shows that he has been set aside to be a faithful soldier in the king's army. His duty is not to side with the king's enemies. Neither is it the duty of the Christian - his calling is to serve the God who has put His seal on us.

This seal grows. It grows in proportion to the growth of Christ's image on the soul. It goes, if you like, deeper and deeper into the heart. God will sanctify to this end every affliction, temptation and spiritual experience. And these will deepen and enlarge this seal upon the soul.

God has also given us the earnest of the Spirit in our hearts. What is this? The same thing exactly as the seal itself. The effectual call, or the work of grace in regeneration is from one point of view the seal of God on the soul of man, and from another it is to be the *earnest* given the soul by God. What is involved in the work of regeneration anyway but God giving us a holy taste and appetite, a foretaste, of these things that His people will enjoy for all eternity? An *earnest* is what gives weight and authority to a promise, just as Hezekiah received the evidence of a miracle to confirm the promise of God to him. Be sure you have the miracle [of regeneration] - if you haven't got the miracle you have not received the promise.

74. RENEWED INWARDLY

For which cause we faint not, but though our outward man perish, yet the inward man is renewed day by day
(2 Corinthians 4:16).

At the beginning of this verse the apostle states the attitude of Christians to the trials which confront them in this world. In relation to these trials they do not give way to despair or pessimism. That they have experience of intense suffering is evident from the apostle's assertions in this chapter itself. Why was their attitude so hopeful in the midst of all these? Because they were persuaded that everything was to work for their spiritual well-being here and hereafter, and would redound to the glory of God.

The apostle speaks here of two men who make up one man. This is applicable to every Christian individually. Who are they? The outward man and the inward man. And what he says about them is that they experience something simultaneously - the outward man perisheth, but the inward man is renewed. Not only so, but in the light of Scripture we shall see that there is a connection here, and that the perishing of the outward man has an effect on the daily renewing of the inward man.

Who is the outward man? This means man's body, as containing the breath of natural life, and which is subject to natural death in accordance with a natural law. The perishing of the outward man means the weakening of the body, resulting in the continued loss of physical strength, and which if it continues unchecked will ultimately end in natural death. This weakening, or perishing, is brought about by certain forces inevitably, whether singly or conjointly. There is, for instance, the advancement of old age as one of these forces, or the passage of time which limits the length or age of human life in this world. Old age is an irresistible agent in bringing about this perishing of the outward man.

There is also sickness, disease and violent injury inflicted on the body, such as Paul himself was accustomed to receive from the enemies of the Gospel. The main reason for the perishing of Paul's outward man at this juncture was undoubtedly the sufferings inflicted upon him by his persecutors because of his loyalty to Christ and His cross.

These factors mentioned may singly or together occasion the perishing of the outward man of the Christian. As long as body and spirit are together, suffering, pain, disease, and other things cause the outward man to perish. The experience one has from this perishing of the outward man is in itself depressing and disconsolate, but yet something is taking place at the same time, namely the inward man being renewed day by day.

Who is this inward man? This is the regenerated soul, designated in Scripture as the new man. While Paul was experiencing pain, sickness and decay, there was constant renewal and sanctification taking place within, as he was being made more like God. This can only happen in the soul that has been worked upon by divine grace. As there co-exists in that soul the old man and the new man, so there is the outward man and the inward man. They are there together. And the inward man is constantly being renewed.

As the body and mind of a man are in pain, suffering in this world, facing death, the inward man is receiving grace again and again, made holy, cleansed and prepared for the eternal rest. So that as the body is being prepared for the grave, the soul is being prepared for glory. The pains and wounds of the body draw it nearer to death and the grave; but the soul is renewed by the ministrations of God for the rest of Heaven.

And this is made especially clear as we see that these ministrations which renew the believer's soul sanctify the pains and troubles of the body to him. Does it not say here that our light affliction, which is but for a moment, *worketh for us* a far more exceeding and eternal weight of glory...? That means something that begins here and works constantly until the glory. In it and by it, the Holy Spirit makes the afflictions of the body food for the soul; perhaps it is not the food the believer wishes to eat, but it is the food that he needs. The psalmist said 'thou hast made us to drink the wine of astonishment', his tears were his meat night and day. This is their food - pain and trials, and the fruit of these are seen in the renewing of the soul, working out a far more exceeding and eternal weight of glory.

And how does the Lord do this? Sometimes the Lord ministers to the soul in distress and affliction by giving great blessing and liberty. There are other times which are times of darkness in which the Lord seems to be lost on the believer. We can understand the first of these; but how can the second be to the good of the soul? When a child is separated from his mother, he cries. He wants to be with his own, and behind the pain of the cry is love, love for, and the love of, his mother. The soul that is in darkness has a pain all its own because of conscious separation from Christ. That is how the Lord deals with us, by showing us our need of Christ. The pain is sore, but it works for us an eternal weight of glory.

75. TRUE REPENTANCE

For godly sorrow worketh repentance to salvation not to be repented of;
but the sorrow of the world worketh death
(2 Corinthians 7:10).

There are many kinds of sorrow in the world. That is the result and the fruit of sin, and none of these sorrows carry any hope along with them - only this one can do that. This is a godly sorrow, a sorrow in which there is godliness, and that is according to the mind of the Lord. It is sorrow for sin, that grows out of a knowledge of God, and our relation to Him as His creatures. We can be acquainted with sorrow, and know something of sorrow for sin, without our sorrow being godly. This godly sorrow grows out of a sense of shame and guilt on the part of those who have it. Christ said, 'Blessed are they that mourn...'

What does godly sorrow mean? It does not mean sadness on account of what we have lost, not even a sense of shame for my sin; nor is it remorse for my having destroyed my soul through sin for all eternity. These feelings are not as common as they should be; but they do not constitute saving repentance. Even an unconverted man can have sorrow for something he has done; but it is often only remorse - there is nothing spiritual in it, the Holy Spirit is not in it.

True repentance turns the mind away from one thing to another, away from sin and the practice of sin to obedience to the God against whom we have sinned. That means that this repentance has sorrow, but it also has fear and forsaking in it.

It also has hope in it - repentance is a hopeful grace. It lays hold of God in His law and attributes as a just and holy God, and by it a person sees himself as unworthy and condemned; but it also lays hold upon the mercy of God in Christ. This is the hope that establishes a soul, that makes him forsake sin, and that gives him new obedience.

Repentance is not alone. Fleshly sorrow rises up and accompanies it, and the soul is only too aware of it. It is a pain to the penitent that this is so. It is also possible that we make our repentance a basis of our righteousness. True, saving repentance makes Christ, and Christ alone, the basis of our righteousness. Sometimes the believer is saddened by how difficult it is for him to find real, true repentance in his soul. But we can be sure that only those who are truly repentant are troubled in these ways, and those who are not aware of these troubles and needs are not truly repentant for their sins.

This repentance has desire in it. The mind of the believer is not only aware of personal guilt, and liability to eternal punishment; but his own sin is abominable and offensive to him. He has seen the nature of God; he knows who God is. He agrees with all that God is, and with the relation God sustains to him as a sinner. And more - God gives him no reason to find Him offensive. He shows Himself as a good God, and a holy God; a God who, by His very nature leaves the sinner without excuse for his sin. The penitent comes to see that his sin is only rebellion against a holy and a good God. He is, if you like, on God's side, when it comes to dealing with sin and God's relation to sin.

This sorrow lays hold of God completely. When a sinner sees how good God is to him, despite all that he has done against God, this increases his repentance. It shows that God never gave him a reason to sin against Him, and so his sorrow is increased as he sees the greatness and the holiness of God. He looks on the one whom he has pierced, and he mourns for him. A sight of Christ on Calvary gives him a zeal and desire to forsake sin, to flee from it with the resolve to give full obedience to God.

76. GODLY AND CONTENT

But godliness with contentment is great gain (1 Timothy 6:6).

When Paul speaks here of contentment, of a happy mind, he does not refer to a mind which is naturally inclined to happiness. He means a mind that is satisfied, that is content. And what is contentment? It is the absence of proneness to murmur or complain against testing circumstances. This is not carnal or natural contentment. It is not of nature; it is of grace. It is in fact a state of mind which is the direct fruit of godliness itself.

It does not imply self-complacency or satisfaction with one's self. It is not contentment with one's own spiritual condition; in fact, the attitude of the believer towards his spiritual condition is one of distinct dissatisfaction. The state of mind from which the contentment stated in the text results accounts for the dissatisfaction which exists with one's own spiritual condition. Only those who have the contentment mentioned here also have the dissatisfaction we have spoken of.

It rather means contentment in regard to how the Lord is pleased to arrange and govern the interests of the believer. Sometimes this may be very weary and trying and painful. It does not mean being free from self-blame, 'a comfortable immunity from personal imperfection'. It is rather an awareness that if God were to mark our iniquities against us, we could not stand.

It does not mean either being content with the ways of the world, and not troubling ourselves to protect against it when it affronts God's majesty and His law. There are things against which this spiritual contentment will set us inevitably in opposition. We will be opposed to the evil in our own hearts and to the evil course of this world as a result of the contentment spoken of in our text. You would think that there is not so much contentment after all! But there is - Christ had this contentment. He saw the Father's hand in the cup which He had to drink. He recognised His having to drink it as the Father's will. He opposed the world because the world opposed His Father and His Father's rightful claim. He had not what you would call an easy time, but He had a contented time. He had this spiritual contentment. When He was telling His disciples what He was destined to face, there was an element in it which was very saddening and tragically painful, but there was a hopeful and joyful element in it, and that element was the enduring one. It was all coming to Him direct from the Father's will. It was painful, but the issue was distinctly hopeful.

Christ had this contentment, but He had pain. He endured even the pain of our folly and waywardness and straying. That was really what the cup He drank contained. But we have our own sins. How can we have contentment? In the sense mentioned already - not satisfaction with ourselves or with our sins. But Christ has made atonement for our sins. He has introduced a reconciliation between us and the Father, on which eternal peace between God and us is based when we come to God through Christ. That is a source and justifiable occasion of contentment. Believing in fact is leaving your sins in God's hand to be pardoned for Christ's sake, and that is the most God-honouring act which man's soul can perform.

This contentment will give you an easy life and an uneasy life. Job could say 'Though he slay me, yet will I trust Him'. It was the possession of such a hope which entailed his submission to God in such a trial, and his victory over it. This contentment flows from a recognition that God does not blunder; that He is not a tyrannical oppressor, yea in fact that He is eternal love and goodness, that everything is controlled and directed by eternal and unfathomable love, that He is behind it, that He is merciful and gracious. He has not dealt with us according to our sins. This contentment is based on what we are and we are to become in God's benevolence and inconceivable love. It means leaving things in God's hands to work out His own will.

It is great gain, says the apostle. How is this? Because this reasoning and exercise own the majesty and glory of God, and His sovereign right to act as He alone pleases. It implies an acknowledgement and a reverence of God as He is unfolded in Scripture.

It is an exercise of mind which accords with the thoughts of Christ. Nothing can be healthier and nothing can be more profitable than such manner of thinking. It is profitable now. It sanctifies us. It brings us closer to God, in greater love and reverence. Is that not great gain? Yes, gain in knowledge, in love and in respect of our worship and obedience. When we begin to view things without examining them in the light of God's purpose and grace, it is then we are at our most unspiritual.

77. RUNNING THE RACE

Wherefore seeing we also are compassed about with so great a cloud of witnesses, let us lay aside every weight, and the sin which doth so easily beset us, and let us run with patience the race that is set before us, looking unto Jesus the author and finisher of our faith; who for the joy that was set before him endured the cross, despising the shame, and is set down at the right hand of the throne of God (Hebrews 12:1-2).

The cloud of witnesses mentioned here are those brought before us in the previous chapter. These are witnesses to the power of faith and its work. They had their trials and difficulties, but they were enabled by the grace of God to overcome. We are exhorted to emulate them in running the race set before us by faith.

In order to run that race, we are asked to lay aside every weight, and the sin which doth so easily beset us. Anything which makes sinning a necessity, as it were. If you cannot be engaged in a certain occupation without its laying an inevitable necessity of sinning upon you, then decline to be employed in that occupation. Have nothing to do with it. I heard of people who for conscientious reasons had to give up their occupations because they were expected to tell lies. It was high time for them to do that.

The sin that so easily besets us. The sins to which one is liable. People have different feelings. Some people are extremely envious. Others are covetous. Some people are avaricious. Other people have ungovernable tempers. Others are dishonest. Others have the failing of being liars. Whatever sins people were accustomed to indulge on in the past, they have special reason to guard against such sins. Other people have a tendency to be quarrelsome. Nothing will satisfy them. They will be at war with everybody. These sins are besetting sins. The besetting sin of one may not be the besetting sin of another. Cultivate the spirit of Christ. Look to Jesus as your example. Look to Jesus to make you ashamed of your sin. Look to Jesus to make you heartily hate your sin. Get to hate your failings intensely. Some people hate all failings but their own. Some people make their evil tempers their Bible. They go by their temper, not by the Bible. The wrath of man, however, will not work the righteousness of God.

How do we get these things laid aside? By looking unto Jesus. By cleaving to the Lord. Think of Christ whenever you are tempted to do anything unworthy. The love of Christ prompting us to think of Christ is the best antidote against sin. How often must Christ have to say to people that their own pride is greater to them than the honour of His own name. He may have to say to some that it is a greater thing to them to satisfy their own pride than honour His name, and that they satisfy their own pride at the cost of sacrificing Christ's honour and glory. We should always remember Christ and how great His honour and glory is besides our own pride and our own temper.

How often has Christ to say this to us - You have denied yourself to honour me today. You have sacrificed your pride to avoid dispeace so as to glorify my name. You have curbed your temper to honour me. Remember when you sin that you are giving Christ away. By loving Christ thus you receive grace from Christ Himself. Your stock of grace will be increased, and you will love more and be more inspired to honour Christ more and more.

By our own self-righteousness we try to equip ourselves without coming directly to Christ. We consider it a humiliation to come thus to Christ and admit that we cannot do it without His help. Let us be sincere and honest with ourselves and with Christ, and let us come to Him admitting that we are not equal to these things without His gracious and loving help, and let us come to Him confessing our lapses and failings and forgetfulness of Him, and of the standard of law and duty which He has placed before us. That is what we do by looking upon Jesus. The reason why people are so lacking in this way is that they don't come to Jesus. They don't take the trouble. But if they loved Him as He deserves, and as they ought, they would come. If they had the interests of their own soul at heart, as they should, they would certainly come. If they had Christ's honour in view as they ought, they would certainly come.

What a disappointment to a father to see a son not growing. He hopes and expects his child to grow. What a disappointment if it doesn't happen. It is a disappointment to our Lord if we don't grow. It is in order that we might grow that he converted us, and caused us to be born again. That is why He has put the breasts of the Gospel in our mouth: that we might drink in of the spirit of Jesus, and manifest it in our lives, to strengthen us to perform our duty to God in the world.

Then the exhortation is - 'Let us run'. That implies effort, and earnestness. It is a labour of diligence, of pressing forward, putting every ounce of energy into use.

All who run in this race must run with patience. This requires a certain watchfulness. No-one who runs can be careless or indifferent - the race requires an earnest application and interest. Are you running? The movement of many who profess the Christian faith is more like a carefree stroll than an earnest running. It must be running with patience. These appear on the surface to be two incompatible things. Yet they answer each other well. Running means an earnest and diligent activity on the part of the Christian, which the believer sees as being suitable for him. It must be a hard labour that will deal with sin, and that will run to obtain the prize of the high call of God in Christ, pressing on towards the mark. But you need patience for dealing with the many things that will meet you in the way, and that will try to stop you from running. The corruption of your nature is one; then there are trials, tribulations and chastisements. You are like a boat, heading for shore, and meeting wave after wave in the process. Paul could say 'I keep my body under submission, lest having preached to others I myself should be a castaway'.

This running is kept on by looking upon Christ. Upon His commands. Upon His holiness. Upon His hatred of sin. Upon His example. Upon the Glory which He will finally bestow on those who thus run. Patience is also derived by looking upon Him. How He put up with trouble Himself. How He endured suffering, He who did not need to endure it. But He endured it for the joy set before Him in the Father's approval of and satisfaction in His work, and in the fruits resulting therefrom in the redemption of those whom He loved from everlasting. The consideration of these aspects will promote our sense of how it becomes us to be patient, sinful, undeserving creatures who pass through suffering for our personal sanctification.

What is the race set before us? It is our whole life in this wilderness on our journey to eternity. Does it become us to sleep? Were we awakened in order that we might sleep soundly again? Did not our sleeping almost deliver us into hell, and notwithstanding how near we went to hell, are we to provoke God by sleeping again simply because we hope that God pardoned us? The day of death will be here soon enough. What if the sins of sleepiness and indifference that some who are credited to be saints indulge in now, and which they carry on in an unrepentant spirit will pain and trouble them with deep sorrow and regrets and misgivings and fears on the brink of death. Let us be up and doing for Christ and let us love Him ardently, and glorify Him with our lives. Let us look upon Him now if we wish to look upon Him eternally. If we don't look upon Him in this world here, how do we expect to be looking upon Him throughout Eternity? Let us therefore be wise.

78. CONFESSION OF SIN

If we confess our sins, he is faithful and just to forgive us our sins,
and to cleanse us from all unrighteousness (1 John 1:9).

There are three thoughts in this text: the confession of sin, the consequence of that confession - forgiveness and cleansing from all unrighteousness - and how God is faithful and just in forgiving.

The teaching contained in these words is one which pervades the whole of God's truth, both in the Old and New Testaments, namely that there is an inseparable connection between confession of sin and forgiveness. Where the former is, the latter must inevitably also be there. That is, true confession is inevitably followed by forgiveness. That teaching is found in the 32nd psalm: 'I have acknowledged my sin unto thee, and mine iniquities have I not hid...and thou forgavest the iniquity of my sin.' The same doctrine is found in the Book of Proverbs: 'he who covereth his sins will not prosper; but whosoever confesseth and forsaketh his sin findeth mercy'. These texts, with the one before us, establish beyond question the fact that it is a scriptural doctrine to declare that if a person truly confesses his sins, he will as surely find forgiveness.

But it ought to be the anxious concern of everybody who confesses his sins that his confession should conform to that particular confession which the Lord acknowledged as true confession, and in consequence of which forgiveness is extended to the party who confesses. For example, there is a clear case of untrue confession in the life of Pharaoh. He admitted to Moses that he had sinned, and he appeared genuinely penitent and contrite when he made that confession, and he soon asked Moses to pray for him, so that the plague which had come as a judgement upon him might be taken away. This was obviously a deceitful move on his part. He confessed having sinned, out of sheer necessity, brought upon by the embarrassing situation in which he was placed; and not because he was at heart sorry for anything which he had done, and by which he had displeased God. He had not actually hated or repented of his sin, the sin which offended the Lord, but he certainly hated the chastisement with which the Lord had afflicted him in punishment for his transgression.

Pharaoh's confession was merely a temporary expedient which was designed to procure liberty for him from the disaster and ruin which his sins had brought upon him. He did not hate sin at heart, and his confession of sin was certainly done most grudgingly. All the insincere and hypocritical confession of sin in the world has definite and distinct points of kinship with that of Pharaoh. They all as a matter of fact partake of the same character, though the circumstances which evoke them may not be entirely similar. Still the underlying motives are the same.

The confession with which the Lord is well pleased is that which is the outcome of true repentance, and which includes in it a true sense of sin. It implies an acknowledgement of the fact of sin itself, and a realisation of its true nature; in other words, a true sense of the sinfulness of sin. It is then seen to be an offence against the holy dignity of the Most High. The soul in consequence, overwhelmed with shame and self-abasement, prostrates himself before God in humble and heartfelt confession, which comes spontaneously from the heart, for the dishonour which he has cast upon the glory of the Creator, upon the glory of the Lawgiver, and King of all intelligent beings.

The Lord is seen in a new light, as sin itself is also seen in a new light, and the guilty soul takes God's side instinctively against himself, and confesses his transgressions without any mental restraints. We have this consciousness of self-guilt exemplified in David's confession as we find it in the 51st psalm. There in his confession he justifies God and condemns himself. 'Against thee, thee only have I sinned...'

The confession is now being made out of zeal for the glory of God. It is not a confession that is reluctantly wrested from the soul. It is made willingly and spontaneously and ungrudgingly. It is only an enlightened and renewed sinner that finds it easy to make confession of sin to God. In all other cases it is forced, and is wrung from them unwillingly, even though God knows all about it already.

Besides, seeing the confession arises from a hatred of sin, it implies a desire to be rid of sin itself. Its presence is now a burden, and a pain to the soul, and consequently the specific object of the person who confesses sin truly is not mere pardon, but entire holiness as well. In this confession of sin there is not merely a petition for forgiveness, but for cleansing as well. When a patient consults a doctor, his ultimate object in so doing is to be cured from whatever malady he suffers. He has not to confess his illness as guilt to the doctor; he merely wants a cure. Sin, however, is guilt, and when we confess it we confess it as such. But then we also discover it as disease, and we shall not only be content to confess it as guilt but to confess it as a disease.

Ah, but is Christ Himself not the great physician, and when we come to Him we confess this disease of sin as guilt and disease. So when we come to Christ the great physician, we first confess sin as our guilt, but not merely to receive the forgiveness of God in Christ, but also to obtain a remedy from Him as that great physician that will heal us entirely. Not only can He take away our guilt, but heal our souls from the plague of sin itself. It is really when we want our souls perfectly healed and sin entirely expelled from our hearts that we become really so earnest about making confession of our sins before God.

You will notice there is a double promise given at the end of our text to the genuine confessor of sin, namely forgiveness and cleansing. The confession of the genuinely confessing soul includes a petition for both, and the double promise is given. The obtaining of cleansing is as much the burden (if not more) of the confessing as the forgiveness is. Forgiveness indeed is never isolated from cleansing in the case of a soul who truly confesses sin. That is what might be called true evangelical confession of sin. What would forgiveness do for a renewed soul if he had no prospect of being also cleansed from sin? It would be an occasion of weeping and mourning for him. But the promise is that he will receive both.

Now let us consider whether it is the intrinsic merit of our confession which procures forgiveness for us. Is there such merit in our confession as purchases the favour of God's forgiveness for us? Certainly not, even although our confession, when it is genuine, is the fruit or product of the work of the Holy Spirit in our heart.

As you know, the forgiveness of sin is the direct fruit of Christ's death, and only Christ by His death could secure forgiveness for guilty men. Yea, in fact, the conscious need of forgiveness on the sinner's part, which issues in confession, is itself the fruit of Christ's death likewise, because genuine and true confession is produced by the effectual work of the Holy Spirit in the heart. And the efficacious work of the Holy Spirit in the heart is the fruit of Christ's death. So the reason why a person who confesses his sins obtains forgiveness is that he rests upon the finished work of Christ. Ah, but that is faith, and do you mean to say that faith is an element in forgiveness? I certainly do, and I trust I shall be able to prove it. We are told in Scripture that without faith in Christ we can never obtain pardon for our sins. Isn't that so? Yes. But here it says that by confessing sin you will receive forgiveness, then that must mean that the element of faith is embraced in genuine confession. So confession here must be synonymous with faith because you receive through confessing what Scripture declares can only be obtained by exercising saving faith upon the Son of God. It is through the death of Christ that God is just in pardoning us as a matter of fact.

How do we confess sin? We confess original sin, and actual transgressions. There is a tendency on men's part to associate sin merely with actions, and man's outward conduct. That is, when they commit breaches of God's law. But only when we clearly realise the guiltiness of original sin can we confess sin. It is when we come to abhor original sin that we can really appreciate the promise of cleansing given in the text.

It is also to be noted that when we confess our sins truly we are not eager to share the guilt attached to our sins with other people, or with circumstances outside ourselves. We merely take cognisance of the fact that we personally have sinned, because that evil principle was in us to lead us to break God's law. Then our sins become our own sins, and not anybody else's. People are naturally prone to fasten the major portion of the guilt of their sins on other people or other circumstances which tempted or provoked them to sin. This was what Adam did. He blamed Eve and she blamed the serpent. They were both deeply concerned to prove that other people were more to blame for their sins than themselves. Only the effectual work of God's Spirit can save us from this fixing of blame on other people for our own sins.

How may it be understood that God is faithful? He is faithful to Christ His Son. It is this evangelist, John, who records in his Gospel that Christ said that whosoever should come to Him should in no wise be cast out. In confession the soul comes by faith to God and Christ, and as Christ will not cast him out, the Father surely will not.

He is also faithful to the Covenant of Redemption made between the Father and Christ. In that covenant, Christ was promised that He should see of the travail of His soul and be satisfied. And all these must come to Him by confession.

He shall be faithful to the Holy Spirit who enlightened the soul and enabled him to see the glory of Christ and rest upon His merits. The Father will in that way be faithful to the Holy Spirit and faithful to the soul who has fulfilled by the aid of the Holy Spirit the conditions which through the merits of Christ's death entitle him to eternal salvation which is embraced in the obtaining of forgiveness from God. And the God who is faithful is also just, to bestow this precious saving gift of forgiveness through the death of His Son.

JOHN MACKENZIE

on

THE WALK AND WELFARE
OF THE CHRISTIAN

79. COMPLAINT AND DESIRE

Oh that I knew where I might find him! That I might come even to his seat! I would order my cause before him and fill my mouth with arguments
(Job 23:3–4).

The Book of Job is difficult in many ways, yet useful to the child of God in a world of temptation and trials which comes on him to prove him. The Providence of God regarding His people is at times difficult to understand, and it is little wonder though the friends of Job, who came to comfort him, should find offence in the things he said, so that instead of comforting him they added to his anguish. In the preceding chapter, Eliphaz ventures to exhort him, and here we have Job's reply. It expresses the deep anguish of his heart – 'my complaint is bitter; my stroke is heavier than my sigh'. Here he states his intense desire for God; he turns away from men to God.

(1) *His Complaint*

It was sore indeed to be misunderstood, and rebuked by his friends, for expressing himself regarding his sorrow – this caused him to say that his complaint was bitter. His complaint, however, was not so much regarding man's misunderstanding of his condition, but of the condition of his soul.

He was conscious of the absence of God. God had withdrawn from him, and was lost to his consciousness. He had no trace of him; like the psalmist he could say 'I looked on my right hand, and viewed, but none to know me were'. This sense of absence is great and sore to the child of God, and he fears it more than anything else in the world. There is, of course, a sense in which God is never absent – we are constantly preserved and sustained by Him. But to our conscious sense He may be absent, and the soul feels forsaken, sore and miserable.

His complaint arose from a sense of value. There was nothing to him in all the world comparable to the presence of God – Job had lost all his earthly possessions and naturally felt this keenly. But his chief grief is what he has felt he has lost of the nearness of God; this was almost beyond endurance. Augustine tells of a good man who said 'Lord, let us have anything but thy frown, and anything with thy smile'. Here we have the soul's deep longing for God, conscious of the distance from God because of sin and unworthiness.

There is also a conscious ignorance of how and where to find God. 'Oh that I knew where I might find him'. It is a confession of ignorance – he had been looking and searching. Where shall we find God for Job? Shall we not find him in Job's intense desire for Him? In the way in which Job was sustained in his distress? Only the unseen hand of God could uphold him in such times and such straits. Yes, God was present in His sustaining care, in that Job did not collapse under the crushing blows of Satan. Like Peter, sifted by the devil, he is kept by the power of Christ's intercession on his behalf. But Job's God is found specially in Scripture, and there alone Christ is known. We live by faith and not by sight or feeling, though we often do both.

(2) *His desire*

This is to come to God's seat, and order his case before God. What would he not do to secure the sense of God's favour restored to him? Conscious of his own ignorance, he desires restoration and renewal.

He would come to God's seat, that is, to His footstool. This implies humility, to be humble and low, to take a worthy and fitting place before Him, to seek His ear. It means to state his case. No–one knows the importance of stating his case well more than a person on trial. That is how Job feels. He is ready to make his state known to God in a way that he will not disclose it to anyone else.

He says 'I would argue'. Filling his mouth with arguments. What? Argue with God? Yes, says Job, I would own my self ruin, my ill–desert, the sin that caused my trouble. I would plead mercy, the merits of Christ, my desire for Him, and my longing to love Him. I would attend to His word and learn of it. More than ever, and more than anything else, I would wish to recognise the voice of Christ speaking to my soul, and applying the word of truth to me.

80. PRAYER IN PILGRIMAGE

Hold up my goings in thy paths, that my footsteps slip not
(Psalm 17:5).

David was a man of prayer, who learnt its value both in distress and in ease. Many resort to prayer in time of distress, who have no use for it in time of ease. Not so David; he found it a profitable exercise of soul, not a burden, but a means of keeping in touch with God, conversing with Him, and seeking of Him needed supply. This was a prayer in distress, as he sees enemies all around him, seeking his hurt, and he pleads that God will preserve him.

In our text we have a prayer suitable for all occasions, which we might adopt as our own. It is particularly appropriate at a time like this, at the close of a communion season, as we find ourselves facing life with all its unseen implications. On occasions like the communion season, we are sometimes uplifted in thought and feeling above earthly things, perhaps thinking that the times of rejoicing will remain with us for ever. Or it may be that we feel very dejected, and fear that we are not right with God. We may have been anticipating much blessing, and perhaps received little of the expected comfort and joy, and have come to hard conclusions about ourselves. If that is your case, you need not be dismayed. You are not the only one who feels that way. At times it pleases the Lord to deny our desires, for the deepening of our spiritual life, that we may learn to abide His time.

(1) *The Request*

It is obvious, first, from the petition 'Hold up my goings, Lord', that the psalmist regarded God as indispensable to him. He was thankful for God's self–disclosure, and that He is the kind of God He has revealed Himself to be. The believer is thankful for all this, that God is 'a just God and a Saviour', a Saviour who justly calls us to observe his precepts, and also authorises and desires us to commit our way unto Him.

In this prayer, the psalmist desires the upholding of God's strong hand, and was deeply earnest and sincere in this, for he had learnt God's truth in the inward part, in his soul. How different is the case with those who have no conscious need of, or time for, God – who think of Him as a hindrance to the realisation of their pleasures. God would have all solicit His aid.

This man also had deep concerns about his goings, or his steps. He was a man of many burdens; he had a high office in life, which brings its own responsibilities. But he had greater burdens than the affairs of state, and these were the affairs of his soul, his personal relation to God.

He was deeply concerned about the course of his life. Life is made up of steps. David saw himself as a pilgrim, not stationary, but running a race, made up of steps, one at a time. He knew that there is a way that seems right to a man, but the end of it is death. His steps mattered to him, because he knew that a wrong step could ruin all that he ever did. He wanted to bear himself well as one of the Lord's witnesses every day. He knew that the world is not a pleasant or a comfortable place; there are many difficulties, trials and sorrows to encounter, though some find it easier than others, depending on the Lord's Providence in their lives. He wanted to live his vocation to the glory of God and the good of others.

This, then, is a prayer that suits us all. We too have need of divine upholding, guidance and care, that we may walk worthy of our calling in Christ. We should be concerned that our lives will be to His honour and glory. When you reflect on all He has done for you, and means to you, the desire to please and honour Him ought to govern your life.

In what way will He guide His people? He will lead them in the way of truth, which is the way of faith and life. The truth is revealed in His commandments. Those who love Him walk in this way. He will lead in the way of Gospel ordinances. There will be a concern for His cause, for devotion to it, for humility, zeal and steadfast loyalty, prepared to go outwith the camp and bear his reproach. He will lead in the way of spiritual progress, increase in grace and usefulness.

(3) *The Reason Assigned*

Why does he pray thus? The answer is 'That I slip not'. He was obviously afraid of this, and with good reason. He had slipped before, and suffered for it. He was afraid of a repeat, so he seeks preservation. Some are more concerned with the steps of others than with their own, but David was concerned about none as he was concerned about his own. We are all subject to the pressures of evil around us, and the unwary or watchless ones are in danger of being ensnared. We are exhorted to 'watch and pray'.

This is a prayer of conscious weakness. 'Let him who thinketh he standeth take heed lest he fall.' David knows that his standing means nothing. He is unsure of himself. We can slip in our mind, as we dwell on the wrong things. We can slip in word, as we say the wrong things. We can slip in deed, as we do the wrong things. We cannot afford to be sure of ourselves. There is constant need of divine protection and preservation. We need the guidance of God's word and Spirit.

This is the language of apprehension. He was afraid. There are two kinds of fear – the one is harmful, the other useful; the one shows weakness, the other strength. He saw the dangers in the way – outward and inward, by which his own good and witness to God in the world, and his usefulness could be hindered. A candle is not easily kept alight – the smallest puff of wind can blow it out. A lighthouse keeper has as his chief concern that his light will shine. The believer is the same. He is apprehensive; he knows that there are many that are trying to extinguish his light.

But this is also the language of confidence and assurance. He believes that God will accept his request. We need not and must not despair, or be fainthearted – greater and stronger is our God than all who are against us. God's present favour, and abiding presence is of greater value than all the honours in the world. God undertakes the charge, and has the power and the will to execute it, and perfect that which concerns us. Remember his promise – 'Lo I am with you'. This is our privilege; and our duty is to commit our all to Him for safekeeping.

If you are unconcerned, your future prospects are dark indeed. The godless life will end in great ruin. But those who have entrusted their way to God are safe for ever.

81. MERCY SOUGHT FOR SINS CONFESSED

Remember not the sins of my youth, nor my transgressions; according to thy mercy remember thou me for thy goodness' sake, O Lord (Psalm 25:7).

David is the author of this psalm. It is evidently a composition of his old age. Even then his past, with its dark catalogue of sins, is open before his mind. Elsewhere he says 'My sin is ever before me'. Here we see him placing the concern of his soul before God in prayer – he lifts his soul to God. Such is the nature of prayer. There are three petitions in this prayer – that he be kept from shame, that he be instructed by God, and that he be forgiven. It is the last of these that concerns us here.

(1) Confession Made

There are many kinds of confession. Some do it as a habit because others do it; this is mere lip service, without the realisation of true confession in their lives. Others do it because they think confession will secure the divine favour for them, while they delight in sin and long to engage in that which they 'confess'. Sin is the most destructive fact in the world.

True confession arises from a deep sense of sin. David was conscious of his sin. He knew he was a sinner, and was only too aware of his sin. Confession arises from knowledge and consciousness of what we truly are; this flows from conviction, in the light of the Word of God. To David, sin is not a meaningless term. It pressed hard on his consciousness, and on his conscience. He is a sinner of long standing.

That is why he confesses the sins of his youth. He began with these and then went on to those of maturer years. He discriminates between them. Sins of youth – the rash and reckless follies of his young days, when reflection was subordinate to passion. Or it may equally apply to the sins of the youthful believer, when enthusiasm and unbalanced zeal urged him to undertakings for which he was not qualified, and may now regret.

Then there are 'transgressions'. These may be regarded as the more notorious sins committed against knowledge, light, warning, failure to respect the will of God and accept it. This includes unbelief, and a continuing in sin when he knows it to be sin. Of all these, he now makes a full and a free confession; he conceals none.

His sins were evidently painful to him. Sin is bitter to him. His conscience and reason agree with the testimony of God's word in his condemnation. He condemns himself, and is merciless to himself. He censures his life in the light of God's Word. He does not regard the seriousness of his sin as following from the injury done to himself by it, great as that was; nor from the injury done to others, either by act or by example. He views sin in this light because He views sin as dishonouring God. This is his shame. This brought a real sense of shame, sorrow and repentance to his heart. As he viewed sin in the light of God's holiness, goodness and love, his cry is 'My sin! My sin! My sin!'

He stands in a new relation to sin. The sin he loved before, he hates now; He repents of it, renounces it, and longs to be rid of it. He is in a new relation to God. Once he was indifferent to His Being, authority and claims. But now he seeks Him, fears and loves Him, and dreads His silence and absence. This is the state of mind we should seek, confessing because of our sin. Neglect of this is sinful in itself, and injurious to us.

(2) *Mercy Sought*

His prayer is twofold – that God would deal with him in two ways, with a 'remember not' and a 'remember'. He says, 'Remember not the sins of my youth'. That is, hold me not answerable for them. Do not charge them to my account, in number, guilt, nature, or penalty. Here he asks God to do what he could not do himself. But what is impossible with man is possible with God.

He also says 'Remember me according to thy mercy'. This explains the former petition. It gives it meaning and authority, and is based on it. It was this that inspired it. He saw mercy in God, and this justifies his plea that God will 'Remember not his sins'. Mercy means undeserved favour. God alone can thus deal with sins. He is the Father of mercies. He delights in mercy, more than in judgement, which is his strange work. He is rich in mercy. It is undeserved, free, great, infinite in value and worth, lasting. Its exercise is well–pleasing to God. It implies pardon, deliverance, blessing. Thus David not only prays for forgiveness, but for a conscious experience of it. A man may be forgiven and yet not enjoy the joy and comfort of it. He wished for both.

Here David asks for what was already his. But he could not grasp it at that time. There are times in a believer's life when sin gathers around him, and obscures his vision, and he feels as if they were never forgiven. The memory of the past, even days of youth, follows to old age. We may reap in old age what we sow in our youth.

(3) *The Ground of his Plea*

He petitions on this basis: 'For thy goodness' sake'. He dispenses with all other pleas and arguments, and raises his appeal to the fountain of all. He does not base his request on self-merit, repentance, reform, confession, diligence, or even his need. It is not even based on mercy itself, which is only the expression of something behind it. He goes beyond mercy to the goodness of God. God is good in Himself, in His works, in His administration and in His Providence. But this is special goodness, revealed in the cross, costly and enduring.

This is faith in exercise, discerning, appropriating, relishing. Confession is the privilege and duty of all. There is mercy with God, for great sinners. And the Gospel offers hope for those who confess their sins and seek for God.

82. REQUEST AND RESOLVE

Draw me, we will run after thee
(Song of Solomon 1:4).

In the Song we have a dialogue between Christ and the Church. He speaks to her in terms suited to her case, to allure her, and she speaks to Him and pleads His love and favour. Here the church speaks to Christ; evidently matters were not with her as she would wish, and she pleads 'Draw me'. This she desires both for the excellence and preciousness of His name and fellowship, and her conscious need of Him. In the first part of the text, we have a prayer suited for all occasions.

(1) *Her Prayer - 'Draw me'*

There is a twofold drawing spoken of in Scripture - the drawing of persuasion and the drawing of attraction, and both enter into the experience of the believer.

At conversion, the call of grace operates powerfully on the soul, showing the sinner his sin, misery and lostness, and the remedy in Christ, answerable to all his needs. By grace the will is renewed, and the soul is enabled to close in with Christ. Both ideas of persuasion and attraction enter into this - Christ speaks of it in John 6:44 as the Father's *drawing*. They are taught of the Lord, showing them Jesus Christ, whose attraction draws as the magnet the steel, and as the sun draws the flowers to itself.

Believers desire the drawing of Christ continually. All who ever tasted

His love and preciousness desire His constant fellowship, to be kept near Him. This is costly to the flesh - only the indwelling Spirit can keep us so exercised.

The prayer implies interrupted fellowship, a sense of distance. Though bound with Christ in spiritual union, yet she feels afar off. When He is not sensibly near she laments that broken fellowship strains the relation with Him. This is a distance of sense, not of state. There is a ceasing of correspondence for a time - and now the desire for nearer communion.

She dislikes her condition. She feels uneasy, dissatisfied with herself, lukewarm and cold, formal - insensible of His nearness, she is disturbed, and she is left displeased with herself and her present state. When He puts His hand through the lock, she stirs and cries 'But when that thou, O gracious God, didst hide thy face from me; then quickly was my prosperous state turned into misery.'

Along with this, there is an inability to help herself, to correct herself, or to attain the desired nearness with her Lord. She can only cry 'Draw me'. When He hides His face, He alone can restore it, or give the comfort of His presence. This requires a visitation of sovereign grace. It is all of grace, from beginning to end. It is the same who first showed us Christ who can keep Him before us, and discover to us His beauty and glory. This she can never attain without His drawing.

It implies a sense of Christ's value, an esteem of His presence and fellowship. Oh! to feel the attraction of Christ's person and love and presence, drawing out the heart to Himself. This application to Him is an exercise of faith in Him, and He is willing and able to do this for her. She puts it to Him - 'do this for thine own name's sake'. She regards her condition as dangerous without Him.

(2) *Her Resolve - 'we will run after thee'*

She desires restoration for herself and others; hence she changes the terms from 'me' to 'we'.

She says 'we will run'. That is, make haste, willingly, when the heart is enlarged. It is not only a running to Him to close with Him, for hiding, comfort and fellowship, but running after Him, as the forerunner who shows us the way. The Christian life is a race, which we are to run after Him; Christ is the prize that we are to win, and the way of realising Him is the way of His commandments. Heaven is our goal.

To run is to make progress, Christward, in a life of grace and holiness. We must seek this way, in which the revived graces of the spirit give impulses to the inner man. This eager, lively feeling is in opposition to formalism and slowness. There is progress in experience and in knowledge, a desire for improvement and advancement in grace, and be useful to others, influencing, inspiring and helping like-minded ones. Reviving to one incites others to seek the same, seeking His honour and glory.

This shows that she was much in love with holiness, and had an ardent desire for more of it. Oh to be like Him in all things, in order to possess Him. This is the desire of all renewed hearts - 'create in me a clean heart, renew a right spirit within me'; as Paul says 'this one thing I do, forgetting those things which are behind, and looking forward to those things which are before, I press towards the mark, for the prize of the high calling of God in Christ Jesus'.

This humble, pressing desire and resolve characterises true Christians. Christ, and fellowship with Him, is meaningful. In this we need His constant drawing, daily drawn to Christ. We are unsafe without this.

83. A NIGHT SEARCH

By night on my bed I sought him whom my soul loveth:
I sought him, but I found him not....I found him whom my soul loveth;
I held him, and would not let him go ... (Song of Solomon 3:1-4).

This chapter answers well to the exercise of soul which distinguishes true believers in Christ in this world. Here their lot is one of ebb and flow, of cloudy storms and sunlit rays. In this state the soul is often tossed with concern, self-accusation, earnest searching and entreaty, resulting in elevating comfort and praise. Here we see the picture of an exercised soul in quest of the Beloved, the agony of suspense and the resulting issue. Such is a fitting exercise for us all in prospect of a communion season.

(1) *The Condition: 'On my bed in the night...'*
This could be true literally. The psalmist speaks of rejoicing in God 'when I do thee upon my bed remember with delight, and when on thee I meditate in watches of the night'. This is often the experience of God's people. During the night watches they lie awake, pleading with concern over their own case, or that of others, so that their pillows are wet with tears, and longing for a day of visitation from on high. That condition is not easy, but it is profitable, and is often rewarded. Biographies of good men 'bear this out'. But it does not seem to be what is here intended.

This passage speaks of an unhealthy state of soul. It was night, and by this is meant a state of darkness, affliction or trial, the opposite of light and comfort. So it is when Christ is absent from the soul, just as His presence means day. There is such a thing as a night of desertion, when on purpose Christ conceals Himself, for correction and discipline. Or it may be the night of spiritual declension, for which the soul is wholly to blame. Of this there are nights, one after another. This may also answer the state of the Jewish church before Christ, with shadows of the ceremonial law, yet having some knowledge of Christ in types and prophecies. Or it answers to the state of the church in the world to the end of time, as she waits Christ's return; as Paul puts it in Romans 13, 'the night is far spent, the day is at hand'.

This denotes a rather sleepy state - 'in bed', representing sickness of soul, affliction, or rest and sleep. It answers to slothfulness of spirit, carnal ease, spiritual laziness, the opposite of active life. Believers have fits of carnal ease; sloth lays hold of the soul, and it becomes dull and heavy. This state grows in darkness, when Christ is absent. But He does not leave His own long in that state, until He makes them conscious that matters are not right.

Then restlessness takes possession of the soul, because of its condition. Carnal ease and sloth become sinful, and backsliding becomes obnoxious. Self-accusation and remorse set in, and the absent Christ is desired and longed for. The soul becomes sick, and afflicted, and the darkness of night cannot restrain the cry 'Oh that I knew where I might find Him'. Then the soul becomes active, earnest, honest with itself, and honest with God.

(2) *The Carriage - 'I sought him whom my soul loveth'.*
Whom did she seek? Him whom her soul loved. This is the title she gives Him. She was conscious of affection towards Him, notwithstanding her condition. Her sense of His absence inspired anew her love. He had a place in her heart all His own. He stood alone in her esteem, though He was absent - in this case, absence made the heart grow fonder. Even in his lowest condition, the believer has a place and a fondness for Christ which nothing can fill except Himself. There is such a thing as sickness of love through absence, as well as through presence.

She sought him. Awareness of her state, and conscious loss, causes concern and alarm, and she sets out seeking. Though as it were half-dazed, trying to ascertain her case, she prays and seeks, while yet shrinking from the trouble and cost of earnest seeking. The believer, in a carnal frame, may keep up a form of duty, yet, like the state of his heart, it is cold and formal until the form itself becomes so distasteful that he cannot bear it.

She finds him not. Her prayers are not answered as she would wish; her desire is unsatisfied, because she has not sought aright. Any form of seeking will not be owned. One may be seeking in a slothful spirit, shrinking from earnest application, and finding not, yet it is good not to give up. Realising that formality in prayer led nowhere, and becoming conscious of failure, her concern becomes burdensome, and she must shake herself from her bonds. She resolves on more earnest and active application.

So she says 'I will arise'. She applies herself sincerely to active inquiry. Hitherto she sought in secret; now her inward feelings shape her outward conduct, and she resorts to public ordinances, going about the streets of the city. By the city is meant the church, so called because it has citizens, government, laws, watchmen, privileges, unity and order. The streets of the church are its public ordinances, where the citizens engage in business, service, and usefulness. Here she enquires of the watchmen, such as ministers, and all who in prayer and service to God seek to address the spiritual needs of men. She enquires for her beloved. They found her.

Beyond them, however, she must go. They could only direct and instruct, rebuke or encourage. She must go beyond men and means. She thought they would help, and in a manner they did. They showed her her case. But we must not rest in men or means; we must seek acquaintance with Christ.

(3) Possession - 'I found him'

At length her quest is rewarded. What is it to find Christ? That is the important thing.

Some speak of finding Christ, and their speech betrays them. One thing about it is that it is preceded by pain, restless anxiety, earnest seeking. Indeed, he gives the enquiring spirit; the soul learns that it is not an easy thing to find Him. Some say it is, and so it is when it pleases Him to reveal Himself. But until then it is the most difficult thing in the world. Normally His method is to prepare the soul by silence and delay, for closing in with Him on His own terms. Thus He may keep the soul waiting for long, as He pleases to reveal Himself. The soul must learn that by grace we are saved. Wholly by sovereign grace. Even those who find Him must realise that it is easier to lose than find again. This is part of His discipline.

To find Christ is to become acquainted with His Person and character in Scripture, and the place which He occupies in our salvation. To understand Him, and His love, feel His presence, hear and understand His speech. To rest in Him, with soul satisfaction in His finished work as Saviour and Lord. To reflect with delight on His Person, love, work and wealth. Then it is in truth a time of love for us. Lay hold on Him, in an act of faith, love and prayer, with a concern and fear of losing Him.

Take Him - she took her beloved to her mother's house. The church is the mother of us all. She has children, both after the flesh and after the spirit.

It is in the church that the soul is born again, and it is the church which the reborn soul wishes to enrich with his new-found life.

We bring Christ to the church in our estimate of His worth, in commendation of His love and praise of His name. By our spirit, words, walk and witness. By confessing Him and doing service to Him.

Christ is indispensable - no substitute will do. He is to be sought. And He is to be found. And He is to be kept. Do you know Him?

84. DESTINATION AND DELIVERANCE

And the ransomed of the Lord shall return, and come to Zion with songs and everlasting joy upon their heads: they shall obtain joy and gladness, and sorrow and sighing shall flee away (Isaiah 35:10).

The history of Israel is a parable of the history of the church of God in this world. It is distinguished by periods of advance and periods of reverse. In this way God manifested His regard and faithfulness to discipline and prepared His church for the designed end. This chapter points to and promises an era of advance, as a time of reviving and restoration. It answers to the experience of the believer under the Gospel, whereby God brings his people to seek the good and blessing of Zion.

(1) *The Description of the people of God*
They are called the ransomed of the Lord, that is, people whom the Lord has ransomed. It is the doing of the Lord, and it is wondrous in the eyes of His people. To Him all the glory must redound. The word 'ransomed' suggests bondage, and must be understood in that light.

They were in deep bondage. This refers to their experience in the land of Egypt, which was hard and cruel. But that was only a symbol of a deeper bondage, in which the whole of the human race is enslaved. One symptom of it is unconsciousness. They resign themselves to it, thinking they are free. It is bondage to sin, which enslaves men, and holds sway over their whole life, their mind, their heart, their will. The devil by his agents, and sin, as a vile, degrading principle, controls them and they yield to its wiles, walking according to the course of this world.

They are in bondage as far as the law of God, or the covenant of works is concerned. Man violated that covenant, and cannot honour it or fulfil it. Man is guilty, and incapable of discharging his debt. When a criminal resorts to breaking the law, there is a fear of apprehension, and he resorts to hiding, in constant fear of being found out and punished. So man in a state of nature, though unconscious of the cause, is yet restless, in dread of being accountable to God.

But here we have a redeemed people, redeemed by price and by power. The deliverance of Israel from the bondage of Egypt included both. There was a sacrifice of blood, under which they were safe, while judgement came on the Egyptians. The blood represented the price paid on their behalf and credited to them. So the blood of Christ secured redemption for His people. He exhausted the curse, and procured liberation from the liability to punishment.

But they were also brought out by a high hand, by the power of God. This represents the power of the Spirit, which quickens sinners. The Spirit applies the benefits of Christ's purchase, bringing a sense of safety under the blood. Two elements are present here – a sense of bondage, guilt and inability, causing concern in the face of divine majesty. And there is a rest of faith in the mercy and faithfulness of God; the soul that rests in Christ is set free from the bondage of sin and inability through the merits of the death of the Saviour.

(2) *The Way they are on*

This is specified a way of return: 'The ransomed of the Lord shall return'. Three things are told us about this way.

It is a way of holiness. That is, it is separated from the old way. It is a way of dedication to God, consecrated to His use and service.

It is the King's Highway. It is appointed by Him, and on it all His redeemed walk. This is the only way of redemption. There is liberty only through Christ who said 'I am the Way'. By the death of Christ, and the power of the Spirit, the power of sin is broken in the affairs of those who walk this way. It is a way of truth; those who are on it are taught the truth as it is in Jesus.

It is a safe way. Those who travel it, 'the wayfaring men', shall not err in it. They may err from the right way at times, but they will not err on it.

(3) *Their Destination*

They are going to Zion. This was the name of the place God set apart for His worship and people on earth, representing the visible church. Thus believers worship God in the spirit, which they regarded as indispensable to true worship. It is characteristic of them that they seek the Spirit of God to teach, sustain and sanctify them.

But Zion also represents the church triumphant, the rests which awaits the people of God in Heaven; that is, Christ's presence and eternal fellowship, which lies beyond all the bondage of this world.

They shall come to it with joy and gladness. Both are identical, yet distinct. There is joy in hope, and joy in the possession of it. There is gladness for relief and rest. There is thanksgiving and joy. While they are on earth their song is a mixed one, and is not always sung with joy. But the people of God have a song which they always sing.

Sorrow and sighing shall flee away. When they shall appear in the upper sanctuary all shall be righted. All cause of sorrow shall be eliminated. Joy shall be the portion. This is the promise, and it will be fulfilled.

We are all on a journey; the important question is 'What road are we on?' God's people sorrow and sigh under a sense of sin, though they are ransomed. They long for full freedom. They can only flee to Christ for salvation.

85. FEAR NOT

Fear thou not; for I am with thee; be not dismayed; for I am thy God; I will strengthen thee; yea, I will help thee; yea, I will uphold thee with the right hand of my righteousness (Isaiah 41:10).

God's eyes are on His people in distress, and He has a word of comfort for them in season. No doubt these words had particular reference to Israel in the distresses which were about to fall on them, but they equally apply to God's people in times of trial down through the ages to the end of time. While He sternly rebukes and threatens defectors, He assures the needy of present and permanent help. Though suffering for personal and national sins, just as we are at present, God does not delight in afflicting sorely. He sends truth to correct, teach, humble; but He also suffers them not to be tried beyond measure. Here He declares His abiding relation to His church, to comfort and strengthen them for all the hazards of life.

(1) *God's people are subject to fear*

Scripture describes two kinds of fear which apply to them.

First, God's people are God-fearing people. This is something commanded in Scripture, and is proper and becoming the creature before the Creator. No-one can be in a suitable frame before God without this. It is the essence of true piety; it is described as the beginning of wisdom and knowledge, as the fountain of life. This implies a healthy exercise of soul. We are not right or safe without it. It is not fear in the sense of dread, but of respect, reverence and love. It is manysided and shows itself in different ways.

It is revealed in respect and affection for God. It is seen in fear of sin. By nature man loves and delights in sin, and has no quarrel with it. It is man's life. Not so the believer; sin has turned on him, and he is against it. It pains him, shames him and is a burden to him. This fear is seen in a fear of Satan, and the believer has good reason to be afraid of Satan. He is not ignorant of his devices, and feels unequal to the temptations and snares he places in the way. They are also afraid of themselves, their proneness to sin, declension, soiled garments, dishonouring the Lord's name. They fear divine discipline, chastisement, forsaking, His silence. We should be thankful for the discipline of correction, but the flesh shrinks from the cost of it.

But there is another fear which is true of the Christian: the fear of being dismayed, as the text puts it. He is subject to becoming fainthearted, discouraged, ready to give up the struggle. Sometimes the Christian can become fearful to a crushing extent, with a sense of his inequality to the strains and stresses of life, and of the future.

(2) *God says 'Fear Not'*

Now, this does not mean that they should cease from a legitimate and healthy fear, that is, the fear of God, as described above; but they should be free from that fear which is a hindrance, which is needless and which is forbidden.

This kind of fear is slavish. It is not profitable, it is harmful, sinful and arises from unbelief and distrust in God. It may be mistaken for godly fear. Some think it a mark of piety to be fearful and doubting, while all they are doing is feeding unbelief. It is a fear which renders them useless, and helpless to the point of guilt, it is the fear of man, and it brings a snare. Such a fear dishonours God. While godly fear stimulates to the obedience of faith, slavish fear dissuades therefrom.

Here God calls for faith to dissuade from harmful fear. 'I am with thee.' Greater is He that is with and for you, than all those that are against you. Do you believe this? It is a challenge to your faith. He does not promise that there will be no trials, but He promises sufficient grace. He declares Himself to be the God of His people, and He will not be apart from them.

What are you not to fear? Such things as alarm you - the voice of the enemy, your own frailty, adversity, bondage. Your God is faithful. Trust in Him.

We must look up to Him, listen to Him, believe Him and what He says to us. Our fault and shame is that we succumb to fears arising from appearances, and think God is against us. But we should look for the explanation of adversity in the light of God's government of our affairs.

Listen - He says 'I will strengthen you'. We are weak, and He is strong. He supplies the needed strength, by His Word, Spirit and ordinances. He says 'I will help you', by His sustaining grace and tokens for good. He makes the crooked places straight and the rough places smooth. He removes the mountains so that they become a plain. This He does 'by the right hand of His righteousness'. All His dealings with you are in terms of righteousness. 'All his works are truth and righteousness.' And it is on the basis of Christ's righteousness that He deals graciously with them.

Let us seek the true fear of God, which is the essence of piety.

86. IN THE SCHOOL OF CHRIST

And all thy children shall be taught of the Lord;
and great shall be the peace of thy children (Isaiah 54:13).

God had a people in every age with whom He dealt by way of promise and providence. These promises and providences were of two kinds: general, to the church at large. By the church I mean not its visible form, but the subjects of His grace, for the promises are yea and amen to those who are in Christ by covenant relation. The church has put her faith in these promises. There are also promises to individual members of the church, who are in living union with Christ, by which they are sustained to bear the stresses of their lot in life. They have need of this; hence the promises are made personal to them, and they are enabled to appropriate them. Here they are combined, it is for us to consider them for the strengthening of our faith: 'Thy children shall be taught of the Lord'.

(1) *The Subjects of Instruction: 'thy children'*
This may refer to the church itself, and may be a promise to her that her children may be taught of the Lord. So they are, and must be. The instruction needed must be of the Lord.

Or it may be a promise to Christ, to whom a seed is promised. In the highest sense, the members of the church are presented in Scripture as His children.

It is the Lord Himself who instructs them. This refers to the Person of the Father, whose mode of teaching is by the ministry of the Spirit, by His word and by providence. He makes these effective to their spiritual edification and growth. He is a most patient teacher. He knows the frame of His children, and the best means suited to their instruction. He is most effective; though they are slow to learn, and need lessons to be repeated, yet He despairs not and His teaching gradually takes effect. It is more noticeable in some than in others, but ultimately it will prove effectual to all.

He is unerring. Naturally, a teacher may misjudge the capacity of the child, and may rush him on. But the teaching of the Holy Spirit is gradual, step by step, and it is sound teaching. Hence we find ourselves at one with Spirit-taught Christians everywhere.

(2) *The Instruction*

Naturally, men presume to be knowledgeable and wise, while they are ignorant of spiritual truth, and have no spiritual experience. By nature they are in darkness, and in need of divine instruction, that they may be brought to a knowledge of the truth. That instruction is spiritual, and is imparted by means of His Word and Spirit. They are brought to a knowledge of themselves as sinners, self-ruined, and in need of deliverance from sin and its issues. This knowledge is preparatory to God's self-disclosure of mercy, and His provision of salvation in Christ, with whom the sinner is enabled to close in as Saviour and Lord.

Again, the Christian life is a process of instruction. The experienced believer is ever learning. All believers are not equally exercised - some are stagnant by undue cares of the world, others are more devotional, and they learn lessons to which others are strangers most of their earthly lives. They are deep, personal and experimental lessons. They have spiritual experiences of His love and Person. But here the promise is to all of His children, however slow their progress. They shall be taught, because His teaching is necessary to prepare them for glory.

(3) *Their Peace*

Naturally, men are not at peace with God, and He is not at peace with them. God says that there is no peace for the wicked.

But here we have the peace of children, who have been brought into a state of peace with God in Christ, who is the basis of their peace. Then there is the peace of the indwelling witness of the Holy Spirit, in His tokens of favour. God initiates and establishes this peace. 'We have peace with God through our Lord Jesus Christ.' The terms of this peace are acceptance of Christ as Saviour, and the indwelling of the Spirit. It is peace that is great, in its nature, effects and endurance.

This does not mean that they have no dispeace. Indeed, the reverse is true. While at peace with God, they have much disquiet and dispeace with sin, Satan, the world, and above all, themselves. They stand in a broken relation to sin, to the world and to its ways, which often pains them.

The promise to them is 'In this world ye shall have tribulation'. So it was, is, and shall be. However long we bask in the sunshine of divine peace, and some do more than others in their Christian lives, yet disquiet will come; and when it does, it will not be easy to bear. But the end shall be peace, and it shall not end.

87. FOLLOWING CHRIST

And as Jesus passed forth from thence, he saw a man, named Matthew, sitting at the receipt of custom: and he saith unto him, Follow me. And he arose, and followed him (Matthew 9:9).

There are critical moments in the lives of most people, moments when the balance seems to hang in equilibrium, and we cannot tell for a while which way it will turn. There are times when men stand as it were at the parting of two ways, uncertain which way to take. They remain for a season undecided. Such moments, however, seldom last long; indeed, they cannot last long. Choice must be made. And what choice! Whether persevered in or not, it has results. It may determine the whole future history of men in the life that now is, and their destiny in the world to come. The words of our text were addressed by the Lord Jesus to Matthew, while the latter was absorbed in the transaction of earthly duties. Jesus would have men put first things first, hence he challenged Matthew to the biggest decision of his life, a decision which had far-reaching results. It determined the whole future course of his life on earth; it secured for him an indelible place in the Christian church, and an exalted position in the Glory of Heaven. Here we have Matthew's call to discipleship and service. Let us note the two aspects of it.

(1) *An Authoritative Command*
'Follow me.' It was a challenge which could not possibly be ignored or resisted - it had to be obeyed, and indeed was heartily and gladly obeyed. There is a call which can be resisted, and which often is resisted and slighted by men - the general call of the Gospel. But there is also a call which cannot be resisted because it comes with such authority and power that it makes a person willing.

It was a divine call. It came from none less than the Lord and Saviour of men. He uttered the call on His own authority, which is not derived, but self-possessed. The Saviour of man is a Divine Person, God manifest in the flesh. Oh what a wonder this is! The God of heaven and earth in the form of a servant - seeking to save the lost, and calling them back to the service of God. Think of the amazing love that moved Him to intervene in our tragic case. Only that He mercifully undertook to save men, they would eternally perish in their sin. He is the caller, and His call is authoritative, powerful and convincing.

It was a call to one considered low on the social scale. He was a tax-gatherer, perhaps a custom house officer at the port of Capernaum, or an exciseman, or a collector of the land tax. Whichever of these offices he held, his occupation was then regarded as ignoble, especially by the Jews who were the chief sufferers. They looked upon publicans with disdain, disquiet and contempt. They were considered as unpatriotic, traitors, spiritually abandoned, and beyond recovery. A publican from the mere fact of being one had no reputation to lose, so that even if he were somewhat scrupulous, he would get no credit for it. It was a calling of ill-fame, because it was attended with much corruption and temptation. There were few in that business that were honest men. Such was the position that Matthew occupied.

It was a call from a low service to a higher: a call from the ordinary business of life to the service of God, a call from the service of sin and self-pleasing and self-interest to the service of love, obedience and loyalty to Christ. Such is the call that comes to the sinner. By nature he is pursuing the service of sin and self, he has self as his chief end in life, his aim is to please and enjoy himself. To such the divine call comes with authority and power, and they cannot resist because it is a call to higher and nobler service. Matthew may have heard the general call before this. He may have heard of Christ's wonder-working power, he may even have heard for himself the awe-inspiring, arresting and convincing power of Christ's presentation of the Gospel and its claims. We are told that the people heard Him gladly, and Matthew may have been among those glad hearers.

It was an effective call. Christ does not say 'Will you follow me?' He does not ask a favour, but demands a duty, and in truth a duty it was, a duty to himself and a duty to God, and a duty to men. There was much Matthew had to renounce, but he did it gladly and ungrudgingly. We must not suppose that Matthew was unaware of the tremendous implications of obedience to the claims of Christ. Christ never concealed from his disciples the consequences of following Him. He drew no rosy pictures of life, made no reckless promises of earthly eminence. He only dissuaded them from cherishing such thoughts. He would have His followers consider the cost, hence He plainly told them that life would be hard and difficult. Foxes had holes, and the birds had nests, but Christ had no place to lay His weary head on, far less an earthly kingdom in which they could hold positions of eminence. 'If any man follow me, let him deny himself, take up his cross and follow me.' What Christ offered and called to was self-denial, a cross, but at the end of the day a crown of glory. This was real reward, and it more than compensates for all the toil, sacrifices and labour of following Him. His call is effective.

(2) *Personal obedience*
'He arose and followed Him.'

If the religion and call of Christ is anything, it is vitally personal. It is to personal religion that we are called. No sooner did Matthew hear the call than he obeyed. There seems to have been a divine power accompanying the call, which imparted strength of purpose and resolution to the mind, and decision to the will, similar to that implied in the words 'rise up and walk'. When Christ calls He is ready to impart, and indeed does impart strength to obey. Thus it becomes an effective call.

The Gospel is the power of God unto salvation. Not that it implies the force of a mighty convulsion; it is rather the power of rational persuasion of the truth of the Gospel and the loftiness of its claims. It arrests the attention, admiration, trust and love of those who hear it. It becomes a moving and energising force in their lives. The belief and understanding of the Gospel has a profound and determining effect on their lives. So Matthew felt, and he responded, and the reality of the change is made manifest immediately.

We find him preparing a feast in honour of Christ. He not only followed Jesus in the way, but he wanted to bear public witness to the fact. He was not ashamed to own His Lord or to defend His cause. He would have his fellow-sinners and friends know where he stood in relation to Christ, and he would have them come to him and follow him. To this feast he invited his associates in his past life, in the hope that they too might discover in Christ what Matthew saw in Him, and so come under the gracious influence of His amazing personality. It was a feast for Matthew's soul to bring his fellows to Christ, but we may also say that it was a feast for Christ to have sinners brought to Him. There is joy in Heaven over one sinner repenting. But Matthew would not only witness for Christ with his lips; he would do so with his head and pen, for:-

He wrote a Gospel. If he bears personal witness for Christ by seeking to bring others to Him, his pen must also be active. Those beyond the reach of his voice, and the witness of his life, must know the glad tidings; and he ably used his pen to write the Gospel story that in ages to come others might know about Him, and better still, know Him.

Now, what Christ said to Matthew He says to us - 'Follow Me'. This is a challenge to you all this day. The world has its appeal, its calls, its absorbing business. But in the midst of the din of this world's confusion and absorbing business and interests, let us listen to the voice of mercy calling us to repentance and salvation. Who would turn a deaf ear to that? Christ says 'This is the way; walk ye in it'. 'Come unto me, and be ye saved'. There are only two ways - the world's way and Christ's way, the way that leads to Glory and Heaven. May God grant that His word may be a living, life-imparting word to us, that we may respond to His appeal, and know His life.

88. CONFESSIONS

Whosoever therefore shall confess me before men, him will I confess also before my Father which is in heaven (Matthew 10:32).

The life of faith as presented in the context is costly. Our Lord did not conceal the implication of witnessing for Him - the disciple need not expect better treatment than the master - they are sent forth as sheep among wolves. The early Christians met opposition from organised religion, and from the state. Though at times less severe, yet the same spirit was and still is in the world. But while He forewarned of the trials, He also set forth in clear relief the reward of faithful service - He assures of His loving care, and abiding presence to sustain them in trial. At times their loyalty would be severely tried, but here He gives direction as to their relation and obligation to Him. He assigns duty, and proclaims reward. He speaks here of a twofold confession.

(1) *Man's confession of Christ*
While this primarily defined the duty of the disciples, and all preachers of the Gospel to the end of time, yet it clearly sets forth the obligation of all Christians, so that everyone should be persuaded in his own conscience as to his relation to the command of Christ - 'if ye love me, keep my commandments'. Obedience to Christ is the golden rule of love. To confess is to own and affirm a thing true or false, and to stand by what one believes.

To confess Christ implies knowledge of Him. That is, knowledge of who and what He is. This is basic to confession. And this knowledge is deeper than mere theoretical knowledge - it implies appreciation of Him, as understood in the light of His self-revelation. This implies the exercise of faith, an unreserved acceptance of who and what He is, and a conscious love to Him in view of who and what He is. This knowledge of, faith in, and love to Christ expresses itself in open avowal of His Person, deity and humanity, of the doctrine of Scripture concerning Him, His vicarious death, and resurrection, His exalted life. Of the benefits received - what He means to you as Saviour, your wisdom, righteousness, sanctification and redemption. All this is basic to a confession of Christ. These are not matters to be kept to ourselves.

He requires public confession - 'before men'. It was not without reason that He emphasised this duty - we must not be ashamed of Him, or hide our light; He expects us to testify to what He is and means to us. This may be done in several ways.

It may be done *by word of mouth*. As Paul puts it in Romans 10:10, 'with the heart man believes unto righteousness, and with the mouth confession is made unto salvation'. The psalmist said 'I believe, therefore I have spoken' (Psalm 116). In this way we are to affirm our estimate of Him, of what He did for us, and in us, and our gratitude to Him. So in Psalm 66:16 there is the invitation to those who fear God: 'come, hear, I'll tell what He did for my soul'.

Confession may be done *by practical obedience to His word.* That is, bearing out the truth we proclaim, lest our walk contradict our talk. Many there are whose walk is not consistent with what they say, and this should not be so. There must be consistency of walk and word, and loyalty to His honour. There is a story about Sir Robert Peel, one of the great Prime Ministers, that once at a dinner party, when the conversation took to the ridiculing of religion, he got up from the table saying that was no place for a Christian.

Confession also has an eye on the *observation of His appointed ordinances.* These are binding upon all believers, until He comes again. This we intend doing next Sabbath - not because of personal merit or worthiness of it, but because of obligation to Christ. It is the expression of faith in Him, the public confession of Him as Saviour and Lord, and what He did for you and in you. Such confession He desires the believer to make. The fact that this means so little in our day should only spur real believers on to own Him. This is a life witness, borne out daily. It should be our earnest endeavour to promote His cause, in every department of life, at whatever cost.

This is not easy, nor was it ever meant to be. Various elements contribute to the difficulty - personal unfitness and timidity, the temptations of Satan, and opposition from the world. But love and loyalty to Christ surrounds it all. We do not confess Him because it is popular, or that it gives a place or name among men, but in obedience and loyalty to Christ.

(2) *Christ's confession of men*

What a wonder! That He should take note of such sinful, inconsistent creatures as us. Yet He says it is true. 'God's eyes are on the just...' (Psalm 33:18). Christ will confess before God those who confess Him before men.

Now, this is in return for their confession of Him, as an acknowledgement of it. He does not say that He will vindicate them before men by singular tokens of His power. It is true that He did so at times, and He will continue to give tokens of favour, and success and blessing in their conscious experience. He affords them comfort and strength. They have these promises of His personal favour, and attention and supply at all times.

But this is a confession of them before the Father. It would seem as if Christ owns the deeds of loyalty, consistency and service before the Father; there is a recording of this for reward at the set time - not a cup of water is forgotten. It is also evident that the Father takes notice of such: 'the Father himself loveth you, because ye have believed me' (John 16:27). In the discharge of our duty to Him, done entirely for Him and for His glory, He comes to us, melting our heart and revealing Himself. But at length He will vindicate His own before the Most High.

There is much denial of Christ in the world. The wicked deny Him. Good people deny Him. And Christ will deny them. But the believer has a duty - to make Christ known. And that duty will not be discharged in vain.

89. CHRIST IN VIEW

When Jesus came into the coasts of Caesarea Philippi, he asked his disciples saying, Whom do men say that I the son of man am? And they said, Some say that thou art John the Baptist; some Elias; and others Jeremias, or one of the prophets. He saith unto them, But whom say ye that I am? And Simon Peter answered and said, Thou art the Christ, the son of the living God
(Matthew 16:13-16).

Here we see Jesus conversing with His disciples regarding His identity - 'Whom do men say that I am?' It is not that He needed them to enlighten Him regarding current views about Him, for He knew what was in man; but He would elicit from them a confession which puts in clear focus the radical difference between the world's view of Him and the believer's estimate of

Him; hence He goes on to enquire 'But whom say ye that I am?'

This is a matter which ought to be of vital concern to us all; what view do we have of Jesus Christ? What place do we assign Him?

(1) *The World's View of Christ*

The world has false or inadequate views of Him. That there is a great difference of opinion among men regarding Christ is evident from what we read and hear, and it is highly important that we should be clear and straight in our views of Him.

The prevailing opinions current in our own day are stated in verse 14. That He was held in high esteem, by what He said and did, is evident from the fact that they regarded Him as a prophet. Some said 'Elias', some 'Jeremiah'; some said he was John the Baptist risen from the dead. A prophet indeed He was, and greater than all the prophets, because He was the substance of their message, and the subject of their investigation.

The Pharisees and the religious leaders of the day were of a different persuasion. Jealous of His power and influence over the people, they regarded Him as an impostor, objected to His teaching, discredited His miracles, and rejected Him as Messiah. 'He came unto His own, and His own received Him not.' Because of preconceived notions about the Messiah, and because He did not fit in with these, they were so incensed against Him as to ascribe His miracles to Beelzebub, the prince of devils. Such unreasonable blindness and hardness of heart, in the face of real greatness and goodness, showed them, and not Him, to be in league with the powers of darkness. His words and works were alike evidence of His goodwill towards men.

Erroneous views of Christ are still current in the world, despite the fact that they have been proved false by undeniable truth. Many regard Him as merely a good man who has shown us the way to live, suffer and die. Others speak of His claims as unreasonable and incredible. Others speak of Him as a figure in history who has no relevance to the present; they reject the essential doctrines which constitute His relevance to the present and future, that is, His deity, virgin birth, vicarious death and resurrection. To them He is a mere man, well-meaning, but self-deceived, who failed in His ambition because the forces against Him were too strong.

Now, it is a matter of supreme importance what views we hold of Christ. What place do we assign Him? Our views place us either for or against Him. Certain things are clear about Him, which entitle Him to serious regard and consideration. There is, for example, His transparent honesty, selflessness, goodwill towards men, and His obvious mastery of all situations. He was not the creature of circumstances beyond His control; He was discharging a mission to which He was appointed and self-committed. Then you have His claims for Himself and upon man; He asks for attention, confidence, trust and faith as He faces death, claiming the power and right to save men from their sins and restore them to divine favour.

These are matters which cannot be lightly estimated or rejected. Many admit the truth of His greatness, but see no need of Him, and will not come to Him for life. It is possible to have good opinions of Him, and yet not be right in heart towards God.

(2) The Believer's View of Him

Jesus turned His question from the general to the particular - 'Whom do ye say that I am?' In reply we have Peter's confession of faith, and it represents the estimate of true believers down through the ages. Christ had spoken of Himself as the Son of Man, and in reply Peter states the essential articles of sound theology and saving faith, with respect to the Person and Work of Christ.

He says 'Thou art the Christ', the Messiah, the Lord's anointed. This was the official name of Christ, which presents Him in His official relation and work. It designates His office to which He was consecrated through divine anointing. Under the Old Testament, kings, priests and prophets were consecrated to office by anointing, which also signified an endowment which qualified for office. The oil of anointing represented the Spirit of God. Our Lord was the anointed one, who received the Holy Spirit without measure with respect to His manhood, first at His conception in the womb of the virgin, and then at His baptism by John. And He claimed this for Himself when, after His baptism and temptation, in the synagogue of Nazareth, He read Isaiah 61:1 'Behold the Spirit of God is upon me'. He is spoken of as the Lord's anointed (Psalm 2:2; 45:7). It was in virtue of His anointing that He discharged His threefold offices as Prophet, Priest and King. This was His qualification for office, which in all its parts He discharged by the Spirit.

Peter also confesses Him as 'the son of the Living God'. He had presented Himself as the Son of Man; here Peter declares Him to be the Son of God. He was of course a man - we must not lose sight of that fact, because it was in human nature that He discharged the work assigned Him. But He was infinitely more than a man; He was the Son of God, the only begotten of the Father, the God-man, God manifest in the flesh. He cannot be understood in any other light; neither His words nor His works can be understood otherwise.

This view of Christ is divinely given (v 17). He called Himself Son of Man - they recognised Him as Son of God, the Messiah, the God-sent Saviour. This is revealed not by flesh and blood. It is not self-discovered:

no man can say that Jesus is Lord except by the Holy Spirit. This is God-given knowledge, and faith confessing Him as Lord is the gift of God.

This is an abiding question, personal to all. There are weighty reasons why we should ask it of ourselves, lest we be infected with the erroneous opinions of the world about our Lord. I once heard a minister say that it took him twenty years to abuse his mind of the poison instilled in his mind during his College days, as erroneous views of Christ were taught to him. The question demands an answer - what is our estimate of Him? Of His place, person and work?

This confession of faith is honouring to God, and glorifying to Christ, who approves it and appropriates the titles ascribed to Him, and the place assigned Him. He is the rock upon which the church is founded, and which ensures her safety against the powers of hell. Let us never forget that the place we assign Him in time will determine the place He shall assign us in eternity.

90. THE EYE OF THE STORM

And he said unto them, Where is your faith? And they being afraid wondered saying one to another, What manner of man is this! for he commandeth even the winds and water, and they obey him (Luke 8:25).

Great and wonderful things are recorded about Jesus Christ, things which prove him to have been the most extraordinary person who ever walked this earth. His birth was a miracle, His life was a puzzle, except to faith. His death was a miracle. His resurrection was a miracle. But not only was He a miracle Himself; He wrought miracles - He possessed wonder-working power. Here we have a case in point, in the stilling of the storm recorded in our text. Now there are some lessons which we may learn from this story.

(1) *A Fearful Storm*
You are all familiar with storms at sea. Some of you may have had so many of them that you hope they will never be repeated. You have become so used to them that there is nothing unusual or romantic about them. A storm at sea is a dreadful, an awe-inspiring thing. When the angry elements rage, and the sea-billows roar, life and property are in danger.

Yet as good comes out of evil, storms have their uses. They stimulate precautionary measures, they evoke sympathy, and create a sense of brotherhood. In times of danger we cease to be strange to one another, we feel like brothers. It is not merely a case of every man for himself; there is also an element of self-sacrifice to help others. That, I think, is evident from the many stories of heroism current in our day.

But the angry moods of the sea are not the only storms we know. There is the storm of temptation, when we are subjected to the cunning persuasion of the enemy, and the lingering attachment of our sinful nature to sin. Then there are the common storms of disappointed hopes, grief, trials and the afflictions of life, of which we must all know something. There is also the constant conflict between good and evil, not only around us, but of which God's people are conscious is in themselves. These try us, and bring forth the best that is in us, just as much, if not more, than the raging wind and the roaring seas. They may for a time lead us out of our course, and imperil our good things - our good name, associations and health, and they may fill us with a sense of apprehension.

And the end is not yet. There may be worse ahead. Life is not a smooth adventure, and at the end there is the dreadful day of reckoning. There is the danger of shipwreck, and moral disaster if we fail to take the precautionary measures. Life, then, resembles the state of those on the angry sea of Galilee.

(2) A Frightened Crew

There is probably nothing worse in a raging storm than a crew in panic. It sometimes happens that men become unnerved by a sense of acute danger, when hope of safety is almost abandoned. It might be said that such may happen with inexperienced seamen, but hardly ever with the tried and seasoned mariner.

But it cannot be said of those men on the stormy lake that they were inexperienced. They were seafaring men, accustomed to boats, and they had weathered many storms before, and yet they were afraid. There is, of course, a difference between being afraid, and panic. It is possible for a man to be afraid, and yet be unspeakably brave, cool and collected.

But this suggests that there are times when the best of men may be afraid. There is nothing cowardly in being afraid, although it may be cowardly to give way to fear. These men expected to perish; the night was dark, the wind was raging and the sea was coming into the ship. And to add to their dismay, the one in whom they trusted for life and death seemed indifferent to their needs and danger.

They needed not more strength, or more knowledge, or more courage, but more faith. They had faith, but not enough to compose them in their danger. Their sense of danger, however, caused their faith to exert itself. They prayed; and it was their faith that inspired their prayer. Prayer cannot rise without faith - you must believe in a Person able to keep and deliver.

Their prayer secured the intervention of the Lord, who controls the elements. He spoke, and there was a calm. For the truth of this, there is the unanimous evidence of those in the boat. There is no conflict of opinion among them. You know how hard it is for three or four men to relate the same event, and agree on it. But these give evidence of what happened, and their testimony concurs.

We may wonder that the Lord did not intervene sooner, why He allowed them to toil and suffer for so long. Well, why did they not pray sooner? At times the Lord is with His people, and allows them toil and struggle, till they call on Him. He does this in order to impress upon them a sense of dependence. Can we lay claim to the Lord being with us? If not, the calm is not safe, far less the storm. But nothing will harm us if He is there.

(3) *The Sudden Calm*

The Lord heard their cry, and by a word stilled the raging seas. He holds the winds in His fist, and the waters in the hollow of His hand. It is evident that nothing is beyond His control; all events are subject to His order and command.

This is often the experience of believers. When harassed with temptation and trial, under the stress of which they are apt to become despondent, they are suddenly and wonderfully relieved and delivered when they call upon Him. Strange and varied are the experiences of men. Some may have a calm within, while there are storms without; while others may have storms within while all is calm without. Some sleep in the storm, ignorant of the danger, like Jonah; others sleep like Jesus, confident of salvation.

On the voyage of life the presence of Jesus is indispensable for safety. The calm of His presence will help us weather the storms, endure the hardship, survive the danger. If terrified at the prospect of death, how much more will the reality be if Christ be not with us. For if He is with us, who can be against us?

91. THE DUTY OF PRAYER

And he spake a parable unto them to this end,
that men ought always to pray, and not to faint (Luke 18:1).

There is hardly any religious duty so much neglected as prayer, and yet there is no duty that is more important. It is taken as a matter of course, and looked upon as the business of a few. There are some who think and speak as if prayer were a senseless game of old wives, and weak-minded men, and that developed and cultured men have no use for it. Others, while admitting that prayer is of some value, scorn to think that it is only meant for special occasions, such as times of danger, sorrow, or some national emergency. But that was not the view of the Lord Jesus, and He was in a position to know, and could give some guidance in the matter. He says that men ought always to pray, and not faint.

(1) *Prayer is a duty imposed on men by the Lord Himself*

Men ought to pray. There is nothing shameful or unmanly in that, but there is definitely something shameful and unmanly in the neglect of it. God demands, expects and is entitled to some recognition by His creatures. To deny Him this is to dishonour, despise, ignore and disobey Him; and what could be more shameful than that? Surely the God on whom we are absolutely dependent, in whom we live, move and have our being, deserves to be acknowledged and praised, honoured and obeyed.

And yet there are some who do not pray at all. They eat, drink, sleep, rise and enjoy manifold favours from God, and they never pray. They enjoy the hospitality of His Providence, they breathe God's pure air; they experience the healing rays of God's sun, and they never give thanks. They live like the beasts that perish, and behave like creatures without souls.

The reason for this is the havoc wrought by sin in us. The natural bent of our nature has been changed. We have become the slaves of sin. The carnal mind is enmity against God. The desire of the natural heart is to get rid of God, and have nothing to do with Him. Our feeling towards Him is fear, and dread of His holiness and justice.

Another reason is that prayer is not fashionable. It is one of the things that many are ashamed to own. It is far easier for many to stand in the way of sin, and sit in the seat of the scornful than to pray. And why should it be so, when God in mercy has opened the way for our approach to Himself? And when He commands us to pray, and invites us to Himself? Why should we be so slothful, and slow, and indifferent, when He says to us - 'Come, Return, Believe'? It is a privilege and an honour that we are thus called to pray. Men ought to pray.

(2) *Prayer is good for the soul*

There is no other exercise more beneficial. Through it we get into touch with God; it is our mode of communication with Heaven, and can be described as the believer's telephone. Earnest and sincere prayer arrests the ear of God, and God is not only a prayer-hearing but also a prayer-answering God. It was Tennyson who said 'More things are wrought by prayer than this world dreams of'.

There is a meaning in prayer. When we are sad and weary and lonely, or in danger, prayer has a meaning. And God answers prayer very often when we are in straits of some kind. But His answers are not confined to the cloudy day.

In prayer we present our desires to God for things agreeable to His will, in the name of Christ, with confession of sin, and thankful acknowledgement of His mercies. That is the Shorter Catechism definition - a grand little book! It is a beautiful compendium of religious truth, well worth reading. In prayer, then, we present our needs, dangers, sorrows, cares and even our successes and joys to God. And we seek something - we seek favour, acceptance, blessing, guidance, protection and strength, strength to resist temptation and perform our duties.

Prayer is to be offered in the name of Christ. This is our only plea. And if thus offered, we may expect an answer to prayer. Perhaps one of the greatest faults of praying people is that they are not expectant enough. We often pray and never look for an answer. And we should pray always, and never faint nor give in. Even if we have to wait long for an answer. We may be sure of God's answer if we pray aright. Others sought and found not, because they sought not aright.

(3) *In this we have the example of the greatest of men*
(a) Jesus Himself prayed. This is our greatest example.
(b) Believers have always prayed, and were answered.
(c) Some of the greatest men of all time were men of prayer. The men who left an indelible mark on history were great and often in prayer. Men like Augustine, Luther, Calvin, Knox and the great nonconformist preachers in England. And men in the military and political sphere were also great men of prayer - Cromwell, General Gordon, Haig, Lincoln, Gladstone, Lloyd-George, and many more.
(d) This is the greatest thing. Oh, to be men of prayer, that we would have a place among that noble crowd!

92. TEMPTATION TRIALS

And the Lord said, Simon, Simon, behold, Satan hath desired to have you, that he may sift you as wheat: But I have prayed for thee, that thy faith fail not: and when thou art converted, strengthen thy brethren (Luke 22:31-32).

The Lord Jesus knew that the time was approaching when He must offer Himself to finish the work He had undertaken on behalf of the church. With

this in view, He instituted the sacrament of the Supper on the night in which
He was betrayed, and ordered that it be kept as a permanent memorial and
witness of His death. That was no doubt a memorable evening in the life
of the disciples. It was a time of fellowship and edification for them, as they
listened to the precious and soul-affecting truths which were spoken by the
Lord Jesus. After the supper, He addressed the disciples, and told them
plainly that before long their loyalty and faith would be subjected to severe
trial. A time of blessing and refreshment is often the prelude to great trial.
In the words of our text, He addresses Peter, either for himself, or as
representing the rest, 'Simon, Simon, Satan desires to have you...' From
this, several things are clear.

(1) *Believers are subject to temptation*

Of this they are forewarned by none less than the Lord Himself. 'The Lord
said.' His special regard and care for His own are clearly illustrated in that
He warns them of danger. He would not have them to be taken unawares,
and so beforehand He puts them on their guard. There is something in
human nature that resents warning of danger. Evidently Peter did not like
to be warned. It has a disturbing effect on the mind, and somehow men
would rather enjoy the ease than to be concerned about future events, so he
tries to escape from the thought of danger. It is however of the Lord's great
kindness that we are warned, and it is our duty to take heed.

The author of temptations is Satan. He is the tempter; his work is to
tempt in order to secure the fall and ruin of men. His aim is to injure, and
ruin if he can. He seeks and plans to effect his malicious purpose. In order
to this, he takes advantage of opportune moments, he is like a roaring lion
seeking to devour. Never was there a lion waiting more eagerly for his prey
than Satan is for your soul. He desires to have you. Some think that as Satan
is under the control of God, he cannot tempt without divine permission.
That is, of course, true. But it does not necessarily mean that he seeks
permission to tempt. That would make him a praying demon, and worse
still, would mean that God gratifies his desire. I know that he sought
permission to test Job, and that he stood before God to resist Joshua the high
priest. But that is no proof that he actually asks leave of God to effect his
wicked intention. He asked no permission to sin, or to tempt Adam, or to
tempt Christ.

How does he tempt? We are not left in the dark as to this. He tempts in
different ways. Note his cunning dealings with our first parents. It assumed
the form of innocent intention. He launched his assault where he considered
his effort most likely to succeed. And his method is the same still. He places
sin in an attractive light, he appeals to our tastes, tries to obscure our vision

of God, and misrepresent His character. He presents evil as an advantage, a means of achieving commended ends or desired results. He presents God as good, but casts a cloud of doubt upon His veracity. He argues - you have known nothing but good at His hand, and you have no right to expect anything else from Him. He is the good God, and will so deal with you, irrespective of your actions. A very plausible argument indeed, and a very fashionable one today.

Believers are the special objects of his attention. This was the case with Peter and the disciples. They were the subjects of his ferocious assaults and wicked darts. He knows that is all he will have of them, unless he can secure their separation from Christ. In his efforts, he may be encouraged by the example of Judas. If he could get them to renounce Christ, then he should hope to have them.

In his attempts, he takes advantage of trial, suffering, sorrow, and even of your best moments. He attacks where and when he is more likely to succeed. He works on your weakness or weak points. He knows these, remember. His sphere of operation is the old man, your sinful nature, your old self. This is suggested by the terms of our Lord's address 'Simon, Simon', not 'Peter, Peter'. He will not attack you on your strong points, but in the region of your weakness. A boxer tries to get at the weakness of his opponent, in order to sap the energy of the heart. So it is with Satan. He tries to undermine and shake our faith. He aims particularly at our faith in Christ. If he can shake our faith, he will leave us groggy, dazed and helpless.

Christ resembles Satan's temptations to the sifting of wheat. Did you ever see the process of sifting oats from the chaff? That is the idea. The corn and chaff are mixed together in a large sieve. They are all at the mercy of the sifter; only the corn escapes his rough usage through the sieve. So Satan has his sieve - temptation. By this he works on the chaff of your nature, tries to thwart the witness of grace in your heart, tells you that you have nothing but chaff, no grace at all, so as to make you succumb to his wicked wiles.

The devil's sieve is a most uncomfortable and dangerous place. Little wonder though our Lord should teach His disciples to pray that they should be kept from temptation. Rev Mr MacQueen of Strontian, and grandfather of Cameron, Resolis, said he would rather be in the devil's sieve than in the devil's cradle. His cradle may be pleasant, but beware lest he lulls you to sleep in carnal ease - the sleep of death.

(2) *Believers are preserved in temptation*
The temptations or sifting of sinners are known to the Lord. They are all subject to His divine supervision. He suffers not that they be tried beyond measure; He says, 'this far, but no further'. As Peter himself says, 'The Lord

knoweth how to deliver the godly out of temptation'. Why He suffers them to be tempted at all is, of course, determined by an all-wise counsel. We may wonder why the Lord suffers His own choice ones to be buffeted by the arch-enemy of God and man. It puzzled David when he saw the wicked prosper, and the godly subjected to trial. But when he viewed the problem in the light of God, he was able to say 'It was good for me that I was afflicted'. It seems clear that these are permitted for the training, correction and development of Christian character. They ultimately work out an exceeding and eternal weight of glory.

The Lord saw that Peter had much to learn, and much to lose, or renounce, in order to progress further in the Christian life, attain to more exalted views of God's way of salvation, and be of more service to the church at large. He was too self-confident, and too self-reliant. There seemed to be too much of the old self clinging to him, and he must learn to put this aside and become an entire debtor to sovereign grace. No doubt there was an element of sincerity implied in his assertion 'though all forsake thee, I will not'. But evidently he relied more on himself than on divine support. Now he must learn that all is of grace, that he could not stand the fires and onslaughts of hell on his own.

The special cause of the believer's safety is Christ's intercession. He secured reconciliation by His death, and His exalted life is the pledge, efficient and effective cause of their salvation, sanctification and glorification. That is clear from Romans 4:20 and 5:10-11. He ever liveth to make intercession for them. He exercised this right to intercede on earth, in the case of Peter and the disciples. He interceded on the cross. 'I have prayed for thee', in particular, and for the church at large. He has the cause of individuals at heart, as well as that of the church at large. Believers shall always stand in need of His intercession. It is the bulwark and pledge of their eternal safety; it is our great guarantee of eternal blessedness.

Christ's intercession has particular reference to their faith. By faith they are saved; by faith they live. The just shall live by faith. The exercise of faith is essential to their growth, perseverance, endurance and comfort. It is a grace which gives much glory to God, much comfort, strength and joy to the soul. Hence the devil strikes at their faith, to blur and weaken it. He tempts them that they have no faith, or if they have, that it is not the right kind. But Christ prays that their faith will not fail. They may fail themselves, but their faith must not, and shall not fail, though it be tested and shaken. There are some respects in which their faith cannot fail.

It must not fail in its roots in the soul. It is a divine principle, implanted in the soul in the day of regeneration, and therefore cannot fail. No doubt its exercise may be subdued, hindered by ourselves and Satan, but it cannot be obliterated. Neither the sin of your nature, nor the efforts of Satan can subdue faith. When matters seem hopeless, it will reassert itself, and triumph over all hindrances.

It must not fail in its objective operation. Faith must have an object. Its seat is in the soul, but its object of action is outside us. Its object is Christ, and God in Christ. Faith is the capacity of seeing, trusting and using the Saviour. Of the conscious exercise of it, the soul may not always be aware, but nevertheless it clings tenaciously to Christ. It will not let Him go, for Christ is to faith what life is to man. Despite the fiercest onslaughts of hell, the believing soul clings to Christ as its only hope, and finds satisfaction in Him, of which Satan cannot rob him. So satisfied is he with Christ that he desires no other Saviour.

It must not fail in its final influence. Peter was never to be a better believer, or a more ready confessor than after his trial. Christ was to be more precious to him than ever before, and his witness and usefulness were to be consequently more conspicuous. We have only to read his memorable witness before the Sanhedrin, the story of which we have in Acts 4, to see this. Besides, his faith was to have a better and more deciding influence on himself. It was to mould and shape his life in a manner hitherto unknown to him.

(3) *The Duty Assigned to Him*

Peter was not only protected and preserved, kept by the power of God unto salvation, he was to be converted, or *restored*, as the word ought to be rendered. Peter was already converted, but he was to go through a period of real soul trial, in which his faith was to be severely tested and strained. He was to stumble in the dark, and behave as if he had no grace or faith, but he was to be restored, recovered from this lapse - restored to conscious favour and to his former composure, strength, relation and loyalty.

We nowadays hear men speak of second conversions. But there is no such thing. Such language is due to hazy, indefinite and unscriptural views of the dealings of God with the soul. A believer is regenerated and converted only once, but he may be restored countless times in his lifetime. Conversion in the text means restoration to renewed favour and fellowship. Here then was a promise of restoration after his temporary lapse.

Thus recovered or restored, Peter was to strengthen his brethren. This duty was emphatically stated, and appointed for Peter. It was a necessary duty. The brethren needed it, and they needed a strong leader too. Peter was suitable to discharge this duty, and he must not shirk it. After emerging, shattered and strained from the conflict and trial, Peter would naturally hesitate to act or take the lead; he would rather feel inclined to take an obscure place in the company - a back seat, as it were. But our Lord would not have it so.

Peter would be better qualified for this duty than ever before, and therefore more able to comfort, encourage and strengthen others. He had learnt much about himself, and his own weakness, to stand in conflict with the foe, and the sinfulness of his nature, but he had also learnt much about the Lord and His loving care, His preserving grace, and His sustaining power. He was to repent bitterly. All this would prepare him for the duty assigned to him. It is when one has had a soul trial and a soul deliverance that he can speak words of comfort and encouragement to others.

Again, perhaps the Lord appointed Peter's duty beforehand so that the disciples would not be slow to respond to his counsel. They probably knew of his inconsistency, his sad lapse, and they might question his right to teach or give comfort; or take the lead among them. To avoid this, Jesus says, 'when thou art converted, strengthen thy brethren'. Here is the duty of all Christians.

Let us warn ourselves by the warning given to Peter. It is the devil's desire to have us. He is bent on this. We are weak. Let us remember the source of deliverance. Christ is the living Lord and the intercessor. Let us look to Him.

93. THE GRIP OF DEATH

And he that was dead came forth, bound hand and foot with gravecloths: and his face was bound about with a napkin. Jesus saith unto them, Loose him, and let him go (John 11:44).

When the Lord does anything, He acts in a manner worthy of Himself. It could not be otherwise. Here we see Him in face of the seeming impossible, transforming the impossible into reality. Man is helpless in the presence of death. All we can do is weep and sympathise with the bereaved, and then bury our own dead out of our sight. And when it comes to ourselves we are more helpless still. Death cannot be averted, it is a must with us all. But here was one who showed Himself to be Master of death, and strange it was that having done so, men should regard His power a sufficient cause for desiring to get rid of Him. What a reflection of the human heart! The words of our text were addressed by the Lord Jesus to those who stood by as witnesses of the miracle of bringing Lazarus alive. From this we may learn many suitable lessons.

(1) *A Man brought to life*

This was not the first miracle of its kind; at least two others were brought to life in this way. And there may have been more, of which we are not told. Many other things Jesus did in the presence of His disciples which are not recorded. It would seem that the raising of Lazarus was the most wonderful of these miracles, because of the attendant circumstances, which reflect the glory of Christ, if only we will have the spiritual vision to see.

He had been dead four days, buried, already corrupted and considered loathsome, and therefore deemed beyond recovery. Whatever hope there is for those who are nearly dead, there seemed none for this. There was no question about his death - all who were present knew it, they had buried the cold, dead corpse, bearing the stench of death.

But he was raised from the dead. It was evident to all that this was a notable miracle, of which Jesus was the author. In this, Christ gave a twofold view of Himself. He showed Himself *as a man*, capable of sympathy and sorrow. He wept. Whether we take this as sympathy with the sisters, or sorrow for the effects of sin, as manifested in the ignorance and hardness of men, and here in face of the wages of sin, which is death, it showed him a man, capable of the deepest feelings of our nature.

He also showed Himself as the possessor of power and authority, explicable only in terms of *His deity*. It was an act identical to creation. The power of raising the dead is second only to the power of creation, as it is the calling back to life of that which existed in life, whereas creation was bringing into existence and form what had no existence before. Both are acts of God alone. Men have made wonderful inventions, and have great power, but men do not possess either creating power, or raising power.

Christ only spake the Word. With a loud, clear voice, He commanded 'Lazarus, come forth'. He spoke with authority peculiar to Himself, and power accompanied the command to effect His will. He called Lazarus by name to distinguish him from the other dead who were buried there. And Lazarus, consequently, came alive, and came forth from the grave. Soul and body became united at the command of Christ, and Lazarus instantly came alive and came forth from the grave, the abode of death. This was not a different Lazarus, but the same Lazarus who had been buried.

The miracle may be taken to resemble a twofold event. It is a parable of that which happens in the spiritual resurrection of men dead in trespasses and sins. At the call of Christ they are regenerated to life. The sinner is so deep in the death of sin as to be unconscious and helpless, dead and so loathsome as to be beyond life and hope. But when Christ commands, the word with power imparts life, so that the soul begins to breathe, and feel, and hear, and see, and speak, and walk.

But this is also a symbol of the general resurrection of the dead, at the day of judgement, when according to Matthew 24:31; John 5:28-29; 1 Corinthians 15:12-19 and 1 Thessalonians 4:16, the dead will be called to life and judgement in the great and solemn day of the Lord.

(2) Here was a living man in the bonds of death
He was clearly alive. This was evident to all around. He had come out of the grave, and yet the symbol of death was clinging to him - he was a living man in the garments of death, from which he must be liberated. He was bound, head, hands and feet, as was the custom. He was therefore in need of being released. He could no more unbind himself than he could raise himself. Jesus could by a word release him entirely, as he did with Peter in prison, and with Paul and Silas from chains. But it pleased Him here to employ human means, so that by handling him they would be the more impressed. Now let us apply this, and seek to learn spiritual lessons from it.

He was a blindfolded man. Seeing, but not seeing aright. The napkin about his head hindered his vision and thinking. He was yet to fully realise what had happened. Is it not so with the quickened soul? He sees dimly, he is ignorant, he hears, but he needs instruction. If the quickened soul sees need of anything, it is of a clearer apprehension of things. He needs more instruction.

His hands and feet were tied. There was a conscious inability to effect self release, to act and walk as he should. It is the lesson of inability learnt. Though at Christ's command he came alive and out of his grave, he feels hindered and helpless; he needs assistance, the bands hinder him. What were the bands? What are yours? Perhaps conscious inability to do anything as you would wish. We do not know what feelings Lazarus had, but no doubt he shrank from the attractions of the world. I remember standing by the deathbed of a 24-year-old girl who time and again opened her eyes to say 'Am I still here? O to be with Christ!' So it is that young converts fear the attractions of the world and of sin. Or it may be that they feel unfit for service, religious duties, witness bearing. They see themselves as nothing. Or is it uncertainty? You are not sure where you are -whether alive or not; you sometimes feel as if you had life, and other times as if you are dead. One thing is certain; the dead have no sense of life or death - it concerns them not.

But why were the bands left? Why did not the miracle perfect the deed of unbinding him? Because it was the will of Christ not to do what the church can do. He has entrusted a ministry to His people, and here we have an aspect of it: 'Loose him, and let him go.'

(3) Christ's command concerning him

Christ commanded that he be loosed and let go. That is, the living were to help their bound brother, those in trouble materially or spiritually. Here was one alive, but bound, and the command was twofold.

'Loose him.' This was work for them - perhaps they had helped to bind him; now they must release him. How true this is in ordinary life! There is a man offended by the inconsistency or sins of Christian people - this offence hinders him and binds him. This must be undone. You must show that although sin is in you, you are now alive to God.

We have this illustrated in Scripture. Saul of Tarsus, struck down by God's arresting of him, needed help to walk into Damascus, and needed Ananias to restore his sight and an understanding of the way of salvation. Lydia had her heart opened, but Paul led her to a fuller understanding; the same happened with Cornelius and the jailer. So it is still - the ministry of the Gospel is designed to introduce sinners to the liberty that there is in Christ. This is Christ's command to every preacher and to every believer. Have you some word of instruction or counsel to the seeking soul?

'Let him go.' As if Christ said - 'You have only to help unloose him, and then it is for him to walk, and he will when unloosed'. Let us attend to the bands, find out what it is that binds souls among us. Is it ignorance? Let us instruct. Is it conscious inability? All is done - Christ is all you need. Is it fear? Of publicity? Of religious duties? Of doubt and uncertainty? Well, 'come thou with us, and we will do thee good'. We will instruct you, feed you, strengthen and dress you.

Have you been released? Do you say 'I need more'? or 'I am not sure'? What is it that hinders you? Well, you should seek relief. He is the deliverer Himself, and uses means to untie the bands of his people. Only a miracle of grace can save us! Herein we see the reign of sin and the wonder of grace. Let us seek the resulting relief that we may know the liberty of sons.

94. EXPECTING CHRIST IN OUR FEASTS

Then sought they for Jesus, and spake among themselves as they stood in the temple, What think ye, that he will not come to the feast? (John 12:56).

In this chapter, we have a miracle, and a sermon, and the ensuing result. One might expect the result to be favourable to the person who is the outstanding figure of the chapter, but we find it to be the contrary. The amazing influence and popularity of Jesus only stirred the hatred of his enemies, who resolved to get rid of Him. It is extraordinary that His chief enemies were the religious leaders of His day - the Pharisees, scribes and priests. These met in council, and resolved that He must die.

Our text may be taken as expressing their desire to know His whereabouts, in order that they might apprehend Him. But we must not limit the meaning and significance of the words to the desire of His enemies to know where Jesus abode. We may safely assume that there were many truly devout people present at the feast who were anxious to see and hear the wonderful prophet of Nazareth. And we may take the text as expressing their desire to make His acquaintance. In this point of view the text is suggestive. As a congregation we hope to commemorate the Lord's death on the last Sabbath of the month, and I thought the words appropriate to impress us with the need of soul preparation in view of that solemn occasion. The text suggests three thoughts to my mind.

(1) *That He may not come.*
I believe that there were many present at the feast who were afraid that He would absent Himself because of the hatred of His enemies. The attitude of the Pharisees and the priests to Jesus was well known. They made no secret of their hostility and hatred towards Him. They publicly disapproved of His works and teaching, and they sought to persuade and prevent the people from listening to Him. They had determined to kill Him. The friends of Jesus might reasonably suppose that He would expose Himself to danger. On other occasions He absented Himself because of this.

And have we not reason to fear that He may absent Himself from our solemn occasions for similar reasons? There is much in our world, in our locality, and in our lives, that might prevent Him from honouring us with His sacred presence and blessing.

There is much *in the ungodly, unregenerate world* to prevent His coming into our midst. There is open flagrance and boldness in sin. Indeed, instead of being ashamed of sin, men and women boast of their sins. The mad craze for pleasure has carried our young and old as it were on a tidal wave, and they have lost their sense of proportion. They have no time for personal or private religion, and they pursue the lower pleasures of life as their chief end. They live for these, forgetting that the wages of sin is death.

Again, there is carelessness about the means of grace and the Lord's day. They have no time for church or religion; many never enter a church, and as for the Lord's Day, it is openly desecrated. Sabbath work is so common that men have no qualms of conscience about it. In the name of a supposed necessity, the attraction of double pay leads them to trample the holy day

under foot, forgetting that the curse of God is on every penny that is to be
earned by desecrating the Sabbath.

Again, there is a disrespect for the godly. The Lord's witnesses are
slighted, ridiculed and treated with contempt. They are considered to be
narrow-minded, and living in the past. Those of you who wish your children
to grow up as decent citizens, must take them in hand, lest they be carried
away in the flood of modern indifference to the things that matter.

But there is also much *in God's professing people* that provokes His
displeasure, and on account of which He might remove His candlestick
from its honoured place. There is lack of faithfulness, lack of interest in His
cause and His coming, lack of spiritual discernment, coldness, worldly
conformity, trifling and trafficking in sin.

And is there not much *in the pious believer* that occasions him real
anxiety lest He provokes His Lord to stay away, when he needs the divine
blessing. When believers look into their hearts and examine their lives, they
find much which occasions them real sorrow of heart and penitence of soul.
They mourn over the hardness of their heart, their broken vows, their
backsliding, their lack of wrestling in prayer, their light views of sin. These
and other reasons cause anxiety that the Lord may absent Himself from our
solemn season.

(2) Hope that He will come

In view of what has been said, the prospects seem dark. Truly, if He should
deal with us according to our sins, He would not visit us at all. But there
are certain considerations which stimulate the hope and inspire the prayer
that He might favour us and visit His vine.

Those who wished His presence at the feast of Jerusalem might expect
Him to come because of *His own respect for the law of God.* By that law
it was required that all males should attend the feast of the Passover. Hence
they might expect Him, who showed such unquestioned respect to the law
and to the prophets, to attend. Jesus came to fulfil the law and the prophets,
and in order to fulfil all righteousness, He attended the fixed ordinance with
unfailing regularity. He would be there as a worshipper. Wonderful! He
who was the Eternal Son worshipped His Father as His God.

We too might reasonably expect His gracious visitation notwithstanding
our unworthiness. There is His unchanging character. Mercy is ever the
same; on that His people base their hope and expectation. There is His
promise to be where two or three gather in His name. When God's people
pray for His presence, and wrestle with Him to favour them at such a time,
when they plead His promise and seek His honour in the good of souls and
the increase of His kingdom, He will not fail them.

And then there is the sacrament itself. It is His own institution. He shall be there whether we see Him or not. Oh pray that you may behold His beauty, and enjoy tokens of His regard.

(3) Evidences of His Presence

When He is there, there is a deeper longing for Him - a longing for the presence, and fellowship of Christ. There will be a unity of presence among God's people, and a manifest desire to confer about religious experiences and discuss the Word of God. There will be a spiritual mind, that hates and seeks to mortify sin. There will be a deeper desire for fuller consecration and loyalty to Christ.

In these ways, the believer's conscious experience assures him of the Lord's presence with him at all times and in all things. The Christian's spirit will be conscious of the refreshing power of the Holy Spirit. Feelings will be aroused and centred on divine things. There will be a conscious presence of the Holy Spirit.

Does it matter to you whether Christ comes? Will His absence trouble you? Some will have sweet moments of His nearness. Will we?

95. THE SADNESS AND THE GLADNESS

Jesus saith unto her, Woman, why weepest thou? whom seekest thou? She, supposing him to be the gardener, saith unto him, Sir, if thou have borne him hence, tell me where thou hast laid him and I will take him away
(John 20:15).

There was never a morning like this. An event occurred, the like of which was never heard of before, and which determines the view which men must form of the crucified Christ. Here we read of women, who came early to the sepulchre, and were astonished to find the stone removed, and the grave empty apart from the graveclothes. An angel comforts and assures them that 'He is not here, for He is risen'. They are surprised and evidently did not expect what they found. Here we are told that Mary Magdalene went to tell Peter and John, and with them turned to the tomb, where she lingered, after they left, with one wondering while the other believed, and we read of what transpired at the tomb.

(1) Mary in her sadness

We do not know very much about her - her history is somewhat obscure, but enough is told to keep her name on record for ever. She evidently belonged to a township called Magdala, on the west shore of the Sea of Galilee. Some think she was a woman of ill-fame, a notable sinner, but there is no evidence of that. She has been identified as the woman who was a sinner, who washed the Lord's feet with tears and dried them with her hair. This was surely a deed of which Mary Magdalene was capable, but cannot be proved in her favour; the feet-washer was from Capernaum, while she was from Magdala. She was the subject of a miracle, for out of her the Lord is said to have cast seven devils, as a result of which she became a transformed person.

She was a follower of Jesus, and of the worthy women who ministered to Him of their substance, and was stricken with grief by the cruel treatment her master received. She was among those last at the cross, and witnessed his burial, and with others desired to supplement, or perfect, the embalming, so was among those first at the grave on the resurrection morning. She sees the stone removed, and grave empty, and hears the testimony of the angel.

Her present grief is the empty grave, and her not knowing where the body of Jesus was. She had seen it placed there, but was not there now. She cannot solve the riddle. She assumes that cruel hands, or the gardener, removed the sacred body which she desired to handle and embalm. So after John and Peter returned, she lingers on, looking into the empty grave, and her heart crying out with tears of sorrow.

This answers to the experience of seeking believers, who, when Christ is lost to the senses, and silent, look for Him where He is not - in the grave of past experiences they seek him, weeping. Their feelings are cruelly rent by the tempter, who seeks to convince them that all is lost, a fake and a dream. Yet they seek Him, the same Jesus, who was crucified and buried. But they often seek Him in the wrong place, where they last saw Him, but He is no longer there. They cry 'Oh that I knew where I might find Him' and resolve, that if He is found, He will not be lost to them again.

(2) *Mary in her gladness*
Several lessons may be found here.

Only seekers find. It is true that Jesus finds us first, and moves us to seek Him. Never was He sought otherwise. The finders are ever seekers, enquirers, pleaders.

Christ may be near us, speaking to us, without us knowing it. He may be speaking to our minds and hearts, questioning and instructing and emptying us, before He reveals Himself to us in a convincing manner. It was so with the two on the Emmaus road, and it was so with Mary Magdalene. He may be in disguise as He was here - she thought He was the gardener.

Christ is known only when He reveals Himself. His method of revealing Himself varies, and yet is similar in essence. He employs ways and means suited to prepare us for His self-disclosure. One method is by asking questions, to draw us out to state our motives and desires. He employed this method while on earth ('Whom do men say that I am?'; 'whom say ye that I am?'; 'lovest thou me?'; 'will ye also go away?'). That He does still, through the reading and preaching of His Word. So He asked Mary two questions.

Why weep? Some do not know the reason for which they weep. Jesus would not have it so. He would have her state the why and wherefore of her tears. Sometimes tears are misplaced, like the women who followed Christ to Calvary, in pity, and whom He forbade. It is not pity He wants, but faith and love. In the church there are different kinds of tears. Some weep for common trials. It is as if they alone had adversity, and may be dishonouring the Lord by rebelling in spirit against their portion. Others weep for soul concern. And there is cause! 'Weep for yourselves' - for your sin, guilt, waywardness, declension, unfruitfulness - tears of penitence, self-condemnation and shame. And others weep still for a lost Jesus, as here. They know what they weep for - an absent Lord. They tasted of His love, His fellowship and presence, and are troubled that these are now lost to their consciousness and denied them.

Whom seek ye? Here He is more specific - He focuses the point of their enquiry. Not 'What seek ye?' but 'WHOM?' By these two questions He cleaned out her heart wound, that He might reveal Himself. He would have her name the cause and object of her tears - 'They have taken away my Lord, and I know not'. She had Him all along, and she knew not, in her desire, her longing and her love.

His self-disclosure gladdens the heart. He reveals Himself. He made her aware that He knew her, her case, her sorrow and her desire. Thereby she knew Him. And when He is known, the soul loses itself in Him - He is all, 'Rabboni, Master'. He is appropriated and surrendered to. Love is possessive - she would embrace Him. She is hindered! Why? Did He not ask others to handle Him? Why prevent her? Because she did not need the evidence of the touch to convince her, as they did. She was now to live by faith and not by sight and touch.

To know Christ savingly implies seeing the relations of all the doctrines of His Person and Work - His birth, life, death, resurrection and ascension. These are what constitute Him a Saviour.

(3) *Mary in her Service*

He sent her on an errand to the brethren. 'Go tell.' It is evident that God has a place for the ministry of women. In the Old Testament and New they are acknowledged by God, e.g., Miriam, Deborah, Manoah's wife, the widow of Sarepta who ministered to Elijah. In the New Testament they are countless. This is an honour to women, who was first in sin, now first in service to Himself and His church. And women have room for similar service - they have encouraged and strengthened the servants of the Lord. We must not despise them, or belittle their contribution - they often shame men.

This did not constitute her in office in the church, as an elder or preacher, but in the capacity of a servant to the church, a private ministry, for which she was fitted. Women have often been favoured with unique nearness to God in secret, and have been useful to His servants.

Later in the evening, with Mary present, we believe, He appeared to the gathered company, and they were all glad when they saw the Lord. This was what Mary had longed for, had sought, and now found.

96. CHRIST AND OUR DOUBTS

And Thomas answered and said unto Him, My Lord and my God. Jesus saith unto him, Thomas, because thou hast seen me, thou hast believed: blessed are they that have not seen, and yet have believed (John 21:28-29).

On the evening of the resurrection day, the disciples (and, according to Luke, some others) were gathered together, presumably in that upper room where the last supper had been celebrated. They resorted thither for fear of the Jews. They probably suspected that the great and blessed event which restored their hope would incite the authorities to arrest them, for they had already denied the fact of the resurrection, and had charged the disciples with having taken the body of Jesus.

While gathered together, and we believe, engaged in meditation and prayer, the Lord Himself appeared in their midst and assured them, if that were needed, that He was risen from the dead. But Thomas was not there, and by his absence he missed that first interview with the risen Lord, and some anxious days were to lapse before he was to be favoured with a similar interview. And where was Thomas? We do not know, but we know where he should have been. In the light of what is stated in this passage about him, we notice three different aspects of his experience.

(1) *Thomas in the grip of doubt*

Thomas was one of the disciples. He had been with Christ from the beginning of His public ministry. He had listened to His wonderful addresses, witnessed His miracles, and was profoundly impressed by the Lord's life and teaching. On several occasions he appears in the Gospel story, and his remarks suggest that he was a man who quickly observed the dark and discouraging side of things, and these loomed so large in his view that he readily gave way to moody fear. He was of a despondent temperament. Once, when Christ intimated His intention to revisit the frontiers of Judea, Thomas could see nothing but the worst, even death, so he said 'Let us go and die with Him'. This at least tells us that he could not bear the thought of living without Christ. And again, when Christ, in His farewell address in John 14 said that he must shortly leave them and go to the Father, Thomas sees in the departure of his Master the extinction of his hope. And now, when the Lord is dead and buried, Thomas probably wished to retire into solitude, there to nurse his despondency and doubt.

There is a sense in which his doubts seemed quite reasonable to himself. The Person to whom he had linked his hope and his faith for time and for eternity, had been put to open shame. He was dead and buried, and with Him his hope crashed. The object of his faith was under the shadow and blight of death, and to him death was the end of all his expectations. There could be no benefit from a dead person. And resurrection seemed impossible and incredible.

But his doubts were more unreasonable than reasonable. This is clear from the fact that he discredited the testimony of his brethren. He knew them to be honest and truthful men, and it was unfair and unkind, even cruel, that he should treat their testimony as unreliable. They stated unmistakable evidence - the grave was empty. He was seen alive. Angels had declared that Christ was risen. They saw Him themselves. Then there was their joy - the change in their countenance, and manner. Then Thomas ignored the reference of Christ Himself to the fact. He was indeed blind to the facts. And he required himself what would be no valid proof, even if granted - the evidence of the senses.

(2) *Thomas in the grip of Christ*

There is a deep and profound sense in which believers are always secure. The Lord Jesus assured His disciples that they would never perish. This was true of Peter, for Christ prayed that his faith would not fail, and it was also the case with Thomas, even when he was the helpless slave of doubt.

Thomas, through the persuasion of the disciples, rejoined their company in that upper room where they waited in prayer, meditation, thanksgiving and expectation. They were indeed a happy company, except for Thomas himself, expecting a re-visit from the risen Lord. The trouble with us is that we do not expect anything. It was not so with them, and their expectation was rewarded, the Lord reappeared. Thomas was there, and that was enough - now his doubts are all gone.

He is in the grip of Christ. He is restored and fascinated by the wonder and reality of the Lord's presence. Christ singled him out and invited him to reach out his hand. The words imply a direct rebuke for his unbelief, and unfair treatment of the disciples' testimony. Does he require more proof than they? Will he insist on putting his finger into the print of the nails? Oh no - Thomas is overwhelmed by wonder, joy, love. Yes and by shame too. Who can measure or conceive the depth of his shame for his unbelief. Did he put his fingers into the print of the nails? I do not think so. He was absolutely satisfied. The evidence was convincing. His soul, mind, heart were at rest in Jesus. It was the most glorious moment of his life - the hour of the triumph of his faith - doubt is for ever banished.

Have you had a similar experience? Can you recall a time in your life when you doubted his love, or power, or willingness to save you? When in the time of your despondency you saw the truth of his risen life and power to save, and were able to say 'This is my rest, here still I'll stay, for I do like it well.'

Visits by the risen Christ to His church are not infrequent. That was His promise. 'I will not leave you comfortless. I will come to you.' But remember that He reveals Himself only in the company of friends. We have seen and felt it. See and don't miss it. You should be in your place amongst the friends of Jesus if you wish to see Him. Remember what Thomas missed, and then, through being in his place, what he found.

(3) *Thomas in the grip of faith*
'My Lord and my God.' Doubt has vanished; certainty has taken its place. This has not happened through the natural vision or senses. Such may help faith, but will not produce it. Faith goes deeper than senses. Deeper than what a man sees or hears. In that interview with Christ He calls for the exercise of faith. Christ Himself is the object of faith. Faith rests upon Him, and appropriates all His resources.

Thomas is now fully satisfied with the truth of the resurrection, and with it many glorious truths opened up to his soul. Now he sees the meaning of the cross and realises that it was not a calamity but the appointed way in which salvation could be procured for sinners. Now he sees salvation accomplished; sin destroyed, death abolished, Satan robbed of his prey. The Lord is alive.

Here we see faith in exercise - 'MY Lord and MY God'. Faith appropriating, resting, receiving, knowing, adoring, loving. It was a confession of Christ as his portion - 'whom have I in heaven but thee'. Such faith is indispensable to the saving of the soul. Beware of asking natural vision, or miracle, or material evidence. Blessed are those who believe, and have not seen.

97. PETER IN THE PASTOR'S HANDS

He said unto him the third time, Simon, son of Jonas, lovest thou me? Peter was grieved because he said unto him the third time, Lovest thou me? And he said unto him, Lord, thou knowest all things; thou knowest that I love thee. Jesus saith unto him, Feed my sheep (John 21:17).

Peter had already seen the risen Lord. There had been that interview on the resurrection morning, on which the seal of secrecy is impressed. There were two other interviews when Peter along with the other disciples received the Lord's benediction - the first, alone; the second, in company. On this, the fourth meeting of which there is record, Peter is restored to his office and usefulness in the church. The scene is by the sea of Tiberias, after the Lord had revealed his identity through the miraculous catch of fish. They were seated round a meal, listening eagerly to what He said, and then Christ turned to Peter and addressed him with a threefold question, designed to elicit a confession which is a measuring rod for all believers to the end of time.

(1) *The Master's questioning*
The question was 'Lovest thou me?' It bears on love to Christ. Now this concerns all believers as well as Peter. This is the real test of discipleship. He does not enquire about other essential graces, such as repentance, godly sorrow, faith, hope etc. He is chiefly interested in our love - in the state of our heart. For if the heart is right, all other feelings will be in order. If not, all is in vain. This is Paul's view in 1 Corinthians 13. This is a distinguishing mark of a believer. And if any man love not the Lord Jesus Christ, he is accursed.

It is evident that the Lord requires our love. Napoleon once asked 'What is it that a man expects most of his friends?' The answer is this - love. He asks for it, and He gets it. It is the response of the renewed heart to His own love - we love Him because He first loved us. He desires it. There is nothing

He desires of us more than this. Men often seek friendship of superiors in ability, station and influence. Christ, on the contrary, looks down to seek our love who are unworthy of his attention even if we were sick with love to Him. He values it. More than any service you can render, because it gives to Him His proper place. It is His reward; it pleases Him, honours Him and delights Him because it shows a corrected heart; hence the Father loves them and delights in them (John 16:27).

The degree of love is enquired into *more than these*. 'What is it that is supreme in your affections? These - or Christ?' This is a matter for inquiry. Opinions differ as to the meaning of this.

Some think that Christ meant the boats and the nets, on the grounds that they were nearby and were their means of livelihood. It is supposed that when Peter went out fishing that night, he was resolved to adhere to his former calling, because he felt the Lord had no further use for him. This view is plausible and possible. There were cases of men turning away from Christ for the sake of loaves and fishes. Besides, men prefer the course of least resistance, and their own comforts, to the extent of neglecting the Lord's command and work. This is a cause for self-examination.

Others think that He meant - 'lovest thou me more than thou lovest the disciples?' Love to the disciples is legitimate, and commanded. The standard measure is 'As I love you', and it is not possible to exceed that. That cannot be the point, because love to the church implies and presupposes love to Christ, and is indeed inspired by it. Only in proportion to our love to Him can we love the disciples, and as we see Christ in them.

Probably the true sense is 'lovest thou me more than they love me?' On a former occasion, Peter had professed the most ardent affection for his Master, and I believe he was honest, but he was too self-confident, and perhaps boastful and daring in saying 'though all should forsake thee, I will not - even to prison and to death'. Within a few hours he furnished an illustration of human frailty by a threefold denial. And now the Lord desires to elicit from him a confession of non-comparison. He addressed him by his old name, Simon, to remind him of his weakness. Is he now confident in himself, still daring and boastful? Will he now put himself forward as he had formerly done?

The reason for this was that he might be restored to office. Three times he had denied his Lord, by which he belied his former profession. This must now be obliterated by a threefold confession of real soul affection. At the first interview he was assured of a full and free pardon, and now, on the basis of his love, he is to be confirmed in office. Thus he enquired not merely about the measure of love, but its real centre.

(2) *The Reply of the disciple*

'Thou knowest that I love thee.' Three times the question is asked, and three times Peter answers in the affirmative. Yes, Peter loved his Lord, he knew it and felt it, and he could not deny it, although he shrank from using the higher term, yet he loved Him more than ever, more intelligently and with greater cause than before.

'Thou knowest.' Here Peter appeals to Christ's omniscience to witness and judge his heart - the reality of his love. It is a terror to hypocrites that the Lord knows their hearts; they can never cite this omniscience as a witness. But it is a comfort to believers.

He is more careful with his confession now. He weighs his words. Experience taught him not to be too boastful or daring. He no longer pretends to love Him more than others - he would probably give John the greater credit for love and loyalty. He no longer says 'I will die for thee', and yet he did. He would now allow deeds to speak louder than words. He uses milder terms for his affection for his Lord. And Christ is satisfied with this.

It was sincere and honest. He was grieved at the third asking of the question. Perhaps it reminded him of his past conduct - hence, with all earnestness he appeals to the omniscience of the Saviour. This was honouring to Jesus.

Believers are not always able to declare their love, and yet they cannot, dare not, deny it. They are not, of course, of the same strength of emotion - they feel chilled, at times, as if under a cloud, and fear they have come short. This is because they look inward rather than outward. They consult feelings rather than the principle of love. You do not study your feelings to infer your love to your friend, wife, parent, child. Love is a principle which determines the attitude of mind, heart and life towards the loved one. We do not bother with inference in such cases - our feelings are not always of the same strength, yet our love manifests itself. But you say, 'Look at my sins, my evil heart'. If Peter looked only to that, he too might question his love. True, a sudden fall like Peter's is less heinous than a worldly, selfish life. It is said that ants eat up the carcase of the buffalo sooner than the lion - it is true of our sins also.

But when God is near, it is easier to trace and confess. You may shrink from claiming higher attitudes of love, but you can at times honestly say with Peter - 'I love thee', and with the psalmist, 'I love the Lord'. This reveals itself in action and admiration - such love to Christ delights in hearing of Christ being honoured and His cause prospering.

(3) *The Duty of the Servant*

Here we have a commission given to Peter. It is stated in the form of a duty
- 'feed my lambs' and 'feed my sheep'. Both lambs and sheep need feeding.
Both are the objects of the shepherd's care. Lambs require special feeding
- the first elements of knowledge, the milk of the word. Those of more
mature experience and knowledge require stronger food, and ought to be led
deeper into the truth, and into God's dealings with the church.

Peter was qualified for this. What a minister he would be! He had the
experience, knowledge and the necessary grace for the work. He knew
himself. He knew his Lord, and he knew the operation of grace in his own
soul. He knew what was suited to the flock of Christ. He could speak from
experience and knowledge, and thus feed both the lambs and the sheep.
Food had to be prepared and distributed, and Peter was equal to his charge.
We have only to read his sermons and epistles to see how he could feed, and
the matter with which he fed the flock.

There are duties for all who love the Lord, and privileges of service too.
All are not called to be preachers, but they are called to obedience and
service, to help the weak and cheer the strong in the way and in their fight
with evil. Share your knowledge, experience and confidence with others.
Our failings and unworthiness must not silence us - it did not prevent or
silence our Lord. It is our privilege and duty to follow Him. Love to Christ
constrains us to further service. Let us abide near Him. Let us speak often
to Him. Let us seek His company, and that of His acquaintances.

98. A LIFE TRANSFORMED

And he trembling and astonished said, Lord, what wilt thou have me to do?
And the Lord said unto him, Arise and go into the city,
and it shall be told thee what thou must do (Acts 9:6).

Here we have an account of the conversion of Saul of Tarsus, afterwards
known as Paul the apostle. That there is such a thing as conversion is a fact
of human experience attested by the Bible, and the change it effects in the
lives of men.

Conversion is not a thing to be ashamed of, or dreaded, as if it were to
deprive you of the joys of life. On the contrary, it is the most blessed and
desirable experience in the world. Indeed, it is the most essential blessing
in life, for if you are not converted you cannot enter the kingdom of God.

What shall it profit a man though he were to gain the whole world, yet lose his own soul?

The text before us covers Saul's past, present and future. We will consider it in its context, and see the wonder, nature and reality of God's grace.

(1) *Saul, the straight man on the Damascus Road*

Let us think of this man's background. He was a young man from Tarsus, a city of Cilicia, the son of Jewish parents. He was educated in Jerusalem, at the feet of Gamaliel, a noted Jewish lawyer. According to his religious persuasion, he was a Pharisee of the strictest sect of his race. In his zeal for the teaching and tradition of the Jews, he was violently incensed with insatiable hatred against Christians, whom he regarded as heretics, or advocates of a false religion. By persecuting them he thought he was rendering service to God. He was, in his own estimation, a straight and upright man.

Here we see him vested with authority from the chief priests and the Jewish Council, or Sanhedrin, to go to Damascus, to seek out and arrest any Christians, and bring them to Jerusalem. Such was his mission. But what happened? He himself is arrested! Suddenly at noon a dazzling light from Heaven shone around him and his companions. A voice personal to Saul spoke to him, charging him with his outrageous conduct.

There is instant prostration. He fell to the ground, and enquired, 'Who art thou Lord?' The voice replied, 'I am Jesus whom thou persecutest; it is hard for thee to kick against the pricks'. These 'pricks' were obviously very personal to him, perhaps they were pricks of conscience which he was suppressing, or the memory and courage of Christians, such as Stephen, and many of whom we have no record at all.

But now he is convicted of his wrongdoing and his ignorance. He trembles with fear. There is no excusing of self. He finds himself sinful, guilty and answerable to Christ. Some have no use or respect for this so-called religion of fear, as if it were a sign of physical or mental weakness. But when God, by His word and Spirit, speaks to men, convincing them of sin, their minds and their consciences consent, and they become concerned as men who are answerable to God.

Now, this is in some degree true in all conversions - there is light and a voice, the Word of God and the Spirit of God are at work. And Saul now owns his sin, acknowledges his sin, and desires reform. God directs him to Damascus.

(2) *Saul on the street called Straight*

We find him here in real straits. The proud, self-righteous and cruel man is a broken man. He is in real distress, humbled, perplexed, trembling, confused, and at a loss as to what he ought to do. This highly gifted and highly intelligent man finds himself incapable of resolving his dilemma.

All he can do is pray. This is true of converts. They pray. He does so as never before. As a Jew, as a Pharisee, he used to pray in his own way as a religious duty. But now he prays as never before. There is here, in one person, the difference between the prayers of the Pharisee and the publican of Luke 18. As a Pharisee he thought he knew a lot about religion, but now he bemoans his ignorance, and seeks light and mercy.

His prayer is answered. God sends His servant Ananias to release Saul from his bonds. Ananias had heard of Saul, and his purpose in going to Damascus. Ananias was naturally reluctant to respond to the divine direction, till assured by God that Saul was a chosen vessel. So Ananias went, and Saul received his sight.

Saul knew that it was Jesus who had spoken to him on the Damascus Road. Ananias introduces himself as sent by Jesus - 'Brother Saul...' We may be sure that Ananias had much to tell about Jesus, as the Saviour of sinners. What light must have shone into his soul, as he apprehended in Jesus God's way of salvation. A way wholly worthy of God, in harmony with the Scriptures, whereby the righteousness of God is revealed in justifying the ungodly who believe in Jesus.

Ananias also acquainted Saul with what God would have him do and endure for His sake. If he was the means of inflicting suffering upon Christians, he himself must endure much, to bear witness for Christ, and not be ashamed of his hope.

(3) *Saul on the straight Way*

Saul had received ample evidence that Jesus was God's appointed Saviour, and he closed in with Christ, and heartily embraced the will of God - 'what wilt thou have me to do?' What a wonder it must have been to Saul that God so graciously saved him. This was God's way - the very opposite of man's way. The way of mercy and grace.

Saul joined himself to the company of believers, not to arrest them, but to rejoice with them in God their Saviour. He assured them that he was now one of them. This was another evidence of conversion.

He went out and preached Christ as Saviour and Lord. With much ability and power he confounded disputers, whether Jews or Gentiles, proving from the Scriptures that Jesus is the Christ, the Saviour of the world. This was real conversion, the doing of the Lord. Would you be converted?

Young folk, would you? You say, 'yes, but not yet'. But now is His time. The portion of those who reject Him is Hell for ever. Perhaps someone says 'What can I do? I must wait for God's time'. Are you so sure this is not it? He appeals in the Gospel to each and all - 'Return, why will ye die?'

99. JUSTIFIED BY FAITH

*Therefore, being justified by faith, we have peace
with God through our Lord Jesus Christ* (Romans 5:1).

In these words the apostle Paul defines the standing and possession of the believer in Christ - he is justified by faith and has peace with God. Justification is a fact in the believer's life, and it is important that we should have clear views of its nature and implications; otherwise we shall have only hazy concepts of the way of salvation. This doctrine affords the believer a solid basis of hope; it humbles our pride and inspires our gratitude to God, to whom the entire glory in our salvation belongs.

(1) *The Nature of Justification*
This is one of the big words of the Bible, called the article of a standing or falling church.

The basic religious question is our relation to God. How can man be just with God? It is evident that man is at variance with God - this appears from the basic fact of conscious sin and conscious guilt in man, and the cause of guilt is sin. Man himself is incapable of rectifying it, because he is all wrong in himself, and so incapable of good. This the apostle shows in chapter 3. Man cannot righten or justify himself before God. But what is impossible with man is possible with God.

What is justification? It is a judicial, or forensic term, that is, a law term, regarding the state of a person in relation to law. It does not mean to make one holy or righteous. When a judge justifies an accused person, he does not make him a good or upright man; he simply declares, or pronounces, that in his judgement he is not guilty of the charges against him, but is upright in terms of the law relevant to his case. Thus, justification is a declaration respecting the relation of a person to the law, which the judge is required to administer. It stands opposed to condemnation.

But here we have a unique situation. It is not the justification of righteous or innocent persons, but of persons who are proved guilty, and wicked, and are condemned to a great death. How can such be justified? It is humanly impossible - only the innocent can be justified, and the guilty must be condemned. But the apostle declares that God does what man cannot do - He justifies the ungodly, and He does so in a manner consistent with the honour of law.

In God's justification of the ungodly, much more is implied than mere declaration. There is, of course, no deviation from the rule that what is declared to be is presupposed to be. The peculiarity of God's action consists in this, that He causes to be what He declares to be. What God does in this case is, that He constitutes the ungodly righteous, and consequently declares them to be righteous.

In the justification of sinners, there is a constitutive act as well as a declarative act, or, to put it otherwise, the declarative act is also a constitutive act. This is illustrated in Romans 5:17-19. The principles of representation and imputation are as inherent in our justification as in the fall by sin. It is on the ground of the imputation of Christ's righteousness that the ungodly are justified and declared righteous. In that act of imputation they are both constituted and declared righteous.

This is purely an act of grace, completed at once and never repeated. It is distinct from regeneration and sanctification, and yet implies them. This may be illustrated by the respective acts of a surgeon and a judge. The surgeon does something in or on us, the judge is concerned with our legal standing only. So regeneration is inward, while justification concerns our legal standing. Similarly, forgiveness is included in justification, but justification is much more than forgiveness.

(2) *The Basis of Justification*
There could be no justification without a first cause - and this could only be in a manner consistent with law and justice; else God would be acting in an arbitrary manner, which He cannot do.

Our justification is said to be in and through Christ Jesus. He is the alone basis of this act of grace towards guilty men. He, as the surety of sinners, by the ministry of His life, and by His death, secured a righteousness on the grounds of which God can, consistently justify the ungodly. This is clearly set forth in verses 15-21, where the principles of representation and imputation are presented. As Adam represented the race, and his sin became theirs by imputation, so Christ, as surety, represents the church, and his wrought-out righteousness is imputed to the believer in justification. This is declared to be the righteousness of God, inasmuch as God required it, received it and bestows it on the ungodly. Thus, God appears just when He justifies the ungodly.

But there is also an instrumental cause - we are said to be justified by faith. This we have not of ourselves; it is the gift of God, wrought in us by God's Word and Spirit. Faith comes by hearing, and hearing the Word of God. Faith is the act of a quickened, living soul in relation to Christ and His righteousness, as the alone basis of acceptance with God.

By faith we apprehend Christ's accomplished righteousness, so suited to our need, and we receive and rest upon it for acceptance with God as a righteousness which covers us. By this faith we are made one with Christ in His righteousness. As soon as the knot is tied which unites the soul to Christ, the change of state takes place, and the one who was formerly a child of wrath becomes accepted in the beloved.

This faith has a transforming effect. It ensures changed habits, interests and a way of life. Old things pass away, and new things attract.

(3) *The Result of Justification*

We have peace with God. This tells us that apart from Christ, and justification in Him, there is no peace with God. By nature we are alienated from God by sin, and God is at variance with us and says 'there is no peace to the wicked'. But Christ has secured our reconciliation, and in justification a state of peace is established.

There is a false peace which many mistake for the real. Many seek peace in forgetting the wrong, danger and the judgement to come. They find their peace in sin, or in the general goodness of God. Such peace is unfounded.

Here is well-grounded peace. It is 'with God'. He is pacified to us, and we to Him. The overtures of peace began with Him, He instituted the means and declares the conditions of peace. It is legal peace, regarding our legal relation. We have it only in Christ - its basis and channel are through faith in Him.

It is conscious peace. When the believing soul discerns the terms of peace, and embraces them and rests in them, then the mind finds rest, and the burdened conscience is relieved of its sting, and a sense of peace with God pervades the soul.

Christ said 'My peace I give to you'. It is great to feel that the God you knew was against you is now reconciled to you in Christ.

This peace of soul in Christ is accompanied by dispeace! What a paradox, yet true! If in peace with God, there is dispeace with sin, self, the world. The pacified conscience is alive, sensitive, authoritative - it censures and condemns sin. Rather a living conscience disturbing false peace than a dead one, lulling you to sleep the sleep of death. Here then is the standing of Christians in Christ. Do you know anything of it? Rest not without it!

100. LIVING IN THE SPIRIT

*For if ye live after the flesh ye shall die: but if ye through the Spirit do
mortify the deeds of the body, ye shall live* (Romans 8:13).

The apostle is speaking of the privileges of the believer in Christ - freed from
condemnation in Christ, and made a partaker of the Spirit of Christ. This
Spirit indwells them and works in them to will and to do, and attests their
sonship. He then proceeds to speak of their obligation to Christ, not to live
after the flesh but after the Spirit. It is a Christian duty to live a holy and
circumspect life. 'Be ye holy, for I am holy.' The Gospel is a call to
holiness. To urge this, he says in verse 12, 'ye are debtors not to the flesh,
to live according to the flesh'. The reason behind this is illustrated and
enforced by our text.

(1) *Life after the flesh*
There is such a life. 'Flesh' means our sinful nature and tendencies,
according to which men live in an unregenerate state. Sin has alienated man
from God, and enslaved him, and it is a power that works in him, and has
so perverted his nature that it masters him. It is represented as a law which
reigns in his members.

Thus our nature as defiled and enslaved, inclines to sin. That is the
element in which it moves - against God, for the carnal mind is enmity to
God. Led by sinful propensities - there is the idea of the flesh leading, and
sinful man living in pursuit of its cravings, holding to the flesh as the guide
and compass of life. Hence in the experience of such a man, God is not in
his thoughts at all.

Such a life issues in death - 'ye shall die'. There is a sense in which such
a man is already dead - he died spiritually the moment he sinned, and he is
termed dead in trespasses and in sins. When the Spirit of God departed from
him, he became dead spiritually, and so incapable of spiritual exercises, or
of attaining fellowship with God.

In addition, sin made man mortal, that is, subject to natural death. The
seeds of mortality entered his nature by the first sin - oh, what a fruitful seed
sin is! And the carnal life is deepening this death, and hastening it.

The end of sin is eternal death - for the impenitent. God cannot but give
the earned wages, and the wages of sin is death. The service of the flesh then
serves you no good - you are not obliged to live to it - it is an enemy enslaving
and ruining you. If you please the flesh you die. That is the only reward it
gives.

(2) *Life after the Spirit*

This is the believer's life. It is an imparted life. It is not self-attained, but given. The soul of the believer is quickened by Christ through His Spirit. God puts His Spirit in the hearts of His people, and he indwells them. This is what distinguishes them in the world. 'Ye are not in the flesh, but in the Spirit.' This Spirit, then, is in the possession of the believer in Christ. This Spirit enlightens, liberates and attests our sonship, and assists our infirmities.

Yet those who have this life are in constant danger from the flesh. They never saw or realised it before. Though in a state of grace, the flesh is still with them, as another nature. They carry it like a burden which wearies them, hinders their walk and spoils their comforts.

The apostle warns Christians to guard against it, lest it ensnare and enslave them, lest it get occasion against them, or become in any shape an incentive to sin. John warns Christians not to love the world, or the things of the world; so believers are constantly in danger, and must beware. The flesh can do a lot of harm, even if your soul is saved, it can rob you of comfort, joy and usefulness. There is such a thing as a sleeping sickness in the spiritual realm.

Our duty is to mortify the deeds of the body, that is, our sinful inclinations in which our bodies are active, our sinful habits. If we do not mortify, or kill, them, they are likely to kill us. How do we do this? By starving them; by refusing to yield or gratify them, by learning to say 'No'! Sin is meat and sweet to the flesh; this self denial is a slow and painful process. We often get impatient with slow progress, and fear we are losing the battle. Indeed, the more you try to mortify sin, the more fierce it becomes. The more starved a lion becomes, the more it growls and roars for its food. Yet at the same time it is getting weaker. So the more you resist sin, the more Satan will inspire the flesh to sin.

This is possible only through the Spirit. Of ourselves we can do nothing, but the Spirit helps our infirmities. The Spirit helps us to overcome, forsake sin and mortify the deeds of the flesh. This is the power of living in the Spirit. But it is not the Spirit who does this - we do it. By dependence on the influence and power of the Spirit, we can work against ourselves.

The result of this is - 'ye shall live', that is, enjoy the life of which the Holy Spirit is author and sustainer. We have this life now, if the Spirit dwells in us. And we will thrive on it, and increase in the knowledge of Him in proportion as the Spirit dwells in us. This life will shape us and manifest itself in action that is in harmony with the truth.

We shall live and grow in a measure in which we shall be able to mortify the flesh. As sin is mastered, you enjoy divine fellowship. This is progress in holiness. We are apt to think that there can be no progress in holiness in this life, because of the feelings of frustration. But this is the very reason why we must not give up the struggle.

And at last we shall live eternally, in our assigned inheritance in light, where nothing hinders our joy and our song. With the ransomed in all ages around the throne of God and of the Lamb. What then is our present relation to this Holy Spirit? And what are our future prospects? If we live in Him, our life is one of conflict with self; but deliverance is assured.

101. RUNNING TO OBTAIN

*Know ye not that they which run in a race run all, but one receiveth the prize? So run, that ye may obtain (*1 Corinthians 9:24).

These words are an exhortation, clothed in figurative language, to stress the need of Christian diligence and exertion in the heavenward race. The apostle had a glorious prize, an incorruptible crown in view, for the possession of which he aspired. In his quest of it he compares himself to the athletes of Ancient Greece, who had to undergo laborious discipline to fit them for the race and qualify them for the prize. He sought to inspire his readers with a desire and a determination to make sure of being among those who reach the goal and obtain the crown. In the text we have the idea of a race, rules for it, and the prize.

(1) *The Race*
The exhortation to run is addressed principally to Gentile Christians, and the imagery used is derived from the public games with which they were familiar in this day. These were the Isthmian Games, which were celebrated every third or fourth year in the neighbourhood of Corinth, and which were a great attraction for people from all parts of Greece.

These games consisted chiefly in leaping, boxing, wrestling, throwing weights and running. The apostle refers to two of these popular exercises to illustrate his own point. In verse 26 he refers to a fight which he wages, for there is a spiritual conflict which the believer has to wage ere he achieves the goal. It is a conflict, waged within the ambit of his own person, between his carnal nature and the new principle of life bestowed upon him by divine grace. Then he wages a daily conflict with the forces of darkness during his earthly pilgrimage. The arch enemy is like a roaring lion seeking to devour him, or hinder his progress. It is a conflict with spiritual wickedness in high places.

Here he speaks of a race. This was one of the principal and most exciting exercises of these games. Swiftness was regarded as an extraordinary virtue, and great pains were taken in order to excel in it. One reason why this was deemed so valuable an attainment among the ancient Greeks was that it fitted men eminently for war, as then conducted. It enabled them to make a sudden and unexpected onslaught on the enemy, or else a rapid retreat. David in his poetical lamentation for Saul and Jonathan says that 'they were swifter than eagles'. Swiftness was commendable for battle.

In our day we are familiar with the concept of a race. We have heard much about the arms race, the race of business, the race of profit, and now we have the race of battle raging the world over. In this mad race nations lose their independence, the very foundations of civilisation are at stake. And all this is through the greed of industrialists, and dictators who aim at world domination.

But there is another race, of which we hear little or nothing, though it is common to all men. It is the race to eternity. We are all runners in that race, and a momentous one it is. There is not a static moment in our life. It is constant motion towards the unknown. Nothing will arrest it. One generation comes and another goes. Here we have no abiding city. Oh that we sought one to come! It is sad to see men behaving as if they had nothing to gain or lose in view of eternity, forgetting that it is a fearful thing to fall into the hands of the living God.

Here Paul describes the Christian life as a race, a race for spiritual attainments. Surely that is something which should commend itself to us all. We all run the race to eternity, but how few run the race of preparation for it. And it is this race of preparation we are asked to join. The Christian race is fraught with difficulties and dangers. The way to Heaven is not a smooth one, and requires all the energy and diligence at our command. We shall not arrive there with folded arms. There is much opposition on the way, opposition within ourselves - our sluggish carnal nature is a drag and a hindrance, and is in alliance with outward opposition directed by the foul and vicious arch-enemy of man. Thus the enemies are numerous, and the battle at times will be fierce. Remember that if you get to Heaven it will be in spite of Hell. Satan is bent on your ruin. Will you co-operate with him to your own hurt and destruction? So much depends on the Christian race and fight, that we must not relax our efforts. We must work out our own salvation with fear and trembling; and yet no effort of ours can win the day. We must ever beware lest we substitute our own efforts for the Saviour. He must ever remain the foundation on which we build for eternity.

(2) *The Rules for the Race*

For these ancient games the competitors prepared themselves by a long course of discipline and exercise. Nothing was left undone that might help them secure the prize. In these games certain regulations had to be scrupulously observed.

The first was *fitness of body and mind.* This could only by attained by special care, and by abstinence from such things as might render them unfit for the race. They had to be temperate in all things. They had to abstain from such things as might enfeeble their effort, such as wine, luxurious living, and licentious indulgences. They had to keep the body fit, vigorous and supple. The world has furnished no stronger argument for total abstinence than the example of the dedicated athlete.

The next thing necessary for the race was the *utmost exertion.* They had to exert every muscle and sinew and use all their knowledge and skill. They had to adhere to the rules of the race, and avoid doing anything which might disqualify them, and thus lose the prize.

Now, in the race that is set before us, *much more than worldly fame* is involved. It includes the salvation of our souls, and the glory of Heaven which if we lose, nothing will remedy the loss. What shall it profit a man to gain the world and lose his soul? In running the Christian race, the old rules hold good.

There must be *fitness for this race.* We must be spiritually robust. This involves a right relation to God, the only source of spiritual life and strength. This is the first essential qualification for the race. We must give ourselves wholly to Him, and make a right relation with Him the grand business of our life. There must also be self-denial - the laying aside of every weight, and the sin that so easily besets us, the sin to which we are attached, and to which we so readily succeed. Thus there must be abstinence from what would deprive us of spiritual vitality. Abstain from every appearance of evil, that you may enjoy the strength that comes from God. If any man says he has fellowship with God, and walks in darkness, he lies, and knows not the truth. Nor must we allow ourselves to be diverted from our object by the appeals and attractions of the world. We must keep our eyes fully fixed on Christ, as our example, and the source of our strength. He is the ground of our hope. Our eye must be on Heaven as the end of the race.

Then there must be *exertion, or diligence in duty.* Christ said, 'Strive to enter in...' The way is narrow, and the gate to life strait. The going is hard, but the crown is sure to those who persevere to the end. One might think that Christians should rest at ease, on the assumption that they are in God's keeping, and consequently safe for time and for eternity. But Paul says 'Run!' 'Strive!'. We must not rest in present attainments, but strive after a higher and fuller apprehension of spiritual values. The Christian life, therefore is a race, constantly in motion and activity for spiritual advancement, seeking always to be acceptable to God, and enjoy tokens of His regard and fellowship.

(3) The Prize

Athletes run in order to obtain a prize, the prize of fame, honour, gain - to achieve the crown of world recognition as champions in their own sphere. What will the Christian run for?

A crown; but not a corruptible, fading, and uncertain crown, such as one might gain today and lose tomorrow, but a crown that is incorruptible, and shall never be lost if once gained. The blessings of Heaven that shall be bestowed on the Lord's people are often represented under the image of a crown. The lustre of their reward shall never fade, or grow out of date. It represents the attainments and eternal felicity of the redeemed and triumphant church of Christ.

This crown is certain for all who run the race. In worldly games only one out of many gets the prize, but we may all strive in the hope of finding and of being publicly acknowledged in the great day of the Lord. Those who seek, says Christ, shall find. If there is a crown that is sure to all who run this race, why be so concerned and perturbed as if it were uncertain? True believers shall never lose their crown of glory, but they are still urged to 'hold that fast which thou hast, that no man take thy crown'.

The whole passage is designed to show that the way to Heaven is not easy. There are many obstacles in the way, the love of sin, the opposition of Satan, and the enticing snares of the world. The danger of coming short is great. Every moment exposes us to hazard, for at any moment we may die unsaved. This is a dreadful danger. If anything should arouse men, it should be the fear of losing their soul. When men in the career of ambition make immense efforts to obtain the perishing objects of desire, why should we hesitate to make great efforts in order to gain eternal glory?

102. SOUL DUTIES

Wherefore, my beloved, as ye have always obeyed, not as in my presence
only, but now much more in my absence, work out your own salvation
with fear and trembling. For it is God which worketh in you both
*to will and to do of his good pleasure (*Philippians 2:12-13).

The apostle praises the Philippian believers, whom he addresses in affec-
tionate terms, for their obedience to the Gospel, not only when he was with
them, but more so in his absence. He proceeds to exhort them to greater
diligence with respect to their salvation. This was needful because they
were exposed to many dangers, and their only safety is to be in real earnest
in this matter. Salvation is the subject under consideration, and in this
connection the apostle emphasises a twofold work, a work for men and a
work for God – for men a duty, with God it is goodwill.

(1) *The Work of Man*
'Work out your own salvation with fear and trembling.' These are solemn
and searching words, over which men have argued long, some over–
emphasising man's part, and others laying stress on God's part. Both are
here taught: men err when they sever them, and overlook the place Scripture
assigns to both. The truth is that there is no contradiction here at all.

'Salvation' is a comprehensive term, and embraces the whole field of
redemption, in its provision, application and consummation. Here the
apostle means the personal possession of salvation, as a deliverance from
sin, in its demerit, guilt and power. Thus he stresses 'your own salvation'.
It is their personal concern, regarding their possession of and progress in the
life of faith. Some would give men the supreme hand in it, and make it
dependent on man's will and work.

But the apostle does not mean that salvation is of works, that man can
save himself. In the sense of making atonement for sin by satisfaction to law
and justice, man cannot save himself. Nothing is more natural to man than
to suppose he can do something to merit salvation, so he resorts to works.
Scripture, however, makes clear that there is no salvation by the works of
the law (Romans 3:19–25). In this respect salvation is provided in Christ
only, and He is adequate to our needs. Faith in Christ is what is required.

Nor does he mean that man can effect such spiritual and moral change
in himself by self– discipline, so as to make himself worthy of divine
acceptance. Here man is helpless, as helpless as is the leopard when it comes
to changing his spots. Only the Holy Spirit in regeneration can effect such
change in man as to make him an object of God's delight. This He does by

quickening the soul to newness of life, and imparting such graces as faith, love and repentance, so that the soul, by the exercise of these, honours God. It is the Spirit that quickeneth.

But while salvation is not of works, yet in a sense it is to be worked out. The apostle is addressing believers, who had already tasted salvation through faith in Christ, and who are here urged to make greater diligence in making their calling and election sure, that is, to make sure of their salvation and strive to grow therein. Though forgiven in respect of guilt, yet sin is still in them in respect of gain. Though justified, they are not wholly sanctified – there is need of improvement and growth in grace and knowledge. In this there is room for exertion on our part. Sanctification is a work which concerns the believer's life on earth, and though the Spirit is the active agent, they are active agents too. Grace makes them so – as living men they seek to adapt their lives to the Word of God as the rule of their life. Grace is like a sown seed, which grows under favourable circumstances. You plant potatoes which, without due care and attention, would be hindered by weeds. So it is with grace.

Now, this is not an easy matter, because there is power in us which is unfavourable to growth in grace. The old nature is carnal, earthly, lazy, and not disposed to spiritual exercises. The term 'work out' means to give out what is within, or yield thereto, so that it becomes visible. 'Let thy light so shine.' In all this, the powers of the soul find exercise, the mind, the heart, the will, in praying, searching, striving, conflict with self and Satan. Israel had to fight hard and long to gain full possession of Canaan. So must we.

How is this to be done? 'In fear and trembling.' These two words have no place in much current religious life – it is assumed that Gospel liberty means to be rid of these. But that it is not so is here asserted. It is true that perfect love casts out fear, the fear of dread and torment. The fear here required is one of respect and love, and it necessarily accompanies faith. It is to fear God by way of respect and love, so to serve, honour, adore and delight in him. It also means to fear sin and the grieving of the Spirit. It is accompanied by a trembling and distrust of self, arising from a sense of danger. So many have failed and made shipwreck and have succumbed to temptation.

(2) *The Work of God*
Although this comes last here, it is really the first, and is given as the occasion of the former – God works in you. It is an encouragement to real endeavour. It is God who works in you, therefore you must be up and doing. Only for the fact that God works, by the inward operation of His Spirit, we would faint in the fight with sin and Satan.

God works in you. All the glory must be given to Him. He has not only provided salvation for us, and applied it to us, but He works in us to conform us to Christ. He thus produces in us effects which become visible in our conduct and which imply a conscious experience of soul in relation to Him, so that He becomes our delight and desire. He quickens the soul by the imparting of life to our spirit.

In this He works especially on the will. He makes a people willing in a day of His power. Naturally, the human will is enslaved by sin, but the Holy Spirit renews it, so that without compulsion or force it chooses the good. Thus, the renewed soul chooses to be saved in God's way, and embraces Christ as Saviour and Lord.

The renewed will shows itself in degrees agreeable to the inward principle which answers to the requirements of Scripture regarding the believer. He delights in the law of God, loves God's will, and this is accompanied by deeds – by good works. We speak of men who are weak–willed, but this is a will sustained by grace, to resist evil and love the good. In Romans 7 we read 'to will is present with me'. The believer is distinguished by his willing service to Christ.

All this is of the good pleasure of God. This is basic to all His dealings with us. It is of His goodwill that He saved us, and leads and sustains us. He affords us glimpses of favour and love and growth. He thus enables us to do His will, and only such will enter His kingdom. Not all who say to Him 'Lord, Lord', will enter, but those who do the will of the Father will enter. This is the service and aim of the Christian, to please God and not self.

This is costly. But it is all of the Lord, in provision and application. The possession of this salvation makes the soul active and resolute. And this should lead us to strive for higher attainments in the Christian life.

103. SAVED AND CALLED

Who hath saved us and called us with an holy calling, not according to our works, but according to his own purpose and grace, which was given us in Christ Jesus before the world began (2 Timothy 1:9).

In the preceding verse the apostle exhorts Timothy not to be ashamed of the testimony of Christ, or of Paul His prisoner. It was not that he suspected the loyalty of Timothy, but the circumstances were such that a young man might succumb to fear, or shrink from open avowal of the Gospel through the trials he would have to encounter. This was natural, for the Gospel was opposed, and its witnesses persecuted. Paul himself was a prisoner, and Timothy might well fear a similar end. To fortify him, Paul reminds him of the sufficiency of divine power to sustain him, and of his obligations to the God of grace, who bestowed such great blessings upon unworthy sinners. The God in whom he asks him to trust, and not shrink from trial, is the God who saved us and called us. These are the two main thoughts of our text.

(1) *The Saving*

This comes first, and is the basis of the second proposition. The foundation was first conceived, planned and laid before the erection could possibly take place.

The whole is ascribed to God as its author, for salvation is of the Lord. It is God in the Person of the Father to whom the apostle refers. The Bible distinguishes between the origin and means of salvation. The first is assigned to the Father, and the second to the Son. This is clear from Ephesians 1:4,5. Salvation originated with the Father as representing the Godhead, and He is thus said to have saved us. He is an active agent from beginning to end. This removes the objection or view that the Father is unwilling to save sinners, as if He agreed only on the intervention of the Son. Herein the love of God is manifest, that He gave His Son to be the Saviour.

This salvation is ascribed to God's purpose and grace as its cause. The purpose operated from grace, as a gracious purpose; its exercise was not inspired by human merit, or even by human need, but purely by grace. It is all of grace. It arose not from mere necessity; acts of grace may be necessary on earth. The public voice may demand charity and benefits for the poor – the elderly, and the unemployed, for example. Need may be such in society that governments will be forced to take action. But God was under no external compulsion, and could be subject to none. He acted freely and sovereignly in this. No voice solicited His intervention, either in earth, Hell or Heaven. Earth was silent; guilty man hid himself. Hell rejoiced at its success. The only voice heard in Heaven was that of justice saying 'Render thou what thou owest'. For the objects of this gracious purpose were rebels, guilty of rebelling against Heaven. Hence they deserved a just punishment as a reward of their sin, and justice required the infliction of penalty. See then the wonder of grace – oh what grace! This excludes all human merit – it is not of works. Salvation was fixed, resolved and complete in God's purpose 'before the world began'. How foolish to suppose that man can save himself, or merit the favour of God!

God's salvation is ascribed to Christ as its means. In conformity with the Father's will He came to reveal and execute that purpose. Hence He said 'Lo, I come to do thy will, O God'. Christ and the purpose of God are inseparable. Any view that would separate them is wrong. Christ, the

eternal Son, assumed human nature so that in the very nature that sinned –
in human nature – He might effect this gracious purpose, even the salvation
of sinners. This He did by offering Himself a ransom for sinners, the just
in the room of the unjust on Calvary.

The liberty which Christ procured for us is twofold. First, it is achieved
by the payment of a ransom for us. Christ redeemed us from the curse of
the law by being made a curse for us. By honouring the law, and fulfilling
the requirements of justice in bearing the penalty of those for whom He
answered, He paid the ransom. This salvation is thus founded upon the
Person and finished Work of Christ. That is the ground of our liberty. God
pronounced the ransom adequate, and a solid basis of worthy acceptance.

But this salvation is also experienced by the power of the Holy Spirit in
us. This freedom secured by Christ is applied to believers by the Holy Spirit.
They are made partakers of it. It is imputed to them, and put to their account.
Hence they come into possession of freedom from the penal consequences
of sin, relief to conscience and joy in God. They have all the benefits of
salvation from Christ – they are justified, accepted, adopted and sanctified.
These too are the conscious possession of believers. Oh, the liberty of the
soul to whom Christ is precious, and who closes in with Him in the gospel!
But to this we must be called, for there is a distinction between salvation in
Christ and salvation applied and possessed. The first secured it, and it
consists in Him. The call applies it, and it becomes the possession of the
believer.

(2) *He Called us*

This also is of God, for the work is the work of the Triune God. And further,
this work transcends all His other works. Nothing can be compared to this,
in greatness, glory and wonder.

There is a general call to sinners. It is addressed to all under the Gospel.
It is so comprehensive that some may think themselves excluded. It was
proposed first to the Jews, and then to Gentiles. There is now no distinction.
Christ broke down the middle wall of partition. There is now no distinction
of race or class. It is to 'whomsoever will' – 'Look unto me and be ye saved,
all the ends of the earth, for I am God, and none else'. In it God deals with
men as moral agents, who are answerable to Him for its exercise in relation
to His call, as they are sinners. He asks, 'How shall we escape, if we neglect
so great salvation?' Here is the external call of the Gospel to all.

But there is also a particular call to some, by the Spirit. It is mysterious,
secret, persuasive, not audible or visible. Strangely, in the case of Paul
himself the call was audible and visible, but his experience was extraordinary.

It is a personal call. In it, man finds himself addressed by God in his word, through the secret and powerful operation of the Spirit making eternal issues real and solemn to him, so that he feels alone with God. It is the Spirit's personal dealings with individuals. As to time, moment, and means, it is wholly of God.

It is an effective call, arresting, persuasive and drawing. The Spirit convinces of sin and misery, the guilt and defilement of sin. It is also a work of enlightening, as the Spirit enlights the mind in the knowledge of Christ – God's provision of mercy. Man of himself could never discover this. God's way of salvation is the greatest of surprises to the overwhelmed and convinced sinner. This the Spirit reveals. It is an encouraging call.

It is a renewing call, affecting the will. The will must be renewed ere a man can embrace Christ. Its natural bias is away from Christ. But by the renewing power of the Spirit, the soul accepts Christ, and embraces Him, resting on Him for salvation. This is an act of will, a willing embrace. Thus the renewed will has a bias for good, it is now towards God and salvation, made willing in a day of His power. Man has no hand in this; he is active, because acted upon. But his action has nothing whatever to do with his calling, any more than with his salvation in Christ. It is wholly of grace. Oh, what grace on the part of the Spirit who visited your soul in its slavish condition.

It is a holy calling. There is no calling of God which is not holy. The stamp of Heaven is upon all God's works, and is upon this. Its cause is holy – God is holy. Christ is holy. The Spirit is holy. The Word is holy. So the call is holy. And it is a call to holiness, from darkness to light, from sin to God, from uncleanness to holiness. It is a call to holiness of walk and life, a walk worthy of God. 'Be ye holy, for I am holy.' We are called to salvation through Christ. We must have this or perish. You who have felt it and feel it – respond to it in holiness and obedience more and more.

104. EXHORTATION AND COMFORT

This then is the message which we have heard of him and declare unto you, that God is light, and in him is no darkness at all. If we say that we have fellowship with him and walk in darkness, we lie and do not the truth. But if we walk in the light as he is in the light, we have fellowship one with another, and the blood of Jesus Christ his son cleanseth us from all sin
(1 John 1:5–7).

We are drawing near the end of another year, and with it passes another chapter in our lives. What is written is written, and we cannot alter or improve it. But we have a duty regarding the present and future, short or long as it may be. In this connection, the last Sabbath of a year is a vantage point from which we may view the past, assess the present, and anticipate the future. It is a time to reflect and consider the way we have been led, and seek renewed strength for the tasks ahead. As individuals and families, we have much to be thankful for. There may have been things which were not pleasant, bitter and hard things, but none that are uncommon to men, and we can bear witness to a sustaining providence, during the dark and steep parts of the road.

The outstanding event of the year has been the cessation of hostilities. That is an inestimable blessing to the world at large, but it is a deliverance which has imposed new and great responsibilities upon the victorious nations. And it ought to be a matter of earnest prayer that they may prove worthy of this trust. May He who holds the sceptre of the universe be acknowledged in the counsels of men, that their decisions may be influenced by the fear which is the beginning of wisdom.

With the end of the war we had hopes of a return to sanity on the part of our people generally, for during these war years there had been a marked deterioration in the national and social life of the nation. But there is no visible improvement, and instead a flood of secularisation has arisen, which endangers the more important relationships of home life. Throughout our land we hardly hear of anything but organisations, which are calculated to take up the time and energy which ought to be devoted to the higher concerns of life. Family life, which ought to be a source of real delight, seems to be to many a burden from which they want to escape, and seek relief in dramatic performances, and such like. It is to be feared that people have succumbed to the call of the world, and are indifferent to higher issues. They live as if God had no right to a place in their thoughts or lives, except for an hour or two on Sunday. Even that sacred day is desecrated, and its privileges neglected, as if it had no binding authority or value. The entire week seems to be devoted to the pleasures of sense. What have we to say to a world thus occupied? Here it is - we have a message from God, upon which the hope of man depends.

(1) *The Message is Given*

It is not a man-conceived message, which had its origin in the brain and in the affirmation of a genius. It is from God. Who can by searching find Him out? None. Yet we are not called to worship an unknown God, but one who is revealed and declared to us in His holy truth.

This message was *received*. We have heard of Him, says John. That is, we heard of the Lord Jesus, the faithful and true witness, the great teacher sent from God. The apostles received their message from Him. When He sent them out to preach the word, He told them what to say. After the resurrection, and before the ascension, He told them plainly what they should teach. No man has seen God at any time, the only-begotten Son, He has declared Him. Again, in His intercessory prayer He says 'I have manifested thy name unto them whom thou didst give me.' Christ is thus the author of the message.

This message is of *a declarative nature* - its message is about God. It declares that He is light. Not a light - not even the light, but light. That means that He Himself is the source and fountain of all light that is in the world. It was He who called light to shine in darkness, saying, 'Let there be light'. This represents revelation or illumination - 'whatsoever doth make manifest is light'. Light is diffusive, penetrating, searching. And is not the revelation which God gave of Himself all this? He revealed Himself, He was not discovered. We are dependent for the measure of our knowledge of God on the revelation He gave of Himself in Christ, and upon Christ's declarations concerning Him. 'No man can know the Father save He to whom the Son shall reveal Him.' Again, the light of revelation shows us the evil that is in the world, and in us.

Light is also an emblem of knowledge. God is the omniscient One, that is, He is all-seeing and all-knowing. All things are open to the eyes of Him with whom we have to do. He is familiar with all that occurs in the world, and with the details of our lives. Nothing is hidden from His searching gaze. O consider the indescribable greatness of God, and the vastness of His knowledge, when it is said that His eye sees and beholds the sons of men full well, He sees all from His dwelling place, that on the earth do dwell.

Again, light is the emblem of purity. He is the Holy One, dwelling in light inaccessible. He is said to have covered Himself with light (Psalm 104). Light is the purest of all things. Other things are polluted. The air, earth and water are all contaminated, but the rays of light are uncorrupted. The sun does not contract impurity by shining on the corrupt earth. Well then, God may well be called light. He is of purer eye than to behold iniquity. He is absolutely holy. All He does is in undeviating correspondence with perfect purity. This is what makes Him, like the light, full of goodness. Nothing is better than light. And nothing is better than the holy love, and rich mercy of God.

In Him is no darkness at all. He is the essence of true perfection. Darkness is the very opposite of His nature, and has no place at all in Him. It is excluded from all His acts of government. There is nothing in Him, or about Him, that dims the pure splendour of His character. He is beyond the possibility of error, beyond making a miscarriage of justice. Now this is a truth that is often forgotten. Many live as if God were darkness, and in darkness. This is not the biblical view of God. The view we ought to cherish is that God is Light, and in Him is no darkness at all.

(2) *The Message Exposes*

If it declares what God is, it exposes the terrible deception to which men may be subject. 'If we say that we have fellowship with him, and walk in darkness, we lie and do not the truth.' It is not what we say but what we prove by the way we walk, and by our conversation, that matters, and that determines our character and our relation to God.

Some may claim fellowship with God who have no right to. They know nothing of what fellowship means. They have mistaken views and notions of it. They are religious, have a good estimate of themselves, that they are as good as the next person. They are morally upright and correct in their behaviour. They are interested in every good cause, and they see no reason why God should be displeased with them.

Yet they walk in darkness. Their conduct contradicts their profession. They are in darkness and their walk is in keeping with that darkness. I represents the life of sin. They hardly see any harm in anything because they do not view it in the light of God and His truth. The true nature of anything is borne out by light, but the sinner will not see by the light, or walk by the light. He will not come to the light, lest his deeds should be reproved. We cannot enjoy fellowship with God if we walk in darkness. For what fellowship hath light with darkness? What communion hath Christ with Belial? Such a profession is a lie.

Those who make such a false claim lie and do not the truth. The truth is absent and the lie predominates. Not that they are habitual liars in the ordinary sense. It is simply that their life is a life of inconsistency. It implies the concealing of something which cannot bear the light. It is a practical lie. It is not what we say, but the life we live that proves where we stand. It is a life of deception, a life which says 'I am rich', but is poor, naked and blind.

(3) *The Message Assures*

The assurance is given in these terms: 'if we walk in the light, as He is in the light, we have fellowship with one another, and the blood of Jesus Christ his Son cleanseth us from all sin.'

There is such a walk as walking *in the light*. It implies that those who walk thus actually have light, and are described as children of light because they have become light in the Lord. It implies illumination by the Spirit of God. They have light on themselves as sinners, sin-ruined and helpless.

They have light on God, as holy, just, good and merciful. They have the light of the word as a lamp to their feet and a light to their path. But this lifestyle is defined as walking 'as He is in the light'. That is, it is the same kind of light as God is. It is not the same, of course, as to measure or degree, but of kind. All who have this light love holiness and hate darkness. They are not ignorant of darkness, but are conscious of it.

They have fellowship with God. All believers share this fellowship. They are one in Christ Jesus. It is the fellowship of oneness and union with Christ. But the conscious enjoyment of this fellowship is conditioned to a holy and circumspect walk.

There is, of course, also the fellowship of believers. This belongs to all of God's people. They are fellow-heirs of the grace of life, partakers of the heavenly calling, redeemed by the same blood, justified by the same grace, sanctified by the same Spirit.

To such there is assurance of cleansing. They are conscious of their need of it, and freely admit it. They confess their failures and uncleanness. They pray 'Create in me a clean heart, O Lord'. Ah yes, their great need is holiness.

What is the cure for their condition? The blood of Christ. Blood refers to life, or to what is of value. It signifies the value and efficacy of Christ's offering as adequate to secure and apply salvation - complete salvation - from sin. It cleanses from all sin, and cures the heart of the love of sin. It cleanses the conscience of its guilt, the life of its practice and the soul of its burden. It robs sin itself of its power. Charles Simeon, when young, read in a book that the Jews knew what they were doing when they transferred their sin to the head of the offering. The thought occurred to him: 'What! May I transfer all my guilt to another? Then God-willing I will not bear it any more.' We can say:

> God laid my sins on Jesus,
> The spotless Lamb of God;
> He bears them all, and frees us
> From the accursed load.

Here, then, is a message to correct and fortify us for the way. The world has nothing to offer but temporary gratification, that can only end in misery and death. But Christ offers all that can be desired - inestimable blessings here, and eternal felicity hereafter. Oh what prospects of brightness await the child of God!

Scripture Index